The Art of Salad Making

Carol Truax

BANTAM BOOKS
TORONTO · NEW YORK · LONDON

A NATIONAL GENERAL COMPANY

THE ART OF SALAD MAKING

*A Bantam Book / published by arrangement with
Doubleday & Company, Inc.*

PRINTING HISTORY
Doubleday edition published 1968
Bantam edition published May 1971
2nd printing
3rd printing
4th printing
5th printing
6th printing

*Bantam Books are published by Bantam Books, Inc., a National
General company. Its trade-mark, consisting of the words "Bantam
Books" and the portrayal of a bantam, is registered in the United
States Patent Office and in other countries. Marca Registrada.
Bantam Books, Inc., 666 Fifth Avenue, New York, N.Y. 10019.*

PRINTED IN THE UNITED STATES OF AMERICA

The Soup and Sandwich Cookbook

Carol Truax

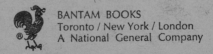

BANTAM BOOKS
Toronto / New York / London
A National General Company

for Marguerite

THE SOUP AND SANDWICH COOKBOOK
A Bantam Book / published March 1973
2nd printing

Published simultaneously in the United States and Canada

Bantam Books are published by Bantam Books, Inc., a National General company. Its trade-mark, consisting of the words "Bantam Books" and the portrayal of a bantam, is registered in the United States Patent Office and in other countries. Marca Registrada. Bantam Books, Inc., 666 Fifth Avenue, New York, N.Y. 10019.

Printed in the United States of America

Contents

SOUPS

SANDWICHES

part one

SOUPS

In Praise of Soup

"Soup of the evening, beautiful soup," sang Alice's friend, the Mock Turtle, in Wonderland.

"Je vis de bonne soupe," said Molière.

Anybody anywhere can live on good soup.

There's nothing better than soup.

For getting a meal off to a good start, there's nothing better.

For the mainstay of the lighter meal of the day, there's nothing better than soup and a sandwich.

For winding up a happy evening, there's nothing better than soup—hot soup on a cold night, chilled soup in balmy weather. Molière might call it a Soup Soiree.

Nothing is easier than soup. These recipes prove it. You'll read them conscientiously and find there's plenty of leeway. It's not like a soufflé to be measured and timed carefully and worried over for fear it will fall. Soup recipes are delightfully flexible, which adds to the fun.

You can entertain yourself, please your friends, and save money by using your ingenuity and your leftovers, in equal parts, to produce delectable surprise soups. Almost any leftover vegetable, buzzed in the blender with a liquid, plus inspired seasoning, equals a gourmet delight. Yesterday's gravy and the remains of the roast it came with, go around together in the blender with tasty companions, such as

3

onions, parsley, celery, or garlic, to make a smooth meat soup. Don't throw away the water or broth you simmer your vegetables in. This flavorful liquid does so much more for any soup than water can.

Remember when there was always a stockpot a-simmer at the cozy, warm back of the kitchen range? Into it went all the odds and ends too good to throw away: the chicken neck and wing tips, the chop bones, the beef ribs, the lamb shank, celery tops, lettuce leaves, flavorful parsley stems, green ends of scallions, young pea pods, tomato skins, trimmings of almost any vegetable. Stewing together they amalgamated into a rich basis for almost any kind of soup.

Even if the coal range has gone to the dump heap, you don't have to relegate your scraps to the same fate. Simmer them together for an hour, strain, refrigerate or freeze, and your soup starter is ready for you.

With such a good start, you can go many places, and you can't go wrong. Beautiful soup is bound to be your reward.

i

Cream Soups

The cream of the crop—the crème de la crème—that's cream soup. Sturdy enough to live on, light enough to whet the appetite, cream soup can be all things to all men. It needn't be filling; it needn't even, these days, be made with cream, though it is always the delightful creamy texture that distinguishes these soups. There are several ways of building up that special creamy smoothness.

The classic method starts with a roux, which is flour gently cooked in butter till it begins to be tinged an appetizing pale beige. Into this mixture a liquid—skim milk, milk, or cream—is gradually stirred. Such a roux adds a delicate special flavor and beckoning aroma of its own to the dish.

Egg or egg yolk is another thickener, stirred in at the last moment when boiling has subsided.

A third thickener, now much in vogue, is a puree of the soup's basic ingredient, which enhances the flavor and keeps down the calories as it enriches the texture. Leftover pureed peas or spinach are all ready for tomorrow's soup. You can make your fresh puree in a sieve or food mill, or, still more efficiently, in your blender. Pieces of the cooked chicken meat buzzed with some broth produce the proper consistency in the finished product. From asparagus to zucchini, any cooked vegetable with a little of its liquid is buzzable.

If at the last moment you'd like your soup slightly thicker, you may stir in a little flour, cornstarch, or arrowroot, smoothed in a small quantity of cool liquid. French cooks think, and I think so too, that a little butter, added just before serving, pulls the suave brew together and makes it perfect.

Two hundred years ago, there was a traveling footman who bragged that he was never out of a job. The English milords vied eagerly for his services, because he knew the flavorsome secret of making Queen of Scots Soup. In his last years he published the recipe. No wonder his services were sought after, because the dish he founded his fame on was the queen of cream soups, crème à la reine, Königinssuppe, or in plain English cream of chicken soup. Modern technology gives this delicious soup a doubled savor by the use of the blender.

CREAM OF CHICKEN SOUP

1/2 cup minced celery
3 cups chicken broth
2 tablespoons butter
2 tablespoons flour
3/4 cup cream
Salt
1 tablespoon chopped parsley (optional)

Cook the celery in broth until very tender. Buzz in a blender or force through a coarse sieve. Melt the butter, stir in the flour, and add about a cup of the broth. Return this mixture to the broth and boil 2 minutes. Stir in the hot cream. Add salt to taste. Add parsley if you wish.

Serves 4.

VICHYSSOISE

8 to 10 leeks
3 tablespoons butter
4 medium potatoes, peeled and sliced
4 cups chicken broth
1/4 teaspoon white pepper
Salt
2 cups heavy or light cream
1 to 2 tablespoons curry (optional)
Chopped chives

Chop the white parts of the leeks and sauté in the butter until softened but not brown. Meanwhile boil the potatoes until soft. Drain and mix with the leeks. Add 2 cups of chicken broth and simmer a few minutes. Buzz in a blender. Add remaining broth, pepper, and salt to taste; chill. Just before serving add the cream and curry (optional), and garnish with chopped chives. Reheat if you wish to serve the soup hot.

Serves 8.

SHORTCUT VICHYSSOISE

6 scallions, chopped
1 onion, cut up
2 tablespoons butter
1/2 cup water
1/2 teaspoon salt
1/4 teaspoon white pepper
2 (10 1/2-ounce) cans potato soup
2 cups chicken broth or 2 cups water plus 3
   chicken bouillon cubes
1 cup cream
Minced chives (garnish)

Sauté the scallions and onion in butter. Add water, season with salt and pepper, and simmer for 15 minutes until softened. Buzz in a blender with the potato soup and broth. Return to heat and add the cream. Serve hot or chilled. Garnish with chives.

Serves 6.

COLD CHICKEN TOMATO SOUP

3 cups chicken broth
1 (10 1/2-ounce) can tomato soup
1 cucumber, diced
1 small onion, chopped
1 cup half-and-half
1/2 teaspoon dill
1 tablespoon minced parsley
1/4 cucumber, sliced thin

Combine the chicken broth, tomato soup, diced cucumber, and onion; buzz in a blender. Pour into a bowl and add the half-and-half, dill, and parsley. Adjust seasoning—the amount of salt will depend upon the seasoning in the soup. Chill. Serve with a few slices of cucumber floating on top.

Serves 6.

CREAM OF TOMATO SOUP

2 (10 1/2-ounce) cans tomato soup
3 cups milk or half-and-half
1 tablespoon sugar
1 teaspoon salt
Dash nutmeg
1/2 teaspoon oregano
Whipped or sour cream (optional garnish)

Combine the ingredients in a kettle and heat together. Serve with a spoonful of cream.

Serves 6.

CREAM OF MUSHROOM SOUP

1/2 pound mushrooms
1/4 cup butter
1 teaspoon minced onion
2 (10 1/2-ounce) cans chicken broth or consommé
1 teaspoon salt
1/4 teaspoon pepper
2 cups cream

Reserve 6 even-sized mushroom caps for garnish. Sauté the mushrooms in 3 tablespoons butter with the onion for 3 to 4 minutes. Do not brown. Add chicken broth and salt and pepper. Simmer for 10 minutes. Buzz in a blender. Reheat and add the cream. Meanwhile, sauté the caps in butter and serve the soup garnished with the caps, either whole or sliced.

Serves 6.

CREAM OF SPINACH SOUP

1 small onion
3 tablespoons butter
3 tablespoons flour
3 cups milk
2 cups finely chopped or pureed cooked spinach
1 teaspoon salt
1/8 teaspoon pepper
1/8 teaspoon rosemary or basil (optional)

Sauté the onion in butter in a saucepan. When clear, but not brown, add the flour. Stir in the milk slowly and any liquid from the spinach. When slightly thickened, add the spinach and salt and pepper and rosemary or basil. Heat.

Serves 4 to 6.

VARIATIONS

CREAM OF BROCCOLI SOUP

Substitute 2 to 3 cups chopped cooked broccoli for the spinach.

CREAM OF CELERY SOUP

Substitute 2 cups diced, cooked celery for spinach.

CREAM OF PEA SOUP

Substitute 2 cups cooked peas for spinach.

CREAM OF CORN SOUP

Substitute 2 cups cooked corn, cream-style or whole kernel, for the spinach. Use pinch of curry in place of herbs.

CREAM OF VEGETABLE SOUP

Substitute 2 cups any chopped leftover or canned vegetables. Substitute 1 tablespoon parsley for other herbs.

CREAM OF LETTUCE SOUP

2 tablespoons butter
2 tablespoons cornstarch
4 cups chicken broth or part water
1 head firm lettuce or 2 heads soft lettuce
1 cup heavy cream
Salt

Melt the butter and stir in the cornstarch. Add broth or water and bring to a boil. Add the cut-up lettuce and simmer for 30 minutes. Buzz in a blender. Reheat, adding cream. Season with salt to taste.

Serves 4 to 6.

CREAM OF CUCUMBER SOUP

2 large cucumbers
1/4 cup butter
2 tablespoons flour
2 cups chicken broth or water
1 quart milk or half-and-half
1 teaspoon salt
1/2 teaspoon white pepper
Whipped cream (optional garnish)
Chopped chives (optional garnish)

Grate the unpeeled cucumbers on coarse grater. Sauté in butter for 2 to 3 minutes; add flour and broth or water. Stir until smooth. Add the milk or half-and-half, salt, and pepper; bring to a boil. Serve hot or cold topped with whipped cream or chives or both.

Serves 8.

CREAM OF CUCUMBER MINT SOUP

4 cucumbers
1 onion, minced
3 to 4 tablespoons butter
3 cups water
1 teaspoon salt
3 tablespoons flour
3 cups half-and-half
2 tablespoons minced fresh mint

Peel and slice the cucumbers. Sauté the onion in 2 tablespoons butter until clear but not brown. Add cucumbers, 2 cups water, and the salt. Cook a few minutes until cucumbers are just soft. Mix the flour with remaining water and add to the mixture. Bring to a boil, then buzz in a blender. Return to pot. Add the half-and-half and the mint; reheat and add remaining butter. Also good served chilled.

Serves 6.

CREAM OF ASPARAGUS SOUP

2 pounds fresh asparagus or 2 boxes frozen
  asparagus
2 cups chicken broth
1 pint heavy cream
1/2 teaspoon salt
1/4 teaspoon pepper
2 to 3 tablespoons butter
2 to 3 tablespoons flour (optional)

Cook the fresh asparagus until very soft in salted water to cover. Cut off the tough ends and return to pot and cook until liquid is reduced to half. If using frozen asparagus, double the amount of water given in package instructions and cook until very soft. Strain and reserve the liquid. Buzz asparagus in blender with 1 cup of the water it was cooked in. Put into a pot with remaining water and chicken broth, bring to a boil, and stir in the cream. Add salt and pepper. If the soup is thick enough, add butter just before serving; if you want it thicker, make a roux by melting the butter and adding the flour, then a cup of the soup. Add roux to soup and boil 2 to 3 minutes to thicken.

Serves 8.

WATERCRESS SOUP

2 cups chopped watercress
3 scallions, minced
1/4 cup butter
3 tablespoons flour
1 quart milk
1/2 teaspoon salt
1/4 teaspoon pepper

Sauté the watercress and scallions in butter for 5 minutes. Blend in the flour; add the milk, salt, and pepper; simmer until thickened.

Serves 4.

AVOCADO CHICKEN SOUP

1/2 cup minced onion
1 cup thinly sliced celery
3 tablespoons butter
1 teaspoon salt
2 1/2 cups water
2 (10 1/2-ounce) cans cream of chicken soup
2 ripe avocados
Thin slices lemon or avocado (garnish)

Sauté the onion and celery in the butter until transparent; do not brown. Add the salt and water and simmer for 5 minutes. Add the chicken soup, blend thoroughly, and bring to a boil. Remove from heat. Cut the avocados in halves, remove pits, and peel. Sieve or rice the pulp; you need 2 cups of puree. Add to the warm soup and reheat. Serve at once, garnished with lemon or avocado slices. This soup is also good served cold.

Serves 6 to 8.

CHILLED AVOCADO CREAM CONSOMMÉ

1 small avocado
Juice 1 lemon
1 teaspoon grated onion
1 cup sour cream or light cream
1/2 teaspoon salt
Dash Tabasco sauce
2 cups consommé
Minced chives or parsley
Lemon wedges or slices

Peel the avocado and mash through a sieve. Stir in the lemon juice immediately. Stir in the onion, cream, salt, and Tabasco sauce. Refrigerate until ready to use. Just before serving, break up the consommé (which has been refrigerated for at least 12 hours) and lightly fold in the avocado mixture. Garnish each serving with chives or parsley and serve with pieces of lemon.

Serves 4.

ALMOND CREAM SOUP

1/2 pound blanched almonds, chopped fine
1 quart chicken broth
2 cups half-and-half
1/2 teaspoon salt
1/2 teaspoon sugar
1/4 teaspoon white pepper

Stir the almonds into the chicken broth. If you want the almonds very fine, buzz in a blender with 2 cups of the chicken broth. Simmer almonds and all of the broth for 15 minutes, add half-and-half and seasoning to taste. Reheat but don't let the soup boil. Like most cream soups, this may be served cold, perhaps topped with a sprinkling of coarsely chopped almonds.

Serves 6 to 8.

VARIATION

WALNUT CREAM SOUP

Proceed as for almond cream soup, substituting 1 cup crushed walnuts for the almonds. Add 1/4 cup sour cream if you wish.

CLAM STEW

1 medium onion, minced
1/2 cup minced celery
1/4 cup butter
2 (8-ounce) cans minced clams
1 quart milk
2 tablespoons Worcestershire sauce
3 tablespoons flour
2 tablespoons minced parsley

Sauté the onion and celery in butter until soft; do not brown. Stir in the clams with their juice, milk, and Worcestershire sauce. Heat. Stir in the flour, which you have mixed with a little water, and cook until thickened. Add the parsley; ladle into cups, bowls, or a soup tureen. Serve with pilot biscuits or crackers.

Serves 6 to 8.

CLAM SPINACH SOUP

1 box frozen chopped spinach
2 (8-ounce) cans minced clams
1 quart milk
1/2 teaspoon salt
1/4 teaspoon pepper
Pinch of basil
2 tablespoons butter

Cook the spinach following package directions. Add the clams with their juice and buzz in a blender. Add the milk. Return to heat and season with salt, pepper, and basil. Just before serving, add the butter a little at a time.

Serves 6 to 8.

EASY LOBSTER BISQUE

2 tablespoons butter
2 teaspoons minced parsley
2 teaspoons minced onion
1/2 pound lobster meat or 2 (5-ounce) cans, cut in small pieces
2 tablespoons flour
1 cup water or fish stock
2 cups cream or half-and-half
1 teaspoon salt
Dash cayenne
2 tablespoons sherry or brandy

Melt the butter, add parsley and onion, and cook until onion is transparent. Add lobster, cook 2 to 3 minutes while stirring. Stir in the flour. Add water or stock and simmer 3 to 4 minutes. Add cream or half-and-half, salt, and cayenne; bring to a boil. Add the sherry or brandy and serve.

Serves 4.

CREAM OF CRAB SOUP

1 onion, finely chopped
1/4 cup minced celery
3 tablespoons butter
2 tablespoons flour
1 teaspoon salt
1/8 teaspoon white pepper
2 cups chicken broth
2 cups crab meat
3 cups half-and-half
1/2 cup heavy cream

Sauté the onion and celery in butter about 5 minutes until soft but not brown. Stir in the flour, salt, and pepper; add the broth slowly while stirring. Add crab meat and simmer 15 minutes. Add hot milk and cream to the soup; reheat for 1 minute, but do not boil. Cover. Let stand 7 to 10 minutes before serving.

Serves 8.

EASY CRAB BISQUE

2 cups chicken broth
1 (10 1/2-ounce) can mushroom soup
1 cup half-and-half
1/2 pound crab meat
3 to 4 tablespoons sherry

Put all of the ingredients except the sherry in a soup pan and heat but do not boil. Stir in the sherry and serve at once.

Serves 6.

EASY SALMON SOUP

1 (1-pound) can salmon
1 (10 1/2-ounce) can frozen potato soup
2 cups milk
1/2 teaspoon salt
2 tablespoons minced parsley or chives

Flake the salmon and put it with its liquid and the potato soup in a kettle. Simmer 5 minutes and with a fork smooth any lumps in the potatoes. Add milk, salt, and parsley or chives. Simmer for 1 minute.

Serves 4 to 6.

Clear Soups

A clear soup is seldom the star turn but very often is an important curtain raiser to an outstanding gustatory performance. Its unemphatic perfection is frequently called on as a prelude to a party dinner.

There is nothing better than a good homemade broth. It is worth every bit of the time it takes, if you have the time. Chicken comes along faster than beef, and with chicken backs and wings packaged on every counter, these ingredients are easy to get. If beef bones are not in sight, your butcher will produce them. Be sure to ask him to throw in a veal knuckle. If you're lucky, he will.

Clear vegetable soup made at home is very special. You can start with a convenient bunch of "soup vegetables" from the supermarket and add what you especially fancy, such as shallots, zucchini, and tomato. One vegetable may dominate the soup if you like. Try mushroom broth, clear beet borsch, or tomato bouillon. Don't hesitate to serve commercial broths from cans, packages, or jars. Do pep them up, do combine them, and always season them to taste. Broth makes a basis for many another soup. Here is where the prepared product, skillfully blended, is invaluable.

On a hot day a chilled soup whisked onto the table meets with instantaneous success. Cold clear soup appears in jellied form. A good homemade stock needs almost no added gelatin; that veal knuckle does the trick. Chicken broth needs gelatin to stay stiff and sparkling at table. Some canned consommé can be chilled into jelly in the refrigerator. Be sure to find the word condensed or jellied on the label. Lemon is an addition to clear soup—a slice floating in the hot bowl, a wedge at the side of the cold cup. A dollop of whipped cream or sour cream is pleasing on any clear soup, hot or cold. Red caviar enriches consommé madrilene, black caviar enhances jellied chicken broth in company with sour cream and chives, a very festive touch indeed.

Variously garnished, hot or cold, clear soup is an unassertive, appetizing starter that prepares for gourmet fare to follow.

BEEF BROTH

4 pounds lean beef
2 tablespoons butter
1 veal knuckle or marrow bone
2 quarts water
1 (1 pound) can tomatoes
2 bay leaves
3 carrots, cut into thick rounds
2 stalks celery, cut up
2 onions, coarsely chopped
6 sprigs parsley
1 tablespoon salt
1/2 teaspoon coarsely ground pepper
1/4 teaspoon paprika
Minced parsley (optional)
Lemon slices (optional)

Cut the meat into cubes and brown in butter; add bones and brown lightly in a soup kettle. Add 1 quart of water and simmer for 2 hours. Add the remaining ingredients including the 4 cups of water. Simmer 2 hours. Cool, strain, and chill. Remove fat from the top. Reheat to serve, adding some minced parsley and a slice of lemon if you wish.

Serves 8.

CONSOMMÉ WITH SHERRY

1 quart consommé or beef broth
2 tablespoons sherry
Chopped watercress or parsley

Heat the consommé or broth, add sherry, and serve topped with chopped watercress or parsley.

Serves 4.

EASY COLD RED CAVIAR MADRILENE

2 (13-ounce) cans madrilene
3 ounces red caviar
6 tablespoons sour cream
Minced chives
1 lemon

Put the madrilene into 6 soup cups. Stir a sixth of the caviar into each. Chill until firm. Top each cup with 1 tablespoon sour cream. Sprinkle with chives. Put a lemon wedge on the side of each serving.

Serves 6.

CHICKEN BROTH

1 (3 1/2- to 5-pound) hen
2 teaspoons salt
3 quarts water
1 cup chopped celery with leaves
1/2 cup chopped carrots
1/2 cup chopped onion
3 sprigs parsley
1/2 bay leaf

Cut up the chicken and simmer covered in the salted water for about 2 hours. Add remaining ingredients and simmer another hour until chicken is very tender. Skim as you cook. Reseason to taste. Strain and chill. (Save the chicken to use some other time.) Remove fat. If you wish the broth more clear, add 1 slightly beaten egg white and the crushed eggshell and boil for 2 minutes. Let stand and then strain.

Serves 8.

CHICKEN CONSOMMÉ ROSA

3 cups tomato juice
3 cups chicken broth
Pinch sugar
Salt to taste
Minced parsley

Mix the tomato juice and chicken broth; add sugar. The amount of salt will depend upon the seasoning in the juice and broth. Serve, hot or cold, topped with a little parsley.

Serves 6.

LEMON CHICKEN BROTH

1 1/2 quarts chicken broth
2 eggs
3 tablespoons lemon juice
1/2 teaspoon salt
1/2 teaspoon pepper

Heat the broth. Beat the eggs and lemon juice together. Pour some of the hot broth slowly into the egg mixture while stirring. Add to the rest of the broth and reheat for 5 minutes. Do not let the soup boil. Season to taste, adding a little salt and pepper.

Serves 6.

VEGETABLE BROTH

5 carrots, cut up
1 large onion, chopped
2 turnips, cut up
1 cup diced celery
2 leeks or 4 scallions, chopped
2 tablespoons butter
2 quarts water
2 teaspoons salt
1/2 teaspoon pepper
2 sprigs parsley
1/2 teaspoon thyme

Cook the vegetables in butter until lightly browned, about 10 minutes. Add water, salt, pepper, parsley, and thyme; simmer for 2 hours. Strain.

Serves 6.

TOMATO BOUILLON

2 cups chopped, peeled tomatoes or 1 (19-ounce) can tomatoes
2 cups beef broth
1 small onion, minced
2 cloves
1/2 teaspoon salt
1/2 teaspoon sugar
1/2 teaspoon freshly ground pepper
Minced parsley

Simmer all ingredients together for about 10 minutes. Remove cloves and adjust seasoning. Strain if you wish. Serve topped with a little minced parsley.

Serves 4.

TOMATO JUICE SOUP

4 cups tomato juice
2 scallions, minced
1 bay leaf
1/2 teaspoon celery salt
1 (10-ounce) can consommé
1/2 cup red wine
1/2 teaspoon sugar
1/2 teaspoon salt
1 teaspoon lemon juice

Put the tomato juice in a large pot with minced scallion, bay leaf, and celery salt. Bring to a boil and simmer 5 minutes. Add the consommé, wine, sugar, salt, and lemon juice. Adjust seasoning to taste. Reheat.

Serves 6.

CLEAR MUSHROOM SOUP

1 small onion, minced
3 tablespoons butter
1/2 pound mushrooms
5 cups water and 5 beef bouillon cubes or 5 cups beef broth
2 tablespoons sherry or 1 tablespoon lemon juice

Sauté the onion in butter until clear but not brown. Add thinly sliced mushrooms and cook about 5 minutes. Add water and bouillon cubes or broth. Just before serving, add sherry or lemon juice.

Serves 6.

CUCUMBER LETTUCE SOUP

2 cups diced, peeled cucumber
1 large head firm lettuce
3 pints chicken broth
1 teaspoon salt
1/4 teaspoon white pepper
1 tablespoon minced onion

Combine cucumber with the lettuce, which has been cut up. Add the broth. Put into a saucepan with salt, pepper, and onion. Simmer for 10 minutes. Buzz in a blender and reseason to taste. Serve hot or chilled.

Serves 6.

FISH BROTH

2 to 3 pounds fish plus bones, skin, and scraps
1 quart water
1/2 onion, chopped
1 small bay leaf
3 sprigs parsley
1 tablespoon lemon juice
1 cup white wine
1 tablespoon salt
Few peppercorns

Put all the fish in water with onion, bay leaf, parsley, and lemon juice. Boil for 20 minutes; add wine, salt, and peppercorns, and simmer 15 minutes more. Strain.

Serves 4.

CLAM BROTH

1 cup minced clams
3 cups water
2 cups clam juice
1/4 teaspoon pepper
Dash cayenne
Whipped cream (optional)

Heat clams and water together for 15 minutes. Strain, add clam juice, and season to taste with a very little pepper and cayenne. Serve with a dollop of whipped cream on each serving.

Serves 6.

Clear soups are time-consuming and difficult to make; the canned ones are quite satisfactory, used undiluted. Canned soups, dehydrated soups, and frozen soups are generally of fine quality.

These soups are particularly delicious if given a personal touch. Add a tablespoon of sherry or Madeira to consommé, float whipped cream on hot clam broth, grate a bit of cheddar cheese into any clear broth. A slice of lemon or lime floats well on turtle soup. Garlic or plain croutons enhance almost any soup, homemade or bought.

Try combining two different cans instead of using two of the same kind. The marriage of soups is much more happy than either one without a mate. Try some of the following unions:

Take equal parts of:	Add a little:
Consommé and chicken broth	Grated cheese
Consommé and tomato juice	Slice of lemon
Consommé and milk	Minced parsley and basil
Consommé and madrilene	Thin slice of cheese
Consommé and tomato soup	Garlic croutons
Consommé and clam juice	Sour cream with dill

Consommé and chopped canned mushrooms	Sherry
Chicken broth and clam broth	Lemon slices or whipped cream
Chicken broth and beef broth	Beaten egg
Chicken broth and cream or half-and-half	Curry
Consommé but only 1/3 Madeira wine	Minced parsley

Substantial Soups

Hearty soups in their time play many parts. They introduce a light meal, they are the mainstay of lunch or supper, and they step forth solo to form many a special repast.

The Soup Soiree demands a substantial dish. Bouillabaisse ladled out of a steaming tureen caps any evening activity. A gumbo with rice hits the spot. On a hot night, cold gazpacho with its assorted toppings satisfies as it refreshes.

Soup *plus* suits everybody for lunch or supper: soup and a salad for sophisticated palates, soup and dessert for the children, soup and a sandwich for everybody. There is nothing as comforting as a hearty hot soup—a good, old-fashioned vegetable beef soup full of succulent soup meat and vegetables, a thick pea soup afloat with frankfurter rounds or hunks of ham, a creamy chowder full of fish.

A hearty soup is a boon to menu making. What goes better before a lamb chop than leek and potato soup? What heralds an omelet better than oxtail? What better precedes a light fish dish than black bean soup?

Certain hearty soups have traditional garnishes. You can't imagine that black bean soup without a slice of lemon and chopped or sliced hard-cooked egg afloat on it. Chowders are improved by being topped with crumbled crisp bacon. With split pea soup you can pass a bowl of toasted croutons, to be sprinkled and consumed before they wilt, or fried croutons so hot they sizzle as they are spooned on.

Don't forget to look in other chapters for hearty soups. A cream soup can be hearty when it is made of corn, potato, or chicken. All the peasant soups are designed for lusty appetites and so are America's great chowders.

CHICKEN GUMBO

1 4-pound hen
1 tablespoon salt
2 quarts water
1/2 pound ham, diced
1 cup celery, diced
1 tablespoon bacon fat or butter
1 bay leaf
2 tablespoons chopped parsley
1/2 teaspoon thyme
3 cups sliced okra, boiled 10 minutes, or 1 package frozen
2 tablespoons filé powder
5 cups cooked rice, hot

Cut up the hen and boil in salted water until tender, about 2 hours. Remove chicken; set broth aside. Cut chicken into large bite-sized pieces. Sauté the ham and celery in fat or butter; add the bay leaf, parsley, and thyme. Cook a few minutes. Add this and okra to the chicken broth. You need about 6 cups of broth. Simmer 10 minutes. Add the chicken and reheat. Just before serving, add the filé powder. Serve on rice in soup plates.

Serves 6 to 8.

VARIATION

CHICKEN OYSTER GUMBO

Heat 18 large or 24 small oysters in their broth for 2 to 3 minutes. Pour the hot oysters and broth into the soup just before serving.

Serves 8.

TURKEY SOUP

Turkey carcass
2 quarts water
1 large onion, cut up
3 carrots, cut up
3 stalks celery with leaves, cut up
1/4 cup chopped parsley
1 bay leaf
Leftover gravy
2 cups raw fine noodles or rice
Leftover bits of turkey meat
1/4 cup sherry (optional)

Break up the carcass and put into a large soup kettle with water, onion, carrot, celery, parsley, and the bay leaf. Add any leftover gravy. Simmer for 2 hours. Strain and chill. Remove fat and reheat. Add noodles or rice and bits of turkey. Cook 15 minutes. Season to taste. Add sherry if you wish.

Serves 6 to 8.

SPLIT PEA SOUP

Ham hock or bone
2 quarts water
1 onion
2 cloves
1 bay leaf
1 pound quick-cooking split green peas
Salt
Leftover ham, cut-up
1/2 cup cream

Boil the ham hock in water with onion, cloves, bay leaf, and peas for 1 hour. Remove ham hock or bone and cloves, and buzz peas in a blender with a little of the broth. Return to remaining broth. Season with salt to taste. Add a little cut-up ham and the cream, and reheat.

Serves 8.

VARIATIONS

PEA BEAN SOUP

Substitute white pea beans for the peas.

LENTIL SOUP

Substitute lentils for the peas. Leave them whole or buzz half of them in the blender.

RED KIDNEY BEAN SOUP

Substitute kidney beans. Puree some or all of the beans or leave whole.

PEA SOUP WITH FRANKFURTERS

1 1/2 cups dried split peas
1 large onion, chopped
2 to 3 carrots, chopped
1 1/2 quarts ham or tongue broth or 1 1/2 quarts
    of water and 1 ham hock
1 bay leaf
1/4 teaspoon pepper
Salt
3 frankfurters
2 cups water

Cover the peas, onion, and carrots with the liquid
in which you have cooked ham or tongue or use
water and a ham hock. Use enough liquid to be sure
the vegetables are covered. Add the bay leaf and
pepper. Cover and simmer until peas are tender,
about 1 hour. Season with salt and additional pepper
to taste. Simmer the frankfurters in 2 cups water for
10 minutes and add the water to the soup. Slice the
frankfurters and serve in the soup. If you used ham
hock, remove it and cut off bits of ham from the
bone and add to the soup.

Serves 8 to 10.

BOULA

3 pounds fresh green peas or 3 boxes frozen
  green peas
4 cups turtle soup
1/4 cup sherry
1/2 teaspoon salt
1/4 teaspoon freshly ground pepper
1/3 cup cream, whipped

Cook the peas until very tender in a little salted water. Buzz in a blender with a little of the water they were cooked in until smooth. You may drain and force them through a fine sieve if you prefer. Add the turtle soup and heat; add sherry, salt, and pepper. Adjust seasoning to taste. Divide into 8 oven-proof soup bowls and top each with a spoonful of whipped cream. Put the bowls under the broiler for 2 to 3 minutes until the cream is lightly browned.

Serves 8.

SHORTCUT BOULA

1 (10 1/2-ounce) can pea soup
1 can turtle soup
2 tablespoons Madeira or sweet sherry
Cream, whipped

Heat the two soups together and add the Madeira. Put into individual cups or casseroles, top with whipped cream, and brown under the broiler for a few minutes.

Serves 4.

BLACK BEAN SOUP

3 cups dried black beans
3 quarts water
1 ham bone
4 slices bacon or 2 ounces salt pork, diced
2 cloves garlic
1 large onion, chopped
1 teaspoon salt
1/4 teaspoon pepper
1/4 cup sherry
Slices of lemon
Slices of hard-cooked egg

Soak the beans in water with the ham bone for 8 hours. Add bacon or salt pork and garlic. Simmer in the same water for two hours. Add the onion, salt, and pepper; cook 1 hour. Remove ham bone and buzz soup in blender. Just before serving, heat, add sherry, and garnish with slices of lemon and egg.

Serves 8.

SHORTCUT BLACK BEAN SOUP

2 (10 1/2-ounce) cans black bean soup
3 cups water
1 onion, quartered and stuck with 4 cloves
1/4 cup sherry and/or 2 tablespoons lemon juice
1 chopped hard-cooked egg
1/2 lemon, sliced thin

Mix the soup with water, add onion, and bring to a boil. Shut off heat, add sherry or lemon juice, and serve at once topped with chopped egg and lemon slices or pass the egg and lemon separately.

Serves 6.

LEEK AND POTATO SOUP

4 to 6 leeks
3 tablespoons butter
6 new potatoes, peeled and cut up
1 1/2 quarts water
2 teaspoons salt
Garlic salt (optional)

Cut up the leeks and sauté in butter until softened. Add potatoes, salt, and a quart of water. Simmer for 1 hour. Mash the potatoes into the liquid. Add 1 to 2 cups more water to achieve the consistency you want. Adjust seasoning and add garlic if you wish.

Serves 6.

SHORTCUT BORSCH

1 (1-pound) can beets
1 large onion, chopped fine
1 clove garlic, crushed
3 tablespoons butter
2 cups water
3 bouillon cubes
1 tablespoon lemon juice
1 teaspoon salt
1/4 teaspoon pepper
4 tablespoons sour cream

Buzz the beets in a blender with their liquid. Sauté the onion and garlic in butter for 3 minutes. Combine the beets, onion and garlic, water, bouillon cubes, lemon juice, salt, and pepper; bring to a boil. Serve topped with a tablespoon of sour cream on each serving. Serve hot or cold.

Serves 4.

PUMPKIN SOUP

1/2 medium-sized pumpkin or 3 cups canned pumpkin puree
About 1 quart lightly salted water
2 teaspoons salt
1/4 cup butter
1 teaspoon sugar
1/4 teaspoon white pepper
1 quart milk

Cut up the pumpkin flesh and boil in lightly salted water just to cover until tender. Force through a sieve or buzz in a blender. You will need about 3 cups puree. Combine the puree, butter, sugar, salt, and pepper in a pan; simmer for 10 minutes. Pour in the milk and simmer for 3 minutes more.

Serves 6 to 8.

SHORTCUT MINESTRONE

6 slices of bacon
1 small onion, chopped
2 stalks celery, chopped
1 tablespoon chopped parsley
1 (1-pound) can kidney beans
1 can (8-ounce) spaghetti sauce or (6-ounce)
   tomato paste
1/2 cup rice
6 cups beef broth or consommé
1/4 head cabbage, shredded
1 cup thin elbow macaroni

Sauté the bacon, remove, and set aside. Add onion, celery, and parsley to drippings; cook until soft. Add this mixture, beans, spaghetti sauce or tomato paste, and rice to the broth. Simmer covered for 10 minutes. Add cabbage and macaroni and cook 10 minutes more. Just before serving, add the bacon, crumbled.

Serves 8.

BLENDER GAZPACHO

1 (14 1/2-ounce) can tomato juice
1/2 Spanish onion
2 cloves garlic
1 teaspoon salt
1/4 teaspoon pepper
1/2 teaspoon basil
1/4 cup olive oil
1/2 green pepper, cut up
2 cucumbers, cut up
2 tablespoons bread crumbs
3 cups cold water or broth or half of each
Cracked ice or ice cubes

Mix all ingredients except water and ice in a large mixing bowl. Half at a time, buzz in the blender, adding 1 cup of water or broth to each blenderful. Stir in the remaining liquid and chill. Serve with a little cracked ice or an ice cube in each serving.

Serves 6.

COLD CUCUMBER SOUP

3 cups diced cucumbers
1/2 cup minced green onions
1 cup diced raw potatoes
3 cups chicken broth
1/2 teaspoon curry powder
1/2 teaspoon salt
1/4 teaspoon white pepper
1/2 teaspoon dry mustard
1/2 cup heavy cream
Minced parsley or mint

Combine the cucumber, onions, potatoes, chicken broth, curry, salt, pepper, and mustard in a saucepan. Simmer for 10 to 15 minutes. Buzz in a blender or force through a sieve. Chill. Add the cream and garnish with minced parsley or mint.

Serves 6.

SPECIAL CRAB PEA TOMATO SOUP

2 cans (8-ounce) crab meat or 1/2 pound fresh crab meat
4 ounces sherry
2 (10 1/2-ounce) cans pea soup
1 (10 1/2-ounce) can tomato soup
2 cups light cream or half-and-half

Pick over the crab meat, pour 2 ounces of sherry over it, and let it stand for a few hours in the refrigerator. Combine the pea soup, tomato soup, and cream or half-and-half in a saucepan. Heat and stir. Add the crab meat and sherry; reheat thoroughly. Just before serving, add remaining sherry. If soup is thicker than you want, add a little hot milk.

Serves 6 to 8.

SALMON TOMATO BISQUE

1 (1-pound) can salmon
1 (10 1/2-ounce) can tomato puree
2 tablespoons minced parsley
2 cups water
1 medium onion, minced
2 tablespoons butter
2 tablespoons flour
2 cups half-and-half
1/2 teaspoon salt
1/4 teaspoon white pepper

Put the salmon and its liquid into a saucepan with the tomato puree, parsley, and water. Simmer for 15 minutes. Meanwhile sauté the onions in butter for a few minutes over medium heat, blend in the flour, and add the half-and-half gradually while stirring. Cook for 5 minutes. Add this to the salmon mixture, season with salt and pepper, and cook 3 minutes. Adjust seasoning as some salmon is saltier than others.

Serves 6 to 8.

SALMON POTATO BISQUE

1 (1-pound) can salmon
2 (10 1/2-ounce) cans frozen potato soup
3 cups milk
2 tablespoons minced parsley
2 tablespoons minced chives

Put the salmon and its liquid and the potato soup in a saucepan. Break the salmon up with a fork and smash any lumps of potatoes. Add the milk and simmer for 10 minutes. Strain if you wish. Add parsley and chives. Serve hot.

Serves 6 to 8.

BUTTERMILK SHRIMP SOUP

1 pound cooked shrimp
1 small onion, minced
1/2 teaspoon salt
1/4 teaspoon pepper
1 1/2 quarts buttermilk
Paprika

Chop the shrimp. Sprinkle with minced onion, salt, and pepper. Heat gently with the buttermilk. Garnish with paprika.

Serves 6.

MUSSEL SOUP

4 to 5 pounds fresh mussels
2 cups white wine
2 cups water
1 large onion, chopped
2 carrots, chopped fine
1 clove garlic, crushed
1 teaspoon thyme or dill
1/4 teaspoon white pepper
2 tablespoons minced parsley

Scrub the mussels thoroughly and debeard. Put into a large kettle with wine and water and cook only until the shells open. Remove mussels; add the onion, carrots, garlic, thyme or dill, pepper, and 1 tablespoon parsley to the liquid. Simmer, covered, until vegetables are tender, about 30 minutes. Meanwhile remove mussels from their shells. Add half of them to the broth, saving the smaller ones. Simmer 10 minutes; buzz the soup in a blender, half at a time. Reheat with remaining mussels and season to taste. Garnish with remaining parsley.

Serves 6.

EASY FISH CHOWDER

2 ounces salt pork, diced
2 onions, sliced
3 potatoes, diced
1 carrot, sliced
1 stalk celery, chopped
1 bay leaf
1 quart water
1 1/2 pounds fish fillets
1 tall can (13 ounces) evaporated milk
1 teaspoon salt
1/2 teaspoon white pepper
1 tablespoon butter
Paprika

Brown the pork, remove, and set aside. Sauté the onions, potatoes, carrot, and celery in pork fat for 3 minutes. Add bay leaf and water. Cook covered for 10 minutes. Add fish and simmer 5 minutes. Add milk, salt, and pepper; reheat. Just before serving, add butter and paprika. Serve with soda crackers.

Serves 6.

BOUILLABAISSE

6 pounds assorted fish and shellfish, as many kinds as are available: halibut, sole, eel, cod, flounder, sea bass, any white fish; lobster, lobster tails, shrimp, scallops, crab meat, and mussels or clams in their shells.
Fish scraps
1 teaspoon salt
6 cups water
2 leeks or 4 scallions, chopped
1/2 cup chopped onion
1/2 cup chopped celery
3 tomatoes, diced
1/4 cup olive oil
4 sprigs parsley
1 pint clam juice (optional)
3 cloves garlic, crushed
1/2 teaspoon thyme
1/2 teaspoon basil or rosemary
1/4 teaspoon saffron
1 teaspoon grated orange peel
1 cup white wine (optional)

Cut off heads, tails, and skins from the fish; set the pieces of fish aside; add any fish scraps you can buy or the fishman will give you. Cook fish scraps in salted water to cover for 30 minutes. Meanwhile sauté all of the vegetables in olive oil for 5 minutes while stirring. Add to the soup pot with parsley and cook for half an hour. Strain the soup, pressing out all the fish and vegetable juices. Or you may remove the fish heads and scraps and return the vegetables to the strained soup if you prefer. Add the clam juice unless you have 6 cups of broth with real fish flavor, the herbs, orange peel, and fish, which has been cut into large serving pieces. Simmer 10 minutes. Add the raw shellfish and the wine and simmer 10 minutes more. Do not overcook. Taste for salt, there should be enough if you use clam juice, which is very salty. Serve with 3/4-inch rounds of toasted French bread.

Serves 6 to 8.

There are many, many versions of bouillabaisse, which is a fish stew. You must have fish, you should have some shellfish, and you need olive oil, onion, garlic, tomatoes, and herbs including saffron. If you don't have fish to make stock, use water and clam juice, and white wine, or sherry.

Serves 8 to 10.

SHORTCUT BOUILLABAISSE

2 stalks celery, chopped
3 onions, chopped
2 cloves garlic, crushed
1/4 cup olive oil
3 pounds assorted small saltwater white-flesh fish
2 pounds fish scraps
1 tablespoon salt
2 quarts water
parsley sprigs
1/2 teaspoon pepper
1/2 teaspoon saffron or 1 tablespoon Worcester-
    shire sauce and/or 1 teaspoon curry
2 cups canned tomatoes
1/2 pound lobster meat
2 cans (7–8 ounces) wet-pack shrimp

Sauté celery, onion and garlic in olive oil for 5 minutes while stirring. Set aside. Cut off heads, tails,
and skin from the fish; set the pieces of fish aside;
add any fish scraps you can buy or the fishman will
give you. Boil scraps, covered, in salted water with
sauted vegetables and parsley sprigs for 1 hour.
Strain. Mix pepper, saffron, and tomatoes. Cut the
fish in large bite-sized pieces and add. Pour in 6 cups
of the water the fish scraps were cooked in, bring to
a boil, and cook for 3 to 4 minutes. Add the lobster
and shrimp with their liquid and cook 3 or 4 minutes more. Add more salt to taste. Serve with toasted
French bread.

Serves 10.

Mix mates for hearty soups are very successful—use canned, frozen, or dehydrated. Add a topping to suit yourself. Also try combining two cans of one kind with one of another. Experiment!

Take equal parts of:	Add a little:
Consommé and black bean soup	Chopped hard-cooked egg and sherry
Consommé and pea soup	Minced scallions
Chicken broth and mulligatawny	Sherry
Chicken broth and oxtail soup	Worcestershire sauce
Tomato soup and milk	Minced parsley
Tomato soup and pea soup	Sherry and basil
Tomato soup and split pea soup and milk	Croutons
Tomato soup and cream of oyster soup	Dill
Tomato soup and corn chowder	Crumbled bacon
Cream of celery soup and minced clams	Crisp bacon bits
Cream of celery soup and oyster soup	Sliced lemon
Oyster soup and pepper pot	Curry
New England fish or clam soup and milk	Crisp, diced salt pork
Pea soup and mock turtle soup	Sherry

Pea soup and tomato juice	Curry
Green pea soup and milk	Croutons
Chicken broth and onion soup	Grated cheese
Tomato sauce and consommé	Minced chives
Tomato juice and clam chowder	Croutons or crackers
Tomato juice and clam broth	Whipped cream and celery salt
Clam chowder and chicken gumbo	Pilot bread or crackers
Turtle soup but only 1/4 sherry	Minced parsley

iv

Foreign Soups

Every country has a favorite soup. You can take a cook's tour of the world in your own soup kettle. Whether you are a traveler, a reader, or just a cook, borsch means Russia to you, minestrone spells Italy, curry suggests India, kangaroo-tail soup can only come from Australia.

Peasant soups are great. The folk on the land count on the soup pot to provide their chief fare. We can't feel sorry for them; they are getting the best of good eating. Over the years various peoples have developed their own delicious, indigenous dishes made from whatever is at hand, spiced and seasoned with the herbs and condiments they like best—chili in Mexico, tarragon in France, caraway in Germany, sesame in the Near East, soy in the Orient. All are available to us too as we copy these great soups.

Favorite foreign adornments are equally easy for us. Every Frenchman knows it is not real onion soup without its floating round of French bread, toasted and topped with Parmesan cheese. Borsch— Russian, Polish, or American—never appears without sour cream. Vichyssoise, hot or cold, rejoices in a sprinkling of minced scallions or chives. Gazpacho may appear with a choice of minced vegetables— green pepper, tomato flesh, onion, celery—but always it has cucumbers. Grated cheese sharpens the zest of many a foreign soup.

ARMENIAN LAMB TOMATO SOUP

6 cups lamb broth or 4 cups lamb broth and 2
   cups chicken broth
4 large tomatoes, peeled and chopped; or 1
   (1-pound 13-ounce) can tomatoes
1 cup rice
1/2 teaspoon sugar
1 teaspoon salt
1/2 teaspoon freshly ground pepper
1/4 cup chopped parsley
Pinch basil

Put the broth in a soup kettle with tomatoes, rice,
sugar, salt, pepper, parsley, and basil. Simmer covered for 30 minutes. Adjust seasoning.

Serves 8.

BELGIAN CHICKEN SOUP
(Waterzooi)

1 (3-pound) broiler with feet
Veal bones
2 sprigs parsley
2 stalks celery
1 teaspoon salt
1/2 teaspoon pepper
5 cups water
1 cup white wine
2 tablespoons butter
1/3 cup bread crumbs

Put the cut-up chicken including feet, liver, heart, and gizzard in a soup kettle with veal bones, parsley, celery, salt, pepper, and the water. Bring to a boil and skim. Simmer covered for about 30 minutes. Remove the chicken pieces to a casserole and continue to cook the broth for 1 hour. Strain and pour broth over the chicken, add the wine, and cook 30 minutes until chicken is tender. Stir in the butter and the bread crumbs and serve.

Serves 6.

CANADIAN CHEDDAR CHEESE SOUP

1 tablespoon minced onion
2 tablespoons butter
3 tablespoons flour
3 cups beef broth
2 cups milk
1/2 cup grated cheddar cheese
1/2 teaspoon pepper

Sauté the onion in butter for 2 to 3 minutes, add flour, and blend. Gradually stir in the broth and add the milk. Bring to a boil and add the cheese and pepper. Simmer and stir until cheese is all melted. Season to taste.

Serves 6.

CANARY ISLAND EEL SOUP

2 1/2 pounds fresh or frozen conger or other eel
Salt
1/4 cup butter
2 large potatoes, chopped
4 large tomatoes, chopped
2 large onions, chopped
1 quart water
1 clove garlic, crushed
1/2 teaspoon thyme
1 teaspoon salt
1/2 teaspoon pepper
2 tablespoons chopped parsley
1 tablespoon lemon juice

Cut the eel crosswise into 3-inch pieces and sprinkle with salt. Let stand overnight or a number of hours. Rinse in cold water. Skin and sauté in butter for 10 minutes. Add the potatoes, tomatoes, and onion; stir and cook for 3 to 4 minutes. Remove to a soup kettle and add the water. Add garlic, thyme, salt, and pepper; simmer for 1 hour. Add parsley and lemon juice. Serve as is, or remove bones from eel and return flesh to the soup, or strain and serve clear.

Serves 8.

CHINESE EGG-DROP SOUP
(Tan-Tang)

5 cups chicken or beef broth
3/4 cup minced celery
1/2 teaspoon salt
1/4 teaspoon pepper
1 teaspoon sugar
1/2 teaspoon monosodium glutamate
2 tablespoons cornstarch
1/4 cup cold water
1 egg

Put the broth into a soup kettle with celery and seasonings. Simmer for 15 minutes. Smooth the cornstarch with water and stir into the soup. Stir and cook until clear and thickened. Add the slightly beaten egg while stirring rapidly and remove immediately from heat.

Serves 6.

CZECHOSLOVAKIAN BEER SOUP
(Pivni Polepka)

1 quart beer
1 quart water
2 tablespoons sugar
1 tablespoon butter
3 egg yolks
1 cup heavy cream

Bring the beer and water to a boil together. Add the sugar and butter. Cook for 20 minutes. Beat the egg yolks and the cream, then add a little hot beer mixture slowly, stirring steadily. Add this mixture to the beer mixture and heat. Do not let the soup boil again.

Serves 8.

DANISH CABBAGE SOUP
(Brumkaalsuppe)

2 pounds cabbage
1/4 cup butter
1/4 teaspoon salt
1 teaspoon sugar
6 cups beef broth or canned consommé
1/2 teaspoon pepper

Shred the cabbage and sauté it in melted butter while stirring. Sprinkle with salt and sugar; cook slowly for 30 minutes, stirring frequently. The cabbage should be browned. Add the broth or consommé and simmer for 1 hour. Add pepper and adjust salt to taste.

Serves 8.

DUTCH PEA SOUP
(Snert)

1 pound beef shin
1/2 pound pork
2 to 3 pounds pork knuckle
2 quarts water
1 teaspoon salt
1/2 teaspoon pepper
1 pound split peas
2 stalks celery, cut up
3 leeks, sliced
1 pound smoked sausage, sliced

Put the beef, pork, and pork knuckle into a big soup kettle with water, salt, and pepper. Cover and simmer slowly for 2 hours. Remove meat, return bones to pot, add peas, and cook slowly for 1 hour. Strain. Add celery and leeks and cook 1 hour. Cool slightly and skim off excess fat. Add sliced sausage and return a little cut-up beef and lean pork to the soup. Cook for 10 minutes.

Serves 8.

EGYPTIAN LAMB SOUP
(Dügün Chorbas)

2 pounds lamb and bones
1 onion
1 carrot
2 teaspoons salt
2 quarts water
6 tablespoons butter
3 tablespoons flour
2 egg yolks
2 tablespoons lemon juice

Put the lamb and bones in a soup kettle with onion, carrot, salt, and water. Simmer covered for 2 hours. Strain. Mince the meat and return to the broth. Melt 3 tablespoons butter, stir in the flour, add a little soup, and stir until smooth. Add to the broth in the kettle and bring to a boil. Simmer 10 minutes. Beat the egg yolks and lemon juice, add a cup of soup to this while stirring, and return to the soup while stirring. Heat but do not let the soup boil. Add 3 tablespoons butter just before serving.

Serves 8.

ENGLISH MULLIGATAWNY

1 (3-pound) chicken
1/4 pound diced salt pork or butter
2 tablespoons flour
1 tablespoon curry
2 quarts chicken broth or water
1/2 cup diced carrot
1/2 cup chopped onion
1/2 cup chopped celery
1 apple, peeled and chopped
2 cloves
2 teaspoons salt
1/2 teaspoon freshly ground pepper
1 teaspoon sugar
1 cup cream
3/4 cup cooked rice, hot

Brown the cut-up chicken in fried salt pork or in butter. Sprinkle with flour and curry. Transfer to a large pot. Add the broth or water, carrot, onion, celery, apple, cloves, salt, pepper, and sugar. Cover and simmer until the chicken is tender, 1 to 1 1/2 hours. Remove chicken, and when cool enough to handle, pull meat from the bones and cut up. Strain the soup, forcing through a sieve. Add the cut-up chicken to the soup. Add cream. Adjust seasoning and simmer for 5 minutes. Place a heaping tablespoon of fluffy rice in each soup plate and fill with soup.

Serves 8.

FRENCH ONION SOUP
(Soupe à l'oignon gratinée)

4 large onions, sliced
2 tablespoons butter
6 cups beef broth
1 teaspoon Worcestershire sauce or 1/4 teaspoon
  Tabasco sauce
6 toasted slices of French bread
Grated Parmesan cheese

In a soup kettle, sauté and stir the onion rings in
butter until light brown. Add the broth and the
Worcestershire sauce or Tabasco. Cover and simmer
until onions are tender, about 15 minutes. Adjust
seasoning. Toast the French bread slices in the oven.
When ready to serve, divide the soup into 6 earthen-
ware bowls or other over-proof dishes. Place a piece
of toast on each. Sprinkle with cheese and put under
broiler to melt. Or you may pass the toast and
cheese separately.

Serves 6.

GERMAN CHICKEN NOODLE SOUP
(Koeniginssuppe)

2 quarts chicken broth
2 eggs
1/4 cup cream
1/2 pound noodles
Julienne strips of cooked chicken (optional garnish)
Chopped almonds (garnish)

Heat the broth. Beat the eggs with cream and add a little hot broth while stirring. When you have beaten in about two cups of broth, add to the kettle. Add the noodles, cooked in salted water, to the broth. If you have some cooked chicken available, cut into thin julienne strips and add with the noodles. Heat but do not allow the soup to boil. Garnish with almonds.

Serves 8.

GREEK LEMON SOUP
(Avgolemono)

3 pounds chicken backs and wings
1 mild onion
1 stalk celery
2 carrots
2 teaspoons salt
2 1/2 quarts water
1/2 cup rice
3 egg yolks
3 tablespoons lemon juice
Thin lemon slices (garnish)

Put the chicken into a soup kettle with onion, celery, carrots, and salt. Cover with the water and bring to a boil. Skim, reduce heat, and cook for 2 hours. Strain. Add the rice and simmer for 20 minutes. Beat the egg yolks with the lemon juice. Add a little soup slowly to the egg-lemon mixture while stirring. Add to kettle and heat but don't let the soup boil. Serve with slices of lemon on top.

Serves 8.

SHORTCUT GREEK LEMON SOUP
(Avgolemono)

1/4 cup rice
1 quart chicken broth
2 egg yolks
Juice 2 lemons

Simmer the rice in broth until tender, 15 to 20 minutes. Beat the egg yolks and stir in a cup of the soup. Add to the soup while stirring. When soup is hot, add the lemon juice and serve at once.

Serves 4.

HAWAIIAN PINEAPPLE PUMPKIN SOUP

4 tablespoons chopped parsley
1/2 cup minced scallions
1/4 cup butter
2 (9-ounce) cans crushed pineapple
1 (1-pound) can pumpkin
3 cups milk
1 cup water
1/2 teaspoon salt
1/8 teaspoon paprika

Sauté 2 tablespoons parsley and the scallions in butter in a soup kettle until lightly browned. Add pineapple, pumpkin, milk, and water. Bring to a boil and add salt and paprika. Serve garnished with remaining minced parsley.

Serves 8.

HUNGARIAN GOULASH SOUP

1 pound lean beef
1 pound lean pork
1 pound lamb
1/2 pound ham
4 onions, chopped
3 tablespoons butter
2 tablespoons paprika
1 teaspoon salt
1 teaspoon pepper
2 green peppers, diced
2 tomatoes, peeled and chopped
1 1/2 quarts water
4 potatoes, peeled and cubed

Cut the meat into 1-inch cubes. Brown the onions slightly in butter, add meats, and brown, stirring steadily. Add paprika, salt, and pepper; cook slowly 15 minutes. Add green pepper, tomatoes, and water; cook for 40 minutes. Add the potatoes and cook for 20 minutes.

Serves 8 to 10.

INDONESIAN CURRY SOUP
(Sajur Kare)

1 cup diced cooked chicken or beef
1 tablespoon peanut oil
2 teaspoons peanut butter
1 teaspoon curry
3 cups chicken or beef broth
1/2 cup diced potatoes
1/2 cup diced carrot
1 bay leaf
1/2 cup chopped onions
1 cup milk
1 tablespoon butter

Sauté the meat in the peanut oil in a soup kettle.
Add peanut butter and curry. Add the broth and
bring to a boil. Add potatoes, carrots, bay leaf, and
1/4 cup onion. Cover and simmer 15 to 20 minutes.
Add milk, heat, and serve. Garnish with remaining
onion sautéd in butter.

Serves 4.

IRANIAN DILL SOUP

1 1/2 quarts chicken broth
2 tablespoons flour
1/4 cup water
2/3 cup sour cream
2 egg yolks
3 tablespoons fresh dill leaves or 1 tablespoon
    dried dill
1 tablespoon soy sauce

Heat the broth, add flour mixed with water, and boil for 1 to 2 minutes. Remove from heat and slowly stir in the sour cream mixed with slightly beaten egg yolks, dill, and soy sauce. Reheat but do not boil.

Serves 6 to 8.

IRISH POTATO SOUP

4 medium-sized potatoes
1 quart water
2 medium onions, sliced
1 bay leaf
1/2 cup half-and-half or cream or milk
2 teaspoons salt
1/2 teaspoon pepper
Pinch thyme
3 tablespoons butter

Peel and slice the potatoes. Put into a soup kettle with water, onions, and bay leaf. Simmer covered for 45 minutes. Force through a sieve or buzz in a blender. Add half-and-half, salt, pepper, and thyme; cook for 15 minutes. Add butter and serve.

Serves 6.

ITALIAN MINESTRONE

1 cup white beans or kidney beans
2 quarts water
1/4 pound salt pork
2 tablespoons olive oil
1 onion, sliced
1/2 cup diced celery
2 carrots, diced
1 zucchini, diced
1 potato, diced
1 large tomato, peeled and diced
2 tablespoons chopped parsley
1 clove garlic, crushed
2 teaspoons salt
1/2 teaspoon pepper
1/2 small head cabbage, shredded
1 cup thin macaroni or vermicelli or 1/2 cup rice
1 cup Parmesan cheese

Soak the beans overnight or for several hours. Simmer for 1 hour in water with the rind of the pork. Mince the pork and put in a separate kettle with oil. Add the onion and cook until softened. Add celery, carrot, zucchini, potato, tomato, parsley, garlic, salt, and pepper. Add to the beans and water and simmer for 1 1/2 hours. For the last 20 minutes, add the cabbage and the macaroni or vermicelli, broken into small pieces, or the rice. Stir in 1/2 cup cheese and serve. The soup should be very thick. Pass more cheese.

Serves 8.

NORWEGIAN FISH SOUP

1 pound fresh halibut or other white fish
2 pounds fish heads and scraps
1 1/2 quarts water
1 teaspoon salt
1 carrot, cubed
1 stalk celery, cubed
2 tablespoons chopped parsley
2 cups water
3 tablespoons butter
2 tablespoons flour
3 egg yolks
1/2 pint sour cream
1/2 teaspoon pepper
1 teaspoon sugar
Chopped chives (garnish)

Simmer the fish and cut-up fish scraps in 1 1/2 quarts of salted water for 30 minutes. Simmer the cut-up vegetables in 2 cups of water until rather soft but not mushy. Strain the fish stock and return it to the kettle. Cut up the fish and add the fish and the vegetables to the kettle. Reserve the vegetable water. Melt the butter and blend in the flour. Stir in the vegetable water and add this to the kettle. Mix the egg yolks with sour cream. Pour in a little of the hot fish soup while stirring vigorously. Pour this mixture into the kettle, add pepper and sugar, and heat but do not let the soup boil. Serve topped with minced chives.

Serves 8.

POLISH SORREL SOUP
(Zupa Czczawiowa)

4 cups beef broth
2 tablespoons flour
1/2 cup milk
2 cups sorrel or 2 jars baby food spinach and 2
    tablespoons lemon juice
1 egg yolk
1 tablespoon butter
1/2 teaspoon salt
1 cup cooked rice, hot

Heat the broth. Mix the flour and milk and add to
the broth. Bring to a boil. Add sorrel or spinach and
lemon juice. Mix the egg yolk with melted butter
and stir in. Add salt to taste—the quantity will depend upon the seasoning in the broth. Serve over
the rice.

Serves 6 to 8.

PORTUGUESE GREEN SOUP
(Caldo Verde)

6 potatoes
2 quarts water
1/4 cup olive oil
1 tablespoon salt
1/2 teaspoon pepper
Dash Tabasco sauce
3 cups shredded cabbage
2 cups spinach, chopped

Peel and dice the potatoes, cover with the water, add olive oil, and cook until the potatoes are very tender. Mash or put them through a coarse sieve. Return them to the liquid in the kettle; add salt, pepper, and the Tabasco. Simmer about 20 minutes; add cabbage and spinach; cook another 30 minutes. Serve hot or cold.

Serves 6 to 8.

RUSSIAN BORSCH
(Bortsch Koop)

2 1/2 pounds beef shin
3 tablespoons butter
3 onions, sliced
3 carrots, sliced thin
3 stalks celery and leaves, chopped
2 sprigs parsley
2 potatoes
6 cups water or consommé or half of each
1 (1-pound 13-ounce) can tomatoes
10 beets, sliced
1 bay leaf
2 cloves garlic, crushed
2 teaspoons salt
1 tablespoon sugar
8 tablespoons sour cream

Cut meat from the bones and brown in butter in a soup kettle. Add the bones, onions, carrots, celery, parsley, and potatoes. Stir and brown slightly. Add water or consommé or half of each; cover and simmer 1 hour. Add tomatoes, beets, bay leaf, garlic, salt, and sugar. Simmer 3 hours. Cool and remove fat. Reheat and strain. Serve topped with sour cream.

Serves 8.

SCOTCH BROTH

1 pound lamb, cut up
1 pound lamb bones, tied in cheesecloth
2 quarts water
1 cup chopped onion
1 cup diced celery
1 cup diced carrots
1 teaspoon salt
1/4 teaspoon pepper
1/2 cup barley
1/2 cup chopped parsley

Put all ingredients except barley and parsley in a soup kettle. Cover and simmer 1 1/2 hours. Skim. Add barley and cook 30 minutes or until meat and barley are very tender. Remove cheesecloth with bones; season broth to taste. Serve sprinkled with parsley.

Serves 8.

GAZPACHO VARIATIONS

There are almost as many receipes as there are Spanish chefs! All include tomatoes, olive oil, onion, garlic, and usually bread. The ingredients traditionally were pounded in a large, wooden bowl; now we (and the Spanish) use a blender. You may, but need not, serve extra diced vegetables as a garnish.

All Spanish versions have about 1/4 cup olive oil for six servings. Americans use less or sometimes no oil at all.

SPANISH GAZPACHO

2 large tomatoes, peeled; or 1 (1-pound 4-ounce) can tomatoes
1 (14 1/2-ounce) can chicken broth
2 cloves garlic
1 cucumber, peeled and chopped fine
6 scallions, chopped fine
1 green pepper, chopped fine
1 teaspoon tarragon
2 tablespoons wine vinegar
2 tablespoons olive oil
1 teaspoon sugar
1 teaspoon salt
1/4 teaspoon pepper
8 ice cubes
2 cups croutons or 1 cup toasted bread crumbs

Buzz the tomatoes, broth, and garlic in a blender. Stir in the vegetables; add tarragon, vinegar, oil, sugar, salt, and pepper. Stir well and chill. Serve with a few ice cubes in the tureen or 1 in each soup bowl. Pass the hot croutons or bread crumbs. In Spain additional chopped raw vegetables are often served on the side for each person to help himself.

Serves 6.

GAZPACHO ANDALUZ

2 cloves garlic
1 teaspoon salt
1 teaspoon sugar
8 large fresh tomatoes, peeled and chopped; or
   1 (1-pound 13-ounce) can tomatoes
1 cucumber, peeled and chopped fine
3 tablespoons olive oil
1 tablespoon vinegar
3 cups chicken broth
6 ice cubes
Chopped scallions or chopped pitted black olives
   (garnish)

Mash the garlic with salt and sugar and buzz in
blender with tomatoes, cucumber, olive oil, and vinegar. Chill and combine with broth. Season to taste
—the amount of salt will depend upon the seasoning
in the broth. Serve with an ice cube in each cup.
Garnish with chopped scallions or olives.

Serves 6.

GAZPACHO OF SEVILLE

2 cloves garlic
1 teaspoon salt
1 canned pimento
3 tablespoons olive oil
1/4 cup dry bread crumbs
8 large fresh tomatoes, peeled and chopped; or
   1 (1-pound 13-ounce) can tomatoes, strained
1 tablespoon vinegar
2 cups ice water
6 ice cubes
Minced scallions

Mash garlic into a paste with the salt and pimento. Stir in the oil and bread crumbs. Add tomatoes and vinegar and buzz in blender. Add 2 cups ice water and serve with ice cubes in the soup. Garnish with minced scallions.

Serves 6.

SYRIAN LENTIL SOUP

2 cups dried lentils
2 quarts water
1 large onion, sliced thin
1 teaspoon salt
Pinch thyme
1 pound spinach, chopped fine
Juice 1 lemon
Soy sauce (optional)

Soak the lentils overnight in water to cover. Drain and put into a kettle with 2 quarts water, the onion, salt, and thyme. Simmer covered until lentils are tender, about 2 hours. Add the raw spinach and cook 5 minutes. Add lemon juice and a little soy sauce or more salt to taste.

Serves 8.

TURKISH YOGURT SOUP
(Yugurtlu Corba)

3 cups yogurt
3/4 teaspoon salt
3 cups beef broth
1/4 cup butter
1/2 cup flour
1 tablespoon chopped mint

Put the yogurt in a bowl, add salt, and stir in the broth gradually. Stir until blended and smooth. Melt the butter, stir in the flour, and add to the soup mixture slowly. Bring to a boil. Serve garnished with mint, fresh or dried.

Serves 6.

YUGOSLAVIAN FISH SOUP
(Čorba od Morske Ribe)

2 pounds assorted fish plus fish scraps
1 onion, chopped
2 cloves garlic, minced
3 to 4 sprigs parsley
4 tomatoes, peeled and quartered
1 bay leaf
1 tablespoon salt
6 peppercorns
1/4 cup olive oil
5 cups water
1 cup cooked rice
2 cups white wine

Put half the fish and all heads and scraps into a soup kettle with onion, garlic, parsley, tomatoes, bay leaf, salt, peppercorns, oil, and water. Bring to a rolling boil and simmer covered for 30 minutes. Force through a coarse strainer. Add rice and remaining fish, cut into small bite-sized pieces. Add wine and simmer 5 minutes.

Serves 8.

V

Famous American Soups

America need not yield to any country in the world in the matter of good soup. Every region—north, south, east, and west—has a soup to be proud of. Think of Philadelphia pepper pot, Maryland crab soup, New Orleans shrimp bisque, Maine lobster stew, West Coast abalone chowder, Iowa corn chowder, California artichoke soup, Grand Central oyster stew, Marx Brothers duck soup.

Americans are the most inventive people on the face of the earth, and that goes for soup too. From Colonial days, we have been good at inventing soups to make out of our unique regional delicacies, which have put great soups on American tables. They can do the same for your table. You don't have to live in California to make avocado soup or in New England to enjoy clam chowder. Vegetables and fish, fresh or frozen, travel all over, bringing satisfactory ingredients for far-flung regional specialties.

Many of the recipes in this book were invented by an American named Carol Truax. You'll enjoy following them. But you don't have to be a copycat. You're an American too. Why not strike out on your own?

The Truax method is part necessity, part dumb luck, and part inspiration. If unexpected guests make the supply of oyster soup skimpy, it is necessary to stretch it with something. How about a can of cream

76

of celery soup? Celery and oysters prove a happy mating. As an example of dumb luck, try clam spinach soup. This delicious dish might never have been thought of if an opened can of minced clams had not inadvertently found its way into the spinach in the blender.

What, first and foremost, makes a good soup better? Inspiration! Inspiration added wild mushrooms, sautéed with onion and pureed, to beef consommé and created Pennsylvania mushroom beef soup. In Colorado at the Broadmoor Cooking Club, lamb broth, surprisingly, profited by the addition of chopped oysters and became famous as Martha's oyster soup. Use your own inspiration; it will surely lead to equally new and unusual American soups.

NEW ENGLAND CLAM CHOWDER

1 quart soft clams or 2 dozen littlenecks
1 cup water
1/2 cup white wine
4 slices salt pork or bacon
1 onion, chopped
2 potatoes, diced
2 cups water
2 cups half-and-half
1 teaspoon salt
1/4 teaspoon white pepper
Pinch thyme

Steam 1 quart of soft clams or 2 dozen littlenecks with 1 cup water and 1/2 cup white wine. Strain broth and save; chop the clams. Or buy a pint of canned clams and a pint of extra juice. Fry the pork or bacon, remove when brown, and set aside. Sauté the onion in pork fat until lightly browned. Add potatoes and water and simmer 15 minutes. Add broth and cook 5 minutes. Add chopped clams and hot half-and-half. Heat but do not boil. Season with salt, pepper, and thyme. Top with crumbled salt pork or bacon.

Serves 6.

VARIATION

MANHATTAN CLAM CHOWDER

Substitute 2 cups stewed tomatoes or tomato juice for half-and-half in New England Clam Chowder.

NEW ENGLAND FISH CHOWDER

1/2 pound salt pork, diced
2 large onions, sliced thin or chopped
3 pounds fresh haddock, cod, or halibut with heads and scraps
4 potatoes, peeled and sliced thin
1 teaspoon salt
1/2 teaspoon pepper
1/4 teaspoon paprika
2 cups boiling water
1 quart half-and-half
6 pilot crackers

Fry the salt pork until browned, remove with a slotted spoon, and set aside. Brown the onions lightly in the pork fat. Cut up the fish, heads and all. Add the heads and scraps, saving about half of the best fish. Add potatoes, salt, pepper, and paprika. Add the boiling water, cover, and simmer for 20 minutes. Remove large pieces of bone and head. Add remaining fish, cut into bite-sized pieces, and cook 10 minutes. Add half-and-half and bring to a boil. Serve with pieces of pilot crackers in the tureen or soup plates, and the diced pork.

Serves 8.

MAINE LOBSTER STEW

1/3 cup butter
1 pound lobster meat, fresh or frozen
1 cup fish or lobster broth
3 cups half-and-half
1/2 teaspoon Worcestershire sauce
1 teaspoon salt
Paprika
2 egg yolks

Melt 4 tablespoons butter and add cut-up lobster meat. Stir to coat the lobster with butter. Add the broth, hot half-and-half, Worcestershire sauce, salt, and paprika. Heat to boiling point. Beat egg yolks with a little hot half-and-half, add to the soup, stir, and heat. Add remaining butter and serve at once, topped with a sprinkling of paprika.

Serves 6.

RHODE ISLAND FISH CHOWDER

1/2 pound diced salt pork
2 onions
2 pounds fresh firm white fish: halibut, cod, or
    flounder
2 potatoes, diced
2 cups water
1 (1-pound 4-ounce) can tomatoes
2 tablespoons flour
2 teaspoons salt
1/2 teaspoon white pepper
1 pint milk or half-and-half
1 tablespoon butter
Pilot or water crackers

Fry the salt pork until crisp. Remove pork and set it aside. Sauté the sliced onions in the pork fat until light brown; add the fish, which has been skinned, boned, and cut into good-sized pieces. Add the potatoes, water, and tomatoes. Simmer for 10 minutes. Add flour, salt, pepper, and milk. Bring to a boil, add butter and diced, cooked pork, and serve with pilot bread or crackers.

Serves 6.

VARIATION

RHODE ISLAND CLAM CHOWDER

Substitute 2 to 3 cups of chopped clams for the fish.

GRAND CENTRAL OYSTER STEW

3 dozen shucked oysters, with juice
1 cup clam juice
3 cups milk
1/2 teaspoon salt
1/4 teaspoon white pepper
1/4 cup butter
Paprika

Drain oysters and bring the juice to a boil. Add enough clam juice to make 2 cups liquid. Add the oysters to the hot juice and cook 2 to 3 minutes until edges curl. Meanwhile heat the milk with salt and pepper and add to the oysters. Top each serving with a piece of butter and a dash of paprika. Serve at once.

Serves 6.

VARIATION

OYSTER STEW WITH CELERY

Cook 2 stalks of celery, chopped fine, in a little salted water until soft. Add this celery and liquid to the milk.

LONG ISLAND FRESH CLAM SOUP

3 dozen clams, fresh
Water
Clam broth (optional)
3 cups cream
1/4 teaspoon pepper
Dash nutmeg
Salt
2 tablespoons butter

Steam clams in water half to cover, only until they open, about 2 minutes. Drain, reserving liquid. Put the clams aside. Measure the clam liquid and add clam broth to make 2 cups. Put the liquid in a pan and bring to a boil. Poach the clams in the liquid until edges curl, about 2 to 3 minutes. Add cream. Bring to a boil; add pepper, nutmeg, and salt to taste. Add butter and serve.

Serves 6.

VARIATION

LONG ISLAND OYSTER SOUP

Substitute oysters for the clams. Omit nutmeg.

PHILADELPHIA PEPPER POT

1 pound veal stew meat
Veal bone
1 pound tripe, cubed
6 cups water
2 teaspoons salt
1/4 teaspoon pepper
3 onions, chopped
2 carrots, diced
2 potatoes, diced
1/4 cup butter

Put the veal, bone, and tripe in a large kettle with water, salt, pepper, and half the onion. Simmer for 2 hours. Remove bone. Cook the remaining onion, carrots, and potatoes in butter for 15 minutes. Add to the soup and simmer 30 minutes.

Serves 6.

PENNSYLVANIA BEEF MUSHROOM SOUP

1/4 pound dried wild mushrooms
3 tablespoons butter
2 tablespoons flour
3 cups or 2 (13-ounce) cans clear beef broth

Soak the mushrooms in water to cover, about 2 cups, until they are limp. This will take several hours. Reserve the liquid. Chop the stems or buzz in a blender. Cut up the mushrooms or chop coarsely. Simmer for 2 to 3 minutes in the butter. Stir in the flour, the broth, and the reserved liquid; simmer 3 to 4 minutes.

Serves 6.

MARYLAND CRAB SOUP

3 tablespoons minced onion
2 tablespoons butter
1 pound crab meat
1/2 teaspoon salt
1/4 teaspoon pepper
4 cups half-and-half
1/2 cup cream
2 tablespoons Scotch whiskey, bourbon, or gin

Sauté the onion in butter until softened but not brown. Stir in the crab meat (in Maryland it's "she-crab"; anywhere, use fresh crab of either sex, if available). Thaw if using frozen. Season with salt and pepper. Cook gently for about 10 minutes. Add the half-and-half and simmer gently for 10 minutes. Add the cream and heat. Stir in the whiskey or gin. Scotch adds a subtle flavor—gin is frequently used in Maryland.

Serves 6.

GEORGIA PEANUT SOUP

2 cups peanuts
4 cups broth
2 cups half-and-half
1 cucumber, peeled and grated
Salt
Peanut butter (optional)

Buzz the peanuts in a blender with 2 cups broth. Put in a pan with remaining broth and simmer for

10 minutes. Add half-and-half and cucumber. Season with salt to taste—the amount depends upon the flavoring of the broth. Top with a little peanut butter.

Serves 6.

FLORIDA AVOCADO SOUP

2 small avocados
1 1/2 cups chicken broth
1 cup half-and-half
1/2 cup sour or heavy cream
1/2 teaspoon salt
1/4 teaspoon pepper
4 small wedges of lemon

Peel the avocados. Reserve 1/4 of 1 avocado and buzz the remainder in a blender with chicken broth, half-and-half, cream, salt, and pepper. Heat or serve chilled. Top with a few thin slices of avocado and a wedge of lemon on the side.

Serves 4.

EAST COAST CREAM OF SCALLOP SOUP

1/4 cup butter
2 tablespoons flour
1 quart half-and-half
2 teaspoons salt
1/4 teaspoon white pepper
1/4 teaspoon Worcestershire sauce
2 pounds scallops, fresh or frozen

Melt 2 tablespoons butter and blend in the flour.
Add half-and-half. Season with salt, pepper, and
Worcestershire sauce. Add scallops and bring to a
boil. Thaw if using frozen scallops. Remove scallops
to a blender with enough soup liquid to cover; buzz
until smooth. Return to pot and reheat. Add remaining butter and serve at once.

Serves 6.

NEW ORLEANS SHRIMP BISQUE

1/4 cup minced onion
1/4 cup minced celery
2 tablespoons minced carrot
3 tablespoons olive oil
1 1/2 pounds raw shelled shrimp
1 quart chicken or fish broth
1 cup dry white wine
2 tablespoons cognac
1 cup heavy cream
3 tablespoons butter

Simmer the onion, celery, and carrot in oil for 4 to 5
minutes; do not brown. Add the shrimp; toss for
a minute or two. Add the broth and cook 10 minutes
very gently. Thaw if using frozen shrimp. Buzz
shrimp and vegetables in a blender with some of the
soup. Return to kettle. Add wine, cognac, and cream;
heat but do not boil. Add butter just before serving.

Serves 8.

LOUISIANA SEAFOOD GUMBO

2 onions, minced
2 tablespoons butter
1/4 cup flour
6 cups beef broth or consommé
1 (1-pound 4-ounce) can tomatoes
1 bay leaf
2 pounds okra
1 pound shrimp
1 pound crab meat
1/2 pound lobster meat (optional)
2 tablespoons filé powder
1/2 teaspoon salt
4–5 cups cooked rice, hot

Brown the onions in butter in a large soup pot. Stir in the flour and add the broth while stirring. Add tomatoes, bay leaf, and okra. Simmer for 1 hour. Add the peeled shrimp, crab meat, and lobster. Thaw if using frozen. Bring to a boil. Add salt to taste. Add the filé powder, stir gently but do not boil. Serve in flat soup plates with a mound of hot rice in the center of each.

Serves 10.

MARTHA'S OYSTER SOUP

6 tablespoons butter
3 tablespoons flour
3 cups mutton or lamb broth
1 pint fresh oysters with extra juice if available
1/2 teaspoon salt

Melt 4 tablespoons butter and smooth the flour into it. Do not brown. Add the broth. In a separate pan, scald the oysters and juice. Strain the juice into the broth and cut up the oysters, chopping the hard parts into smaller pieces. Add the oysters and heat for 2 to 3 minutes. Add remaining butter and salt and serve at once.

Serves 4.

IOWA CORN CHOWDER

1/4 pound salt pork or 5 slices bacon, diced
12 ears of corn or 2 (1-pound) cans cream-style
  corn
1 large onion, diced
2 potatoes, cut up
1/2 to 1 teaspoon salt
1/4 teaspoon white pepper
6 cups half-and-half

Sauté the pork or bacon until browned. Remove the pork or bacon and reserve. Grate the fresh corn. In a large kettle, sauté the onion and potatoes in the pork fat until very tender; do not brown. Add the corn, salt, pepper, and half-and-half. Boil for a few minutes. Adjust seasoning. Served topped with salt pork bits or crumbled bacon.

Serves 8.

PLAINS RABBIT SOUP

1 (4-pound) rabbit
1/4 pound salt pork, sliced thin
1 quart water
4 chicken bouillon cubes
6 small carrots
4 scallions, cut up
4 turnips, quartered
2 onions, cut up
1 cup canned tomatoes
1 cup whole kernel corn
Salt

Sauté the cut-up rabbit in salt pork for 15 minutes. Add water and bouillon cubes, cover, and simmer 45 minutes. Remove meat from bones, return meat to liquid, add vegetables, and simmer about 20 minutes. Add salt to taste.

Serves 4.

COLORADO BEET SOUP

6 medium beets
2 (13-ounce) cans consommé
Juice 1 lemon
1 bay leaf
2 cloves
1 teaspoon sugar
1 teaspoon salt
1/2 teaspoon pepper
1/2 glass red wine
Sour cream (optional)

Grate the raw beets; combine with consommé, lemon juice, bay leaf, cloves, sugar, salt, and pepper. Simmer 10 to 15 minutes. Strain, add wine, and reheat. Serve topped with a little sour cream.

Serves 4.

VARIATION

CHILLED BEET SOUP

Proceed as for Colorado Beet Soup. Add 2 egg whites while cooking and add 1/2 package gelatin after straining.

CALIFORNIA ARTICHOKE SOUP

4 large artichokes
1 tablespoon salt
4 cups water
4 tablespoons butter
2 tablespoons flour
Pinch nutmeg
2 cups cream or half-and-half
1/4 cup white wine (optional)

Cook the artichokes in salted water to cover until very soft. Reserve 1 cup of liquid. Scrape the edible ends off of the leaves, add to the fonds, and buzz in a blender with the reserved liquid. Melt half of the butter and blend in the flour. Add artichoke puree, salt, and nutmeg. Simmer for 2 to 3 minutes. Stir in the cream or half-and-half. Just before serving, stir in the wine slowly. Add remaining butter bit by bit while stirring. Adjust seasoning.

Serves 4.

MARX BROTHERS DUCK SOUP
(As easy as duck soup)

2 duck carcasses
2 quarts water
2 teaspoons salt
Few peppercorns
1 cup chopped celery
Celery leaves
1 cup chopped onion
3 sprigs parsley
1/2 cup chopped carrots
1 small bay leaf
1 teaspoon grated orange peel
Leftover duck gravy
Leftover bits of duck meat
1 cup wild or domestic rice or 1/4 pound thin pasta
1 chicken bouillon cube (optional)

Break up the carcasses and put into a soup kettle with water, salt, peppercorns, the vegetables, bay leaf, orange peel, and gravy. Simmer for 1 1/2 hours. Strain and chill. Remove fat and reheat, adding bits of duck meat and rice or thin pasta. Use a pasta such as alphabets or small forms or break up the thin noodles or vermicelli. Cook until rice or pasta is done, 10 to 20 minutes. If you need more liquid, add water and a chicken bouillon cube. Season to taste.

Serves 6.

WEST COAST ABALONE SOUP

6 slices bacon, diced
1 large potato, diced
1 large onion, chopped
1 clove garlic, crushed
1 pound abalone, diced fresh, frozen, or canned
2 cups water
1 teaspoon salt
1/4 teaspoon pepper
3 cups milk

Sauté the bacon, remove from pan, and set aside. Sauté the potato, onion, and garlic in bacon drippings until lightly browned. Add the abalone (if you live on the West Coast use fresh), water, salt, and pepper; simmer until abalone is tender. Add the milk and bacon, and reheat.

Serves 6.

WASHINGTON STATE APPLE SOUP

1 1/2 pounds apples
1 quart water
1 teaspoon cornstarch
1 tablespoon cinnamon
1/3 cup sugar
3/4 cup sour cream
Croutons (optional)

Quarter and seed 1 pound of the apples. Simmer in the water for 15 minutes. Rub through a sieve. Mix the cornstarch with a little water and stir in. Bring to a boil. Peel and slice the remaining apples. Add to the soup with cinnamon, sugar, and sour cream. Serve warm or cold. Garnish with croutons.

Serves 4.

Our own famous soups, like any other soup, profit by garnishing. All chowders are improved by a sprinkling of fried bits of salt pork. Oyster crackers or crumbled pilot biscuit are attractive scattered over the soup plates of oyster stew at table. The heavy cream floated on Boula is run under the kitchen broiler to brown. Thin slices of avocado go into the delicate avocado soup before serving.

Vary the garnish as well as the ingredients. Try new ones from time to time: you may find that you too have invented a famous American soup.

Soup on the menu, in short, gives a sense of well-being at table.

part two

SANDWICHES

middle-word

In Praise of the Sandwich

It's fashionable, delectable, portable, packable, sackable, stackable—

Nourishing, saving, appetizing—

Low cost, high energy, universal appeal, wide variety, small effort, large return—

Easy to make and neat to eat.

It's a sandwich!

Who invented this paragon of all the culinary virtues? Was it a household economist saving money? Was it a housewife saving time? Was it a career girl saving effort? Was it a helpmate packing a lunch box? Was it a mother nourishing the children? Was it a chef varying his menu? Was it a gourmet creating a masterpiece?

It wasn't any of these. It was an inveterate gambler—a gambler so dedicated he couldn't leave the gaming table long enough to gulp down a meal. So he reached to the sideboard for a slice off the roast, slapped it between two slices of bread, and there he sat, rolling the dice with one hand and taking his supper from the other.

That was two hundred years ago. The gambler's name was Lord Sandwich. This Earl of Sandwich was First Lord of the Admiralty, and they named the Sandwich Islands (now Hawaii) after him; but nothing has immortalized his name like that simple invention over the hazard table. The noble earl's idea quickly caught on. In no time, every gamester in London would call for a sandwich with his midnight tipple, and fashionable tables offered sandwiches with a dish of tea.

In short, the sandwich jumped immediately into fashion. Before long it was seen to have all those other advantages too.

As Lord Sandwich first demonstrated, a sandwich is the easiest and most convenient meal to make, serve, and eat. It requires no utensils, no gadgets, no kitchen equipment, no eating tools. With a simple knife, you can put it together; and with fingers and teeth, you can eat it.

And everybody does. Everybody likes a sandwich. It's the favorite American meal. The number of sandwiches eaten every day from coast to coast would stagger a computer. Children go for them, matrons nibble them, teen-agers gobble them, gourmets savor them.

And no wonder. They're so good, good, good! Their variety approaches infinity. With limitless permutations of fillings and flavors, a sandwich fan could lunch on a sandwich every day for a year, and then go around again without repeating.

No other dish is nearly as versatile as the sandwich. Scarcely a wedding knot can be tied without dainty sandwiches at the reception. Picnics, cocktail parties, and box lunches could hardly exist without sandwiches. They go with the laborer's beer as perfectly as with the diplomat's champagne. They make a midmorning tidbit, a tea-time treat, a cocktail-hour must, a supper special, a late-party delight, a bedtime snack, and first and foremost, an ideal easy meal. Where would we all be, day in and day out, without that sturdy partnership—soup and a sandwich?

Soup and a sandwich unite to make a meal—at midday, at end of day, on into the night—a perfect lunch, supper, or Soup Soiree. Here hearty soups and sandwiches play their part. A few suggested combinations will give a clue to the possibilities. The following chart is merely a guide, not a rule. Read it, and take off from there!

Cream of mushroom soup	with	Club sandwich
Cream of cucumber soup	with	Tuna salad sandwich
French onion soup	with	Egg salad sandwich
Consommé Rosa	with	Reuben's special
Chicken gumbo	with	Hamburger sandwich
Canadian cheddar cheese soup	with	Ham sandwich
Greek lemon soup	with	Chicken salad sandwich
Vichyssoise	with	Grilled or sautéed cheese sandwich
Irish potato soup	with	Roast beef sandwich
New England fish chowder	with	Watercress or cucumber sandwich
Gazpacho	with	Turkey sandwich
Chinese egg-drop soup	with	Hero Sandwich (French, Italian, or miscellaneous)

Hearty Sandwiches

The first sandwich was man-sized, sturdy rounds of bread with plenty of sliced meat between. That's still a recipe for a hearty sandwich.

Bread is the staff of life and the mainstay of the sandwich. No bread, no sandwich. Luckily the world is full of bread, all kinds of bread. The delectable aroma of baking bread hovers over your own oven or the baker's, scenting the air and making your mouth water. But no longer need you be the baker, except if you choose to for your own pleasure. Every supermarket, every delicatessen tempts you with a limitless variety of delicious breads: white, whole wheat, three kinds of rye, pumpernickel, (black and brown), nut and fruit breads, hard or soft rolls,

Bread is the staff of life and the mainstay of the French and Italian loaves, and many more mouth-watering varieties.

Nowadays you don't even have to slice your bread. It comes neatly sliced—thick, thin, or medium—all ready for the sandwich maker to spread.

As to the meat between the bread slices, that's where planned efficiency comes in. The look-ahead housekeeper plans her leftovers, choosing a heavier turkey or a larger roast than a single meal demands. It makes for economy in buying and for convenience in producing sandwich meals. With ingenuity and flavorful touches such as chutney, mustard relish, or sauerkraut, you have it made—the hearty sandwich, that is.

ROAST BEEF SANDWICHES

Soft butter
8 slices white or light rye bread
4 slices roast beef
Salt
Pepper
2 tablespoons mustard pickle, chopped; or 1 tablespoon mustard

Butter the 8 slices of bread. Put the beef on 4 and sprinkle with salt and pepper. Spread with mustard pickle or mustard. Cover with remaining bread and cut in half.

4 sandwiches.

SLICED PORK SANDWICHES

8 slices of bread
Soft butter
1/2 teaspoon Worcestershire sauce
16 slices roast pork
Salt
Pepper

Spread 4 slices of bread with butter to which you have added the Worcestershire sauce. Cover with the pork. Sprinkle lightly with salt and pepper and top with remaining bread.

4 sandwiches.

CHICKEN OR TURKEY SANDWICHES

Soft butter
8 slices white bread
16 slices chicken or turkey
Salt
Pepper
1 teaspoon curry powder
3 tablespoons mayonnaise

Butter 4 slices of bread and cover with the slices of chicken or turkey. Sprinkle with a little salt and pepper. Mix the curry with the mayonnaise and spread on remaining bread. Cover the turkey with the bread, mayonnaise side down. Cut off crusts and cut in half.

4 sandwiches.

STEAK SANDWICHES

Soft butter
8 slices white or whole wheat bread
16 slices steak
Salt
Pepper
Worcestershire sauce

Butter all 8 pieces of bread. Put the steak on 4 pieces, sprinkle with salt and pepper, and add a few drops of the sauce. Cover with remaining bread. Cut off crusts and cut in half.

4 sandwiches.

If the leftover roast is not sliceable, it is surely diceable. That way lies salad sandwiches, and what a way to go!

CURRIED CHICKEN SALAD SANDWICHES

2 1/2 cups diced cooked chicken
1/2 cup diced celery
1/2 cup diced apple
1/2 teaspoon minced onion
1/3 cup mayonnaise
1 teaspoon lemon juice
1/2 teaspoon salt
1/8 teaspoon pepper
2 teaspoons curry powder
12 slices buttered bread

Mix the chicken, celery, apple, and onion in a bowl. Combine the mayonnaise with the lemon, salt, pepper, and curry. Stir into the chicken mixture. Spread on 6 slices of the buttered bread and top with remaining bread.

6 sandwiches.

HAM SALAD SANDWICHES

1/4 cup mayonnaise
2 teaspoons prepared mustard
1/2 pound ham, diced
2 tablespoons chopped parsley
2 tablespoons chopped celery
Soft butter
8 slices rye bread

Combine the mayonnaise and mustard; add the ham, parsley, and celery; blend well. Butter 4 pieces of the bread lightly, spread with the ham mixture, and top with remaining bread.

4 sandwiches.

HARD ROLL BOATS WITH HAM SALAD

6 crusty long rolls
1/2 pound ham, diced
1/4 cup diced celery
1/4 cup mayonnaise
2 teaspoons prepared mustard
1 tablespoon minced onion or chives
Minced parsley (garnish)

Cut the rolls through lengthwise near the top. Pull out the soft bread from the inside. Mix the ham, celery, mayonnaise, mustard, and onion or chives. Fill the bottom half of the rolls with salad and replace the tops. If they are to be transported, wrap individually in foil or waxed paper and put an elastic band around the middle to hold the top in place. If they are to be served at home, you may leave them open and sprinkle with parsley.

6 sandwiches.

EGG SALAD SANDWICHES

6 slices bacon
1/4 cup chopped celery and/or scallions
6 hard-cooked eggs, chopped
1/4 cup mayonnaise
1 to 2 tablespoons prepared mustard
1/4 teaspoon fines herbs
2 tablespoons soft butter
12 thin slices white or whole wheat bread

Cook the bacon, remove, and dry on paper toweling. Sauté the celery and/or scallions in bacon drippings. Combine the eggs, crumbled bacon, and scallions and/or celery. Stir in the mayonnaise, mustard, and herbs. Adjust seasoning to taste. Spread on half the buttered bread. Cover with remaining bread. If for a party, remove crusts and cut in half.

6 sandwiches.

CHICKEN AND EGG SALAD SANDWICHES

1 cup chopped chicken
4 hard-cooked eggs, chopped
1/4 cup mayonnaise
2 tablespoons melted butter
1 teaspoon lemon juice
1 teaspoon Worcestershire sauce
1/2 teaspoon paprika
1/2 teaspoon salt
12 slices whole wheat bread

Combine all of the ingredients except bread and blend well. Spread on half the bread and cover with remaining bread. Pat top pieces of bread in place before cutting in half. Remove the crusts or not, as you wish.

6 sandwiches.

Suppose there's no meat left to slice or dice. Just because you ate it all up last night at dinner, that's no reason you have to go without meat sandwiches today. There's still the whole gamut of lunch meats —sliced and packaged at the supermarket, ready to slice at the delicatessen.

CORNED BEEF SANDWICHES

2 tablespoons soft butter
2 teaspoons prepared horse-radish
8 slices rye bread
4 to 6 slices corned beef
2 tablespoons mayonnaise
1 teaspoon prepared mustard

Combine the butter and horse-radish and spread on 4 pieces of bread. Cover with the corned beef. Blend the mayonnaise and mustard and spread on remaining bread. Cover the sandwiches and cut in half diagonally.

4 sandwiches.

PEANUT BUTTER AND BOLOGNA SANDWICHES

12 slices dark bread
1 (6-ounce) jar peanut butter
6 large slices bologna
3 tablespoons soft butter

Spread 6 slices of bread with peanut butter. Cover each with a slice of bologna. Butter the remaining bread and cover the bologna, pressing the bread down.

6 sandwiches.

SWISS CHEESE SANDWICHES

2 tablespoons prepared mustard
1/8 teaspoon Worcestershire sauce
1/4 cup soft butter
16 thin slices pumpernickel bread
1 pound Swiss cheese, sliced thin

Mix the mustard and Worcestershire sauce with the butter. Spread on half the bread. Cover with the cheese, top with another piece of buttered bread, and press firmly together. This sandwich packs well and keeps moist.

8 sandwiches.

TONGUE SANDWICHES

2 tablespoons prepared horse-radish
1 tablespoon sour cream
1 tablespoon capers or 1/2 teaspoon prepared
  mustard
Soft butter
16 thin slices pumpernickel or rye bread
1 pound smoked tongue, sliced thin

Mix the horse-radish, sour cream, and capers or mustard. Butter half the bread; spread the other half lightly with the horse-radish mixture. Cover the buttered pieces of bread with tongue and top with remaining bread. These carry well.

8 sandwiches.

LIVERWURST AND CHEESE SANDWICHES

12 slices dark rye or moist pumpernickel bread
Soft butter
12 slices liverwurst
6 slices cheddar cheese
6 slices tomato
6 slices Bermuda onion
Mayonnaise (optional)

Spread 6 slices of bread with butter. Put on the liverwurst, cheese, tomato, and onion. Cover with remaining bread, either buttered or spread with a thin layer of mayonnaise.

6 sandwiches.

SALAMI AND POTATO SANDWICHES

6 slices white bread
3 tablespoons soft butter
12 slices salami
6 boiled potatoes, peeled
2 teaspoons salt
1/3 teaspoon pepper
2 tablespoons mayonnaise
Chopped chives

Spread the bread evenly with butter and cover with salami. Place one sliced potato in the center of each sandwich. Sprinkle with salt and pepper and top with a bit of mayonnaise. Sprinkle generously with chives.

6 sandwiches.

The sandwich that Reuben made, made Reuben's. It was concocted on the principle that two good things are twice as good as one. Traditionally, between generous slices of rye bread goes plenty of thin-sliced kosher corned beef and Swiss cheese, garnished with sauerkraut. Or if Reuben isn't looking, you can pile up any combination of cold cuts, perk it up with coleslaw, and call it a Reuben's à la you.

REUBEN SANDWICH

2 large slices rye bread
Butter (optional)
Sliced corned beef
Sliced Swiss cheese
Sauerkraut

You may butter the bread if you wish, but it is not necessary. Place the corned beef and cheese on one slice of bread, add a generous topping of sauerkraut, and cover with remaining bread.

1 sandwich.

VARIATIONS

For each sandwich you need 2 large slices of rye bread, buttered or not. Instead of the corned beef and Swiss cheese, substitute one of these combinations.

Spiced beef, cheese, and lettuce
Sliced pastrami, sliced cheddar cheese,
and sauerkraut
Sliced ham, sliced Swiss cheese, and coleslaw
Sliced turkey, sliced Swiss cheese,
and sliced tomatoes
Sliced salami, sliced mozzarella cheese,
sliced tomatoes, and lettuce
Sliced roast beef, sliced tomatoes, lettuce,
and mayonnaise

You don't have to be a member of the club to enjoy a club sandwich. Like Mr. Reuben's invention, that nourishing and appetizing combination depends on achieving a happy meeting of several good things —customarily sliced chicken, crisp bacon, sliced tomato, and a middle piece of toast.

CHICKEN CLUB SANDWICH

3 slices buttered toast
Sliced chicken
Salt
Pepper
Sliced tomato
1 tablespoon mayonnaise
Small lettuce leaves
2 pieces crisp bacon, cut in half

Cover a piece of toast with chicken and sprinkle with a little salt and pepper. Cover with the second piece of toast, buttered side down. Add 2 slices of tomato and spread with mayonnaise. Add the lettuce and bacon and top with the third slice of toast, buttered side down. Pat gently in place. Put a toothpick on each of the four sides through the three pieces of toast. Cut the sandwich diagonally both ways, making 4 triangular pieces. Work fast to keep the toast warm.

1 sandwich.

VARIATIONS

TURKEY CLUB
Use sliced turkey instead of chicken.

BEEF CLUB
Substitute sliced roast beef for the chicken.

SHRIMP CLUB
Cover the bottom layer of toast with cooked shrimp, the second layer of toast with sliced avocado and crisp bacon.

Club members with dainty mouths may prefer to leave out the middle toast for a more bitable tidbit, and call it a junior club sandwich.

The advantage of three decks, however, is that the middle deck separates different textures—the crisp from the moist, the firm from the soft. The decks may be slices of bread rather than toast, and for additional variety the kinds of bread may vary, presenting an extra fillip of dark bread contrasting with white for eye as well as taste appeal. Between these decks, the bottom layer may support a salad or a spread, while upstairs may appear crisp slices of cucumber, green pepper, tomato and/or lettuce. Or the bottom and top layers may offer contrasting textures as well as flavors.

CHICKEN SALAD THREE-DECKER SANDWICH

Soft butter
3 slices bread
1/2 cup chicken salad (see page 105)
1 thin slice ham
Mustard
Lettuce

Butter the bread and refrigerate for a few minutes until the butter is firm and makes a coating on the bread. Spread bottom piece with chicken salad, cover with bread, buttered side down. Add the ham, spread with a little prepared mustard to taste. Add lettuce and cover with remaining bread, buttered side down.

1 sandwich.

VARIATIONS

Tuna Salad, sliced green pepper, and lettuce

Salmon Salad, sliced cucumbers, and lettuce

Turkey Salad, lettuce, and split white seedless grapes

Shrimp Salad and sliced tomatoes

Crab Salad, sliced avocado, lemon juice, and lettuce

Triple-decker sandwiches are for hungry men. There are even mightier sandwiches for heroes. The hero sandwich starts with crusty French bread baked short or long, from six inches to six feet. There are daring bakers who don't flinch from baking the six-foot size, which is spectacular to cut up for a party of heroes; but don't try to buy one if you don't have a ski rack to carry it home.

It isn't only the bread that makes a hero, it's what's inside (and that goes for people too). Once you have your French loaf, split it and stuff it full. Don't spare the slices of meat, the various cheeses, the garden sass, the flavorful extras. The original hero sandwich had an Italian accent.

HEROES, ITALIAN STYLE

Italian bread

Soft butter

Provolone or mozzarella cheese

Salami

Ham

Sliced red Italian onion

Sliced tomatoes

Soft lettuce

Mayonnaise

Cut the bread through lengthwise and remove a little of the inside from the lower half. Spread the lower half with butter. Pile up with layers of all of the ingredients. Spread top half of bread with mayonnaise and cover the sandwich. Cut in about 8-inch lengths.

1 sandwich.

FRENCH HEROES

French bread (long loaf)
Unsalted butter
Port Salut cheese, sliced
Smoked tongue, sliced
Sliced chicken
Lettuce
Sliced tomatoes

Cut the bread lengthwise, spread with soft butter, and proceed as for Italian heroes.

VARIATIONS

French or Italian bread or long hard rolls
Soft butter
Tongue, ham, spiced beef, bologna, luncheon
    meats, chicken or turkey, corned beef
Swiss, cheddar, or American cheese
Lettuce, tomatoes, cucumbers, sweet peppers
    (red or green), coleslaw, onions
Mayonnaise or Russian dressing

Proceed as for Italian heroes, using a generous selection of the meat, cheese, and greenery.

hot sandwiches

Hurrah for the hot sandwich! It is so good in winter —a perfect lunch or supper or midnight feast—not only delicious and different but heartwarming. An ordinary sandwich can attain extraordinary variety by the various ways in which it can be given the heat. Grill it, sauté it, or fry it; use a hot filling, add a hot sauce. The simplest way, and the most efficient, draws on that leftover roast with its gravy to produce the universal hot meat sandwich.

HOT ROAST BEEF OR POT ROAST SANDWICH

1 slice toast
Soft butter
2 slices roast beef
Beef gravy

Butter the toast, place the warm beef on the toast, and cover with hot gravy.

1 sandwich.

VARIATION

HOT LAMB SANDWICH
Substitute sliced lamb for beef.

HOT CHICKEN SANDWICH

Warm chicken slices
Mayonnaise
Soft butter
1 or 2 slices toast
3 tablespoons hot chicken gravy or Cheese Sauce

Spread the chicken with mayonnaise on both sides and place on hot buttered toast. Cover if you wish with a second piece of hot buttered toast or leave open. Cover with chicken gravy or Cheese Sauce and serve at once.

1 sandwich.

HOT TONGUE OR HAM SANDWICHES WITH MUSTARD SAUCE

1 tablespoon butter
1 teaspoon minced onion
1 tablespoon flour
1 cup beef broth
1/4 teaspoon salt
1/8 teaspoon freshly ground pepper
1 tablespoon prepared mustard
3/4 pound sliced smoked tongue or ham
6 slices bread

Heat the butter and sauté the onion until softened but not brown. Blend in the flour. Add the broth, salt, pepper, and mustard; simmer several minutes while stirring. Place the tongue or ham (at room temperature, not directly from the refrigerator) on the bread. Spoon the hot sauce over the sandwiches and serve at once.

6 sandwiches.

Grilled sandwiches are cooked, both sides at once, in an electric sandwich grill, or just as easily, on a griddle on top of the stove, turned once with a spatula to brown both sides.

A sautéed sandwich is browned in butter in a skillet or griddle, which adds a delicious brown-butter savor.

GRILLED CHEESE AND BACON SANDWICH

1 slice buttered toast
Sliced American cheese
1 slice bacon

Cover the toast with cheese, cut the bacon in half, and place on the cheese. Broil until the cheese melts and bacon is crisp. Serve open.

1 sandwich.

BROILED BAKED BEAN SANDWICH

2 tablespoons baked beans
1 slice buttered toast
1 slice Bermuda onion
2 slices bacon

Spread the beans on the toast, add the onion, and top with bacon slices that have been cut in half.

Broil about 4 inches from the heat for about 8 minutes until bacon is crisp and beans heated through.

1 sandwich.

BAKED CHEESE SANDWICHES

1/4 pound American cheese
1 teaspoon prepared mustard
Pinch cayenne
1/2 teaspoon Worcestershire sauce
1 tablespoon milk or cream
2 slices bread

Chop or grate the cheese and mix with remaining ingredients except the bread. Spread on both slices of bread and bake face up in a 500° oven for a few minutes until the cheese is puffy and the edges of the bread crisp.

2 sandwiches.

SAUTÉED CHEESE SANDWICHES

2 eggs
1/2 pound cheddar cheese, shredded
2 tablespoons minced chives
1 tablespoon minced parsley
1/2 teaspoon salt
1/4 teaspoon pepper
1/2 teaspoon dry mustard
Soft butter
8 slices bread

Separate the eggs and beat the whites stiff. Combine the yolks with the cheese, chives, parsley, salt, pepper, and mustard. Spread the bread with butter. Fold the egg whites into the cheese mixture and spread on the unbuttered side of 4 pieces of bread. Cover with the remaining bread, buttered side out. Sauté in butter, turning once to brown the bread on both sides.

4 sandwiches.

SAUTÉED HAM AND CHEESE SANDWICH

Soft butter
2 slices bread
2 slices Swiss cheese
1 slice ham

Butter the bread. Place on this a slice of cheese cut to fit the bread, then the ham, and another slice of cheese. Top with the second slice of bread, buttered side down, and press firmly together. Sauté until brown in hot butter, turn with a spatula, and brown the other side. Serve very hot.

1 sandwich.

A similar sandwich, made with two slices of bread as usual, may be dipped in batter and fried in deep hot fat.

BATTER
(For Fried Sandwiches)

2 eggs
1/2 cup flour
1/2 teaspoon salt
1 cup milk

Beat the eggs lightly with a fork and mix in the flour and salt. Blend in the milk.

Batter for 4–6 sandwiches.

FRIED HAM SANDWICHES

8 slices bread
Soft butter
4 slices ham
1 teaspoon prepared mustard
Batter (see recipe, page 120)

Spread the bread lightly with butter. Place a piece of ham on each of 4 pieces of bread. Spread with a little mustard and press top pieces of bread into place. Dip into batter and fry in 380° deep fat until browned.

4 sandwiches.

FRIED CHICKEN OR TURKEY SANDWICHES

8 slices bread
2 tablespoons soft butter
2 tablespoons mayonnaise
4 slices chicken or turkey
Batter (see recipe, page 120)

Spread 4 pieces of bread lightly with butter and 4
with mayonnaise. Place the sliced chicken or turkey
on half the bread and cover with the other half.
Press in place and dip into the batter, covering all
sides. Fry in 380° deep fat until browned.

4 sandwiches.

FRIED MOZZARELLA SANDWICHES

12 slices bread
1/4 cup soft butter
1/2 pound mozzarella cheese, sliced
3 eggs, beaten
1/4 teaspoon salt
1/8 teaspoon pepper
2 tablespoons grated Parmesan cheese

Trim the crusts from the bread and spread with
butter. Place slices of mozzarella cheese on 6 slices
of bread. Cover with the other 6 slices, buttered side
down. Press edges together firmly. Mix the eggs, salt,
pepper, and Parmesan cheese. Dip the sandwiches
in the mixture on both sides and fry in hot fat until
browned.

6 sandwiches.

Toasting is becoming to a sandwich. A sandwich made on hot buttered toast gains an additional dimension if the filling too is heated.

STEAK SANDWICHES

3-pound London broil or boneless sirloin, cut 2 inches thick
1/2 teaspoon salt
1/8 teaspoon pepper
12 slices French or Italian bread or toast
1/3 cup soft butter
3 tablespoons minced sweet onion or scallions
2 tablespoons Worcestershire sauce (optional)

Broil the steak until rare or medium rare and season with salt and pepper. Spread bread or toast with butter. Slice the steak crosswise into strips and place on 6 slices of bread. Add sauce if you wish. Cover with remaining bread or toast.

6 sandwiches.

TOASTED CHEESE SANDWICH

2 slices bread
Soft butter
American cheese

Butter the bread lightly. Cover one piece generously with slices of cheese. Top with a second slice of bread, buttered side down. Toast under broiler until brown, turn, and broil until the other side is brown. Cut in half diagonally and serve at once.

1 sandwich.

TOASTED ROQUEFORT SANDWICHES

1 (3-ounce) package cream cheese
1/4 cup crumbled Roquefort cheese
1 tablespoon heavy cream, sour cream, or mayonnaise
1/4 cup chopped nuts (optional)
8 thin slices white bread

Soften the cheeses and blend together with cream or mayonnaise. Add nuts if you wish. Spread on 4 pieces of bread and cover with remaining bread. Just before serving, toast on both sides.

4 sandwiches.

TOASTED LIVER SAUSAGE SANDWICHES

1/2 pound liver sausage
1 teaspoon Worcestershire sauce
1 teaspoon minced onion
2 tablespoons tomato paste
8 thin slices rye bread

Heat the sausage to soften it and mix with the Worcestershire sauce, onion, and tomato paste. Spread on 4 pieces of bread, cover with remaining bread, and toast on both sides just before serving.

4 sandwiches.

For a change, you can omit the top toast, leaving the filling exposed, and run it under the broiler.

HOT OPEN-FACED CHICKEN SANDWICH

1/3 cup diced cooked chicken
1 tablespoon soft butter
1/8 teaspoon salt
Pinch pepper
Few drops lemon juice
1 teaspoon mayonnaise
1 slice toast
Grated Parmesan cheese

Mix the chicken with 1 teaspoon butter, the salt, pepper, lemon juice, and mayonnaise. Spread on a piece of buttered toast. Sprinkle with grated cheese and broil about 4 inches from heat for 3 to 4 minutes.

1 sandwich.

HOT TURKEY CHEESE FACE-UP SANDWICHES

Sliced turkey
6 slices Swiss cheese
6 slices cooked bacon, cut in half
6 slices buttered toast
6 tablespoons mayonnaise

Put the turkey, Swiss cheese, and bacon on the toast in that order. Top with a tablespoon of mayonnaise on each. Brown under broiler and serve at once.

6 sandwiches.

TOASTED CHEESE FACE-UP SANDWICHES

1/2 cup milk
1 egg, slightly beaten
1 teaspoon prepared mustard
1/4 teaspoon salt
3/4 pound American or cheddar cheese, sliced
8 thin slices bread
Soft butter

Scald the milk in a double boiler. Add the egg, mustard, salt, and cheese. Cook for 15 minutes, stirring frequently. Spread on 4 pieces of bread. Cover with remaining pieces. Spread all sides of sandwiches with a little butter and bake in a 375° oven until brown or toast under the broiler, turning once.

4 sandwiches.

BROILED CHEESE, TOMATO, AND BACON SANDWICH

1 slice white bread
Soft butter
2 slices tomato
Sliced American cheese
2 slices bacon

Spread the bread lightly with butter. Cover with slices of tomato. Add the cheese and then the bacon. Broil until cheese melts and bacon is crisp.

1 sandwich.

When the president of the United States wanted to entertain the queen of England in the real American way, he gave a wienie roast. The Yankee hot dog leads the pack.

FRANKFURTERS (HOT DOGS)

8 frankfurters
8 frankfurter rolls, split in half lengthwise
Soft butter
Relish, mustard and/or sauerkraut

Broil the frankfurters or sauté them for 3 minutes, turn, and cook 3 minutes more. Spread the rolls with soft butter. Toast them if you wish. Place a hot dog in each and garnish with relish, mustard, or sauerkraut or all three.

8 hot dogs.

The president might well have offered the queen a hamburger. American beef leads the herd, and in the form of a hamburger sandwich, it is the most popular dish in the U.S.A.

The ground beef patty, broiled or fried, is usually served on a round hamburger bun. When buns begin to pall, you can substitute toast, or toasted English muffin, or a hard roll.

HAMBURGERS ON BUNS

2 pounds lean ground beef (round, sirloin, or chuck)
1 teaspoon salt
1/4 teaspoon pepper
1 egg
2 tablespoons catsup
1 teaspoon minced onion
1 tablespoon flour (optional)
16 small hamburger buns
Soft butter (optional)

Toss the meat lightly with the salt, pepper, slightly beaten egg, catsup, and onion. If it is a little sticky to handle, sprinkle in the flour. Form into 16 patties. Broil or sauté the patties a minute or two on each side. Put into warmed buns, buttered or not.

16 canapés.

HAMBURGERS ON TOAST

2 tablespoons minced onion
2 tablespoons butter
1 pound lean ground beef (flank, round, or sirloin)
1/4 teaspoon monosodium glutamate
1/2 teaspoon salt
1/4 teaspoon freshly ground pepper
Soft butter
8 slices toast

Sauté the onion in butter and mix with the beef, monosodium glutamate, salt, and pepper. Form into 4 patties and broil or sauté in a little butter for about 2 minutes on each side. Place on 4 pieces of hot buttered toast and cover with remaining toast.

4 sandwiches.

CHEESEBURGERS ON ENGLISH MUFFINS

1 pound lean ground beef (round or sirloin)
1 teaspoon salt
1/4 teaspoon pepper
2 tablespoons tomato catsup or tomato sauce
4 English muffins, cut in half
Soft butter
4 slices mozzarella or Swiss cheese

Combine the beef with salt, pepper, and catsup or tomato sauce. Toss lightly and form into 4 patties. Butter muffins and toast. Place a meat patty on each of 4 muffin halves and broil 2 minutes. Top each patty with 1 slice of cheese and broil until the cheese melts. Top with remaining buttered toasted muffins.

4 sandwiches.

CHEESEBURGERS WITH NUTS

1 pound lean ground beef
1 cup grated sharp cheese
1 teaspoon salt
1/4 teaspoon pepper
1 tablespoon Worcestershire sauce
1/2 cup chopped walnuts or slivered toasted almonds
4 hamburger buns, split; or 8 small buns, split

Combine all of the ingredients except the bread. Blend thoroughly with a fork. Form into 4 patties but do not pack the meat down; it should be loose. Broil for 2 minutes and place the cooked side down on bottom halves of buns. Broil 2 minutes more and top the buns. For small hamburgers, form into 8 patties and use small-sized buns.

4 regular or 8 small hamburgers.

ROQUEFORT HAMBURGERS

2 pounds lean ground beef
1/2 teaspoon salt
1/2 teaspoon pepper
1/4 pound Roquefort or blue cheese
1 tablespoon cream
16 small hamburger buns
Soft butter (optional)

Sprinkle the beef with salt and pepper and toss lightly. Soften the cheese, which should be at room temperature, and blend with the cream. Form the beef into 16 patties and make a slit in the center of each, cutting three-fourths of the way through. Stuff a little cheese mixture into each and pinch the cut shut, using a bit of water. Broil 1 1/2 minutes on each side. Place each in a warmed bun, buttered or not as you wish.

16 canapés.

TOMATO HAMBURGERS

1 pound lean ground beef
1/2 teaspoon salt
1/4 teaspoon pepper
1 small onion, minced
2 tablespoons butter
1/2 cup chopped fresh tomato or drained canned tomato
1/8 teaspoon sugar
4 hamburger buns, toasted

Season the beef with half the salt and pepper. Sauté the onion in 1 tablespoon butter for 2 minutes until transparent. Add the tomato, sugar, and remaining salt and pepper. Simmer to reduce. Make 4 beef patties 1 1/2 inches thick, split them, and put some tomato mixture in between. Pinch the edges together so the sauce will stay in. Broil or sauté in 1 tablespoon butter, turning once. Cook about 2 or 3 minutes on a side. Serve on buns.

4 hamburgers.

SMOKY HAMBURGERS

1 pound lean ground beef
1/2 teaspoon salt
1/8 teaspoon pepper
2 eggs, slightly beaten
2 tablespoons catsup
1/4 teaspoon hickory salt
1 tablespoon flour
4 toasted hamburger buns, split

Mix all of the ingredients except the bread together, tossing lightly with a fork. Form into 4 patties and broil 2 to 3 minutes on each side. Serve on toasted buns.

4 hamburgers.

HOT BARBECUED HAMBURGERS

1 medium onion, chopped
1 tablespoon minced green pepper
2 tablespoons butter
1 pound lean ground beef
1 tablespoon prepared mustard
2 tablespoons catsup
1/2 teaspoon salt
1/4 teaspoon pepper
1 tablespoon vinegar
4 toasted hamburger buns or 4 slices toast

Sauté the onion and green pepper in butter for 2 to 3 minutes. Add the beef, stir, and cook 2 minutes until lightly browned. Add a mixture of the remaining ingredients except bread and cook 2 minutes more until heated through. Serve on toast or toasted buns.

4 hamburgers.

BAKED BEAN AND HAMBURGER SANDWICHES

2 pounds lean ground beef
2 teaspoons salt
1/2 teaspoon pepper
1 tablespoon minced chives
1 tablespoon Worcestershire sauce
1 tablespoon chili sauce
1/4 cup soft butter
16 slices bread
1/2 cup baked beans

Mix the meat with salt, pepper, chives, Worcestershire sauce, and chili sauce. Make into 16 small patties the size of the bread. Butter the bread. Put a patty on each of 8 slices, add 1 tablespoon baked beans in center, top with remaining patties, and press edges of meat together. Broil 5 to 6 minutes. Top with remaining bread and toast 2 minutes.

8 sandwiches.

BEEF TARTARE SANDWICHES

4 slices white bread
2 tablespoons soft butter
1 1/2 pounds lean ground beef
1 teaspoon salt
1/4 teaspoon pepper
2 tablespoons minced parsley
1 tablespoon chopped beets
4 egg yolks

Spread the bread evenly with butter. Divide the beef into 4 portions and put one on each piece of bread, piling it a little high in the center. Sprinkle with salt, pepper, parsley, and beets. Make a slight indentation in the top of each and drop in a raw egg yolk.

4 sandwiches.

portable sandwiches

Every child loves a sandwich. It is his own special thing, and he can eat it in his fingers without being admonished. Furthermore, it is portable. Circumstances permit, he can eat it wherever he is, at his own special play table, walking around the yard, or on a beach towel beside the swimming pool. And it's neat; he doesn't have to be driven to wash his ears after a sandwich, which is more than you can say about corn on the cob.

There isn't any lunch box a child takes to school that doesn't contain a sandwich. Even fried chicken doesn't go sandwich-less; there's sure to be a bread and butter sandwich along.

Lunch box sandwiches can be made in the morning, or the night before, as convenient. Nowadays, when sandwich-size plastic bags are available at such little cost, a sandwich can keep its freshness if it's treated right. Bread dries quickly when exposed to air. Each sandwich should be bagged separately as soon as made, closed airtight, and refrigerated until departure time comes.

You don't have to cudgel your brains to think of what to put in your child's sandwich. You know his likes and dislikes, and within that framework you can concoct a happy variety that will appeal to his taste day in and day out. No use getting too inventive with something he won't eat. You don't want him going lunchless. Save your experiments for the home. There are plenty of nourishing combinations with surefire appeal. And when you're in a hurry, don't forget these children's favorites.

Peanut butter and sliced banana
Peanut butter and jelly or jam
Peanut butter and bacon
Bacon and tomato or lettuce
Ham and chopped egg
Ham and cream cheese

Cream cheese and jelly
Cream cheese and chipped beef
Cream cheese and marmalade
Cream cheese and chopped nuts
Turkey and cranberry jelly
Turkey or chicken and lettuce
Chicken and ham
Creamed chicken on toast
Chicken and chopped celery

TUNA SANDWICHES

1 (6 1/2- or 7-ounce) can tuna
1/4 cup mayonnaise
1 teaspoon lemon juice
2 tablespoons minced celery
8 slices whole wheat bread

Drain and flake the tuna. Combine the mayonnaise, lemon juice, and celery; mix with the tuna. Spread generously on 4 pieces of bread and top with remaining bread. Press top on firmly and cut off crusts. Cut in half.

4 sandwiches.

HAM AND EGG SANDWICHES

3 hard-cooked eggs, chopped
1/4 pound boiled ham, chopped
1/4 cup mayonnaise
Salt
2 tablespoons soft butter
8 slices whole wheat or white bread

Combine the eggs, ham, and mayonnaise. Add a little salt to taste—the amount will depend upon how salty the ham is. Butter 4 slices of bread, spread with the ham-egg mixture, and cover with remaining bread. Press top piece of bread in place so they stick. Cut off crusts and cut each sandwich into 3 pieces.

4 sandwiches.

PEANUT BUTTER AND BACON SANDWICHES

6 slices bread
1 cup peanut butter
4 slices crisp bacon, crumbled
Soft butter

Spread 3 slices of bread with peanut butter and sprinkle bacon over it. Spread remaining bread with butter and pat firmly on top of the bacon. Cut in halves diagonally.

3 sandwiches.

CREAM CHEESE AND NUT SANDWICHES

1 (4-ounce) package cream cheese
2 tablespoons chopped nuts
6 slices white or nut bread
2 tablespoons jelly

Combine the softened cheese and nuts. Spread on 3 slices of bread. Spread jelly over the cheese and cover with the remaining bread. Cut off crusts and cut in half.

3 sandwiches.

CHICKEN SPREAD SANDWICHES

1 1/2 cups minced chicken
3 tablespoons mayonnaise
1 tablespoon cream
1/2 teaspoon salt
2 tablespoons soft butter
8 slices white bread

Blend the chicken, mayonnaise, and cream; add salt
—more salt if needed. Butter 4 pieces of bread with
the chicken mixture. Cover with remaining bread,
pressing top slices firmly in place. Cut off crusts and
cut in half or in thirds.

4 sandwiches.

Children are not the only ones who carry lunch
boxes. Busy executives eat at their desks, secretaries
and teachers in the lunchroom, laborers on the job.
For them, a homemade sandwich lunch can be a
treat. Making it a treat is a challenge to the wife
or mother who packs the lunch box. These hungry
people eat with developed palates, for which it is
a pleasure to create unusual and appealing sandwiches of the portable kind.

HEROS TO GO

Long hard rolls
Soft butter
Filling from your choice of heros (see pages
113–114

Cut the rolls in half lengthwise and remove a little
of the insides. Butter the rolls lightly. Fill the sand-

wiches with a choice of fillings. Cover with tops, wrap in waxed paper, and put an elastic band around each to keep the top in place. These can also be made with French bread if you fit the tops on neatly.

ITALIAN BREAD STEAK SANDWICHES

8 slices Italian or sour-dough bread
8 slices steak
Salt
Pepper
4 slices mild onion
2 tablespoons soft butter
2 tablespoons Roquefort or blue cheese

Use a large loaf of bread so you can make large sandwiches. Cover 4 pieces with steak and sprinkle with salt and pepper. Place a slice of onion on each. Combine the butter and cheese and spread on remaining bread. Cover the steak and press down. Cut in half.

4 sandwiches.

LIVERWURST AND CHEESE SANDWICHES

1/4 cup butter
12 slices rye bread
12 slices liverwurst
6 slices aged cheddar cheese
3 sliced Bermuda onions or Italian red onions

Butter the 12 slices of bread. Lay 2 slices of liverwurst on each of 6 pieces of bread, cover with a slice of cheese, and top with onion. Cover with remaining bread and press top slices in place firmly. Cut in half or, if the rye is very large, into 3 pieces.

6 sandwiches.

SARDINE SANDWICHES

2 (3 1/2-ounce) cans sardines
3 tablespoons minced celery
2 tablespoons mayonnaise
1 tablespoon lemon juice
12 thin slices white or rye bread
Soft butter

Drain and mash the sardines and mix with the celery. Combine the mayonnaise and lemon juice and stir into the sardine mixture. Adjust seasoning to taste. Spread the bread with butter and chill until the butter hardens. Spread half the bread with sardine spread and cover with remaining bread. Cut in half.

6 sandwiches.

To a child, any sandwich is a picnic. To everybody, a picnic is a picnic; whether by the roadside on an automobile tour, out of a knapsack on a hike, or in a boat on the water, sandwiches are in order. You can't even go on a fishing expedition without sandwiches. You can't eat the fish; it isn't marinated.

Barring the squashiest, most sandwiches travel well, whether going to work in the lunch box, or ranging afield in the picnic basket. Whatever the destination, the same portable sandwiches are appropriate. From the individual lunch box, the consumer eats what has been chosen to suit his individual taste. In the picnic basket it would be well to include a variety of sandwiches. Everybody will try a sample of each, and then settle down to work on what he likes best. If you use different kinds of bread for different fillings or cut the sandwiches in different shapes, you'll eliminate confusion. You won't have the picnickers lifting the tops to peek to see whether it's chicken or tuna.

Warning: there's something the open air does to appetites. You'll sell more sandwiches than you think. Don't skimp!

SUBSTANTIAL STEAK SANDWICHES

3 pounds boneless sirloin, cut
1/2 teaspoon salt
1/4 teaspoon pepper
1/4 cup soft butter
1 tablespoon Worcestershire sauce
2 tablespoons minced onion
12 large slices bread

Broil the steak rare or medium rare and slice it diagonally into 1/4-inch strips. Sprinkle with salt and pepper. Mix the butter with sauce and onion and spread it on all 12 slices of bread. Divide the steak among 6 slices and put the other slices on top. Press firmly into place.

6 sandwiches.

BAKED BEAN SANDWICHES

1 (1-pound 1-ounce) can Boston baked beans
2 tablespoons grated onion
3 tablespoons catsup
6 tablespoons butter
14 slices dark bread
7 slices crisp bacon, crumbled

Drain the beans. Mash with the onion and catsup. Butter the bread and spread the bean mixture on 7 slices. Cover with crumbled bacon and top with the remaining bread. Pound the tops in place with the palm of your hand. Cut in half.

7 sandwiches.

There is such a thing as a sandwich that's too hearty. It's called a Dagwood. To make a Dagwood, you raid the refrigerator at midnight. Take all the leftovers you find there, pile them up high between two slices of bread, lubricate liberally with catsup, mustard and/or relish, and eat it if you can. You are sampling the creation of Dagwood Bumpstead of comic-strip fame, America's answer to the inventive Lord Sandwich. For details see the funny papers.

HAM AND CHEESE SANDWICHES

1/4 cup soft butter
3 teaspoons prepared mustard
12 slices dark rye bread
6 slices ham
6 slices Swiss cheese

Blend the butter and mustard and spread lightly on the bread. Cover 6 pieces of bread with a slice each of ham and cheese and top with the other 6 pieces of bread. Cut off crusts if you wish and cut in half.

6 sandwiches.

LIVER LOAF SANDWICHES

1 pound chicken livers
1 sweet onion, cut up
1/2 pound lean pork
2 teaspoons salt
1 teaspoon pepper
1/2 teaspoon oregano
2 tablespoons tomato paste
1/4 cup soft butter
16 slices rye bread
Minced chives or parsley

Preheat oven to 300°. Chop the liver, onion, and pork together; or put through a meat grinder. Add the salt, pepper, oregano, and tomato paste. Blend well. Put into a buttered oven-proof dish and bake in a 300° oven for 1 hour. Chill and slice. Put a slice on each of 8 pieces of buttered bread. Garnish with minced chives or parsley and cover with another slice of buttered bread.

8 sandwiches.

Party Sandwiches

Sandwiches are not only happy at home and welcome as traveling companions but they also are social successes at parties large and small, for tiny folk and tall.

children's parties

Sandwiches are ideal party fare for children. Why try to serve chicken patties, concocting creamed chicken over a hot stove, filling a row of patties, coping at table with awkwardly used forks and stickied fingers? Wouldn't you rather serve something that can be made ahead, brought to table easily and quickly, and eaten tidily without utensils? —in short, a platter of sandwiches.

A tableful of children is a tableful of capricious tastes and uncertain appetites. Children's sandwiches should be made small to fit tiny fingers and little appetites. Then the kids can choose from the platter, sample their choice in a mouthful, and come back for more, while neglected edges on each child's plate will be kept to a minimum. For unformed tastes, keep the sandwiches simple and bland. Serve mustard or relish on the side for the more adventurous to try.

PEANUT BUTTER AND JELLY SANDWICHES

1 cup peanut butter
3 tablespoons jelly
6 slices white bread

Use the peanut butter your children prefer and also choose jelly that they like such as grape, apple, currant, or plum. Spread 3 slices of bread with the peanut butter, which should be at room temperature. Spread jelly over the peanut butter and cover with remaining bread. Cut sandwiches in half, removing crusts or not.

6 small sandwiches.

CREAM CHEESE AND CHIPPED BEEF SANDWICHES

12 slices moist dark bread
1/4 cup soft butter
1 (8-ounce) package cream cheese
8 ounces chipped beef

Spread the bread with butter. Add a layer of softened cheese to half the bread and cover with the chipped beef. Top with remaining bread. Remove crusts or not. Cut in half.

6 sandwiches.

CHICKEN AND HAM SPREAD SANDWICHES

1 cup minced chicken
1 cup minced ham
1/2 cup minced green onions
1/4 cup mayonnaise
12 thin slices bread

Mix the chicken, ham, onion, and mayonnaise. Spread on 6 slices of bread. Cover with remaining bread and cut off crusts. Cut into quarters.

24 small sandwiches.

RIPE OLIVE AND CREAM CHEESE SANDWICHES

1 (8-ounce) package cream cheese
3 tablespoons soft butter
2/3 cup chopped ripe olives
1/4 teaspoon minced onion or chives or 1/4 teaspoon onion juice
1 tablespoon cream (optional)
12 thin slices bread

The cheese and butter should be at room temperature. Combine all of the ingredients except the bread and blend. If the mixture is too firm to spread well, add a tablespoon of cream. Spread the mixture on 6 slices of bread and cover with remaining bread.

6 sandwiches.

TUNA SANDWICHES

1 (7-ounce) can tuna
1 teaspoon grated onion
1/2 cup minced celery
1/2 cup minced dill pickle (optional)
1/4 cup mayonnaise
12 thin slices white or whole wheat bread

Drain the tuna, flake it, and mix gently with the onion, celery, and pickle. Stir in the mayonnaise. Adjust seasoning and spread on half the bread. Cover with remaining bread and pat firmly into place. Cut off crusts and cut diagonally both ways.

24 small sandwiches.

tea parties

No one can give a tea party without dainty sandwiches to nibble. A tea party is likely to be an intimate affair, an inner circle gathering for family and a few friends. When you have put out the snowy tea cloth and the embroidered napkins, the translucent porcelain teacups, the Japanese teapot or the silver tea service, the final touch will be the platter of sandwiches.

Tea sandwiches are the younger sisters of the sandwich family, smaller but not less sophisticated, daintier but not less delicious.

Sandwiches for the tea table must be made on very thin slices of bread. This is an order! Commercial bread labeled "thin-sliced" is not sliced thin. There is on the market a white bread marked "Melba-sliced," which is satisfactory. Party rye provides thin-sliced, conveniently small rounds or squares. Pumpernickel, too, is sliced thin before packaging.

Unsliced bread is not always easy to find. Even bakeries often slice their new baked loaves—thick— before wrapping. However, unsliced bread can be obtained, even if you have to order it. At the delicatessen or your friendly butcher counter, you can have the loaf sliced on the meat machine as thin as it ought to be.

Slicing the bread yourself is the best way, and if you have a serrated bread knife or a sharp butcher knife, it's not very hard. There is even a gadget on the market to enable you to cut a thick commercial slice into two usable thin pieces.

Avoid fluffy breads. They won't cut thin no matter how you go at it. A fine firm texture is needed for successful tea sandwiches.

If you plan to slice the loaf yourself, first either chill it or freeze it. Freezing is better. If you are making buttered sandwiches, remember that a very thin slice of bread is almost impossible to butter. It will shred into holes. Do it the other way. Butter the cut end of the loaf before you cut off each slice. Melted butter may be brushed on, or soft butter spread sparingly.

The simple bread and butter sandwich is traditional for tea, and if it is made with white bread and fresh sweet butter, no sandwich is more delicious.

Small sandwiches with refreshing, unobtrusive fillings in interesting variety highlight the tea table. A cup of filling will spread three full-sized sandwiches, which can be cut into tea-sized dainties.

Spread the bread not quite to the edge. Lay on the upper slice, and slap it down briskly to make it stick. Don't spare the muscle. You can hit it much harder than you think. Neatly stack four of these sandwiches, cut off the edges of all four at once, and cut through to make the shape and size you want, three fingers or four squares or triangles.

It is on such festive occasions that your repertory of piquant sandwich butters comes into its own. To 1/4 pound (1 stick) of creamed butter add one of these flavorings.

1/4 cup minced parsley
1/4 cup minced chives
1/4 cup chopped watercress
2 teaspoons dried fines herbes
1 clove garlic, crushed
1/4 cup prepared horse-radish
2 tablespoons prepared mustard
1/4 cup minced almonds
1/4 cup chopped chutney
2 tablespoons anchovy paste
1/3 cup mashed sardines
1 teaspoon chili powder and 1/4 teaspoon garlic salt
1/4 cup deviled ham and 1 teaspoon prepared mustard
1 teaspoon curry and few drops Tabasco or Worcestershire sauce

CREAM CHEESE ON NUT BREAD SANDWICHES

1 (8-ounce) package cream cheese
2 tablespoons heavy cream or sour cream
12 slices nut or date nut bread

The cheese should be at room temperature. Smooth it with cream. Spread on 6 slices of the bread, cover with remaining slices, and cut in half. If the bread slices are large, cut into 3 portions.

12 to 18 sandwiches.

CUCUMBER SANDWICHES

1 or 2 cucumbers (about 30 slices)
1/3 cup soft butter
2 tablespoons minced parsley
2 tablespoons minced chives
1/2 teaspoon salt
1/4 teaspoon pepper
Very thin slices white bread

Peel and slice the cucumbers. Blend the butter, parsley, and chives. Season with salt and pepper. Cut the bread into rounds the size of the cucumber slices (no crusts). Spread about 30 rounds with the butter mixture and top with a slice of cucumber. Serve open. For a change, substitute 1/4 cup minced watercress for the parsley and chives.

30 sandwiches.

SMOKED SALMON SANDWICHES

18 slices white or light rye bread
1/2 cup softened butter
9 slices smoked salmon
Juice 1 lemon

Spread the bread with butter, cover 9 slices with the salmon, and press into the butter so it sticks. Sprinkle with lemon juice. Cover with remaining bread. Press top slices down firmly and refrigerate at once so the butter will harden and the salmon won't seep into the bread. Cut off crusts and cut in half. For smaller sandwiches cut into 3 finger-shaped pieces.

18 or 27 sandwiches.

WATERCRESS SANDWICHES

1 (4-ounce) package cream cheese
1 tablespoon cream
3 tablespoons soft butter
2 cups chopped watercress
18 thin slices white bread

The cheese should be at room temperature. Blend it with the cream and butter. Stir in the watercress. Spread onto 9 slices of bread and cover with more pieces of bread. Press top bread in place and cut off crusts. Cut into finger-shaped thirds.

27 small sandwiches.

MINCED CHICKEN SANDWICHES

2 cups minced cooked chicken
1/4 cup strong chicken broth
1/4 cup mayonnaise
2 tablespoons minced parsley
1/2 teaspoon salt
16 thin slices white bread

Mix the chicken with broth and mayonnaise; add parsley and salt to taste. Spread on 8 slices of bread and cover with remaining bread. Pat top pieces of bread down hard. Cut off crusts and cut each sandwich into 3 finger-shaped pieces.

24 sandwiches.

CURRIED EGG SANDWICHES

6 hard-cooked eggs, chopped
1/4 cup mayonnaise
1/2 teaspoon salt
1/4 teaspoon pepper
2 tablespoons minced chives or scallions or 1 clove garlic, crushed
1 to 2 teaspoons curry
12 slices bread

Combine all the ingredients except the bread. Spread on 6 slices of bread. Cover with remaining bread and pat the top slices down hard. Remove crusts and cut in half or in thirds.

12 or 18 sandwiches.

When you plan a small tea party is the time to let yourself go and have fun as you prepare your sandwiches. You have the time, and your intended guests provide the inspiration. Unusual fillings and astonishing shapes can be produced to charm the small circle around the tea table.

MUSHROOM SANDWICHES

1/2 pound mushrooms, chopped fine
1 tablespoon minced scallions or onion
3 tablespoons butter
2 tablespoons water
1 tablespoon minced parsley
2 tablespoons mayonnaise
1/2 teaspoon oregano
1/2 teaspoon salt
1/4 teaspoon pepper
8 thin slices white bread

Sauté the mushrooms and scallions or onion in butter for 1 to 2 minutes. Remove from heat and add 2 tablespoons water. Cover and let stand at least 10 minutes. Stir in the parsley, mayonnaise, oregano, salt, and pepper. Spread on 4 slices of bread and cover with remaining bread. Press the top pieces of bread firmly in place. Cut into thirds or quarters.

12 to 16 sandwiches.

EGG AND DEVILED HAM SANDWICHES

4 hard-cooked eggs, chopped
2 (4 1/2-ounce) cans deviled ham
1/4 cup mayonnaise
1 teaspoon prepared mustard
1/8 teaspoon pepper
12 slices rye or whole wheat bread

Blend all of the ingredients together except the bread. Spread on half the bread and cover with remaining bread. Remove crusts or not as you like.

6 sandwiches.

CHICKEN SANDWICHES WITH WATER CHESTNUTS

2 cups diced chicken
1 cup diced water chestnuts
1/4 cup mayonnaise
2 tablespoons soy sauce
2 tablespoons chicken gravy or broth
8 slices bread

Combine the chicken and water chestnuts. Blend the mayonnaise with soy sauce and chicken gravy or broth. Mix with the chicken and chestnuts. Spread on 4 pieces of bread and cover with remaining bread. Trim crusts and cut in half diagonally.

8 sandwiches.

EGG AND SALMON SANDWICHES

1 (7 3/4-ounce) can salmon
3 hard-cooked eggs, chopped
3 tablespoons minced celery
1 teaspoon minced onion
1/2 cup mayonnaise
1 teaspoon lemon juice
12 slices bread

Drain the salmon and flake it. Combine with the eggs, celery, onion, mayonnaise, and lemon juice. Spread on 6 slices of bread and cover with remaining 6 pieces. Pat the tops firmly in place and cut in half.

12 sandwiches.

LIVERWURST PATÉ SANDWICHES

1 pound liverwurst
3 tablespoons minced scallions
2 tablespoons butter
3 hard-cooked eggs, chopped
1 tablespoon tomato paste
1/3 cup mayonnaise
1/2 teaspoon oregano
16 thin slices rye bread

Heat the liverwurst until soft. Remove and sauté the scallions in butter until transparent but not brown. Mix scallions with the liverwurst. Stir in the eggs, tomato paste, mayonnaise, and oregano. Adjust seasoning. Spread on half the bread and cover with remaining slices. Pat top slices in place firmly and cut off crusts. Cut in halves or quarters.

16 to 32 sandwiches.

MINCED HAM AND CELERY SANDWICHES

2 cups minced ham
1/2 cup minced celery
2 teaspoons prepared mustard
1/4 cup mayonnaise
2 tablespoons minced pickle
3 tablespoons soft butter
12 to 16 slices rye bread

Mix the ham, celery, mustard, mayonnaise, and pickle. Either butter the bread or add the butter to the spread. Cover half the bread with the ham mixture, top with remaining bread, and press the tops down firmly. Remove crusts if you wish and cut in half.

12 to 16 sandwiches.

TONGUE SPREAD SANDWICHES

2 cups ground minced smoked tongue
1 teaspoon prepared mustard
2 tablespoons prepared horse-radish
1/4 cup mayonnaise
Soft butter
12 thin slices rye bread

Mix the tongue, mustard, horse-radish, and mayonnaise. Butter the bread and spread the tongue mixture on half the slices. Cover with remaining slices and pat tops on firmly. Cut off crusts and cut in halves or quarters diagonally. You may make these open-faced if you wish.

12 or 24 sandwiches.

TURKEY ALMOND SANDWICHES

3 cups chopped turkey
1 cup chopped toasted almonds
2 drops almond extract
1/2 cup mayonnaise
2 tablespoons parsley
12 slices white bread

Combine all of the ingredients except the bread and spread on 6 slices of bread. Cover with remaining bread. Cut off crusts and cut in half.

12 sandwiches.

Don't be afraid to tackle those fascinating architectural constructions that vary the appearance of the sandwich tray, putting among the conventional flat sandwiches a few three-dimensional forms as accents. They catch the eye, they look as though you had worked your fingers to the bone, and they aren't really very hard at all.

CORNUCOPIAS

12 small square slices bread
3 cups chicken or ham spread (see page 160)

Trim crusts from bread and flatten with a rolling pin. Spread with filling not quite to the edges. Roll each slice into a cone shape, keeping one end cleared. Fasten with toothpicks and refrigerate. Remove toothpicks to serve.

12 sandwiches.

VARIATIONS

Cornucopias may be filled with any kind of spreads such as the mixtures used in mushroom sandwiches, chicken and water chestnut sandwiches, watercress sandwiches, egg salad sandwiches.

ROLL-UPS

12 slices bread
3 cups egg spread (see pages 158–159
3 tablespoons soft butter

Cut the crusts from the bread. Flatten with a rolling pin. Cut pieces in half. Mix the egg spread with soft butter and spread on the bread. Roll up, fasten with toothpicks, and refrigerate. Remove the toothpicks before serving.

24 sandwiches.

ROLLED WATERCRESS SANDWICHES

1 (8-ounce) package cream cheese
2 tablespoons heavy cream
1 cup minced watercress
1/4 teaspoon salt
1/8 teaspoon pepper
12 thin slices white bread
Watercress sprigs

Blend the cream cheese and cream. Stir in the watercress, salt, and pepper. Cut crusts off the bread and spread with the mixture not quite to the edge of each slice. Roll up at once and fasten with toothpicks. Place a sprig of cress in one end if you wish. Chill. Remove the toothpicks before serving. You may cut the bread in half for smaller sandwiches.

12 to 24 sandwiches.

receptions

It is not really a long step from your own small tea table to the formal reception, whether for wedding guests or VIPs. Sandwiches are the fare for fifty, as they were for fifteen. The difference lies in the planning.

You begin with more materials. For fifty people, you will need up to two hundred small sandwiches, which means 125 slices of bread more or less. If you plan some open-faced sandwiches, they take less bread. If you cut fancy shapes instead of quarters, they take more.

A loaf of party rye is cut into about forty slices of bread, making twenty covered sandwiches. Melba-sliced white, with about thirty slices to the loaf, produces sixty small triangles or forty-five fingers. An ordinary sandwich loaf, gadget split, may provide as many as seventy-two fingers, ninety-six quarters. A pound loaf, if you cut it yourself, may produce up to fifty small sandwiches. The label on packaged imported pumpernickel indicates the number of slices. A little mental arithmetic will tell you how many of the various kinds to buy for your fifty guests.

In general, when you figure spreads for fifty, count on six to eight cups of filling for fifty small sandwiches. The following spread recipes are caculated to yield about 2 cups each. Twelve to sixteen small sandwiches. For fifty, get out your computer and tell it to multiply.

In planning a large-scale sandwich operation, you will want to make things as easy as possible for yourself. To save time, skip the buttering step. When butter is needed to bind the ingredients, it is included in the following recipes. Making spreads is a matter of mixing. Combine the ingredients and blend thoroughly. Adjust the seasoning to taste, and you're ready to go.

EGG SPREADS

Mix 4 chopped hard-cooked eggs, with 1/2 teaspoon salt, 1/4 teaspoon pepper, and 3 tablespoons mayonnaise. Add one of these combinations.

2 tablespoons minced parsley, 1 teaspoon minced olives, and 1/2 cup minced cucumber

1/4 cup minced celery, 2 tablespoons minced onion, and 2 tablespoons chili sauce

1/4 pound sautéed and chopped chicken livers and 1 tablespoon minced onion

1/4 cup cooked chopped chicken and 1 teaspoon curry powder

1/4 pound crisp crumbled bacon

1/2 cup minced ham and 2 teaspoons prepared mustard

1/4 cup chopped olives and 1 tablespoon minced pimiento

1/2 cup shredded Swiss cheese and 1 teaspoon prepared mustard

2 (4 1/2-ounce) cans deviled ham

1 (7 3/4-ounce) can salmon (flaked) and 1 teaspoon lemon juice

1 teaspoon fines herbes, 2 tablespoons minced chives, and 1 teaspoon curry

2 tablespoons minced pickles, 1 teaspoon prepared mustard, and 1 teaspoon minced onion

1/2 cup mashed sardines and 2 teaspoons lemon juice

1 tablespoon chopped green pepper, 1 tablespoon chopped pimiento, and 1 teaspoon chili powder

Spread on thin-sliced buttered bread and do not spread too close to the edges. Top with a second slice and press firmly into place. Stack 4 sandwiches at a time to cut off crusts. Slice into 3 or 4 pieces.

CHICKEN SPREADS

To 1 1/2 cups minced cooked chicken mixed with 1/4 cup well-seasoned mayonnaise add one of these combinations.

1/2 cup minced celery and 1 tablespoon minced chives or onion
1/2 cup minced ham and 1 teaspoon prepared mustard
1/2 cup minced tongue and 1 teaspoon prepared horse-radish
1/2 cup crisp crumbled bacon
1/2 cup chopped toasted almonds and 1 teaspoon curry powder
1/2 cup coarsely chopped water chestnuts and 2 tablespoons soy sauce
2 tablespoons minced parsley and 1 teaspoon minced onion
3 tablespoons minced celery and 1 tablespoon fresh or 1 teaspoon dried tarragon

HAM SPREADS

To 1 1/2 cups minced ham, 1/4 cup mayonnaise, and 1 tablespoon prepared mustard add one of these suggestions.

1 tablespoon minced parsley
2 chopped hard-cooked eggs and 1/2 teaspoon garlic powder
2 tablespoons minced celery, 1 tablespoon minced parsley, and 1 tablespoon minced chives
2 tablespoons minced green olives and 1 tablespoon minced pickle
1/2 cup shredded cheddar cheese

Once your spreads are made, you are ready for assembly-line preparation of sandwiches. If you are on your own, lay out a convenient number of bread slices, spread them, top, and smack them down all round. Stack, trim, and cut into small sandwiches as you did for the small tea table.

But why run a lone-wolf operation? Teamwork is so much more fun. Get your gang together, and making the sandwiches can be as much fun as the party. A five-girl assembly line can make two hundred reception sandwiches quicker than Ford can make Mustangs. Worker No. 1 monitors the bread and lays out the slices, Worker No. 2 spreads, No. 3 tops and slaps, No. 4 trims and cuts. Presto! there are your sandwiches.

Of course you will be making several kinds of sandwiches. It will be efficient if Worker No. 4 cuts each variety into a different shape, to be stored separately.

Worker No. 5, mindful that bread dries out quickly, attends to the storing, immediately picking up each cut stack and putting it into plastic or foil.

If space is at a premium in the refrigerator, the sacked stacks of sandwiches may be stored in a cool place and kept moist by swathing them in wet towels over the plastic. If refrigerator space is abundant, sandwiches may be arranged directly onto the serving platters and protected by plastic, tamped down so as to be airtight.

At this stage sandwiches become a fascinating medium for the artistic feminine hand. The appearance of the refreshment table depends upon the presentation of the sandwiches. An attractively arranged platter gives to the eye a foretaste of good things for the palate.

A handsome round plate displays a chrysanthemum in bas-relief if you arrange on it finger-shaped egg sandwiches radiating from the center like the spokes of a wheel and overlapping so that the yellow edges show. If a real chrysanthemum is available, it makes a beautiful center rosette; if not, there is always curly green parsley.

Flowers always make a colorful garnish. Be sure to select varieties that will keep fresh. Small chrysanthemums are ideal. Nasturtiums have an additional claim to fame. They are fun to eat—seeds and leaves and flowers alike—as well as to look at.

Another handsomely garnished platter might feature triangle sandwiches around the outside, then a wreath of cherry tomatoes or green or ripe olives, and the center piled with squares or fingers.

Other gay garnishes are watercress, celery leaves, curly lettuce, feathery fennel. Colorful, crisp, crunchy vegetables give the teeth a change of texture. Try carrot sticks, radish roses, celery curls, zucchini rounds, cucumber fingers.

If platter space is limited, sandwiches may be stacked. It is better to make uneven stacks, so each sandwich can be easily picked up from the plate. Finger sandwiches are effective arranged in a tick-tacktoe pattern, for instance. Pile triangles reversed as in the Star of David, and squares with the corners swirled.

If trays of sandwiches are to be set out buffet style, each tray may present a different kind of sandwich. If platters are to be passed, they should contain a selection of several varieties from which to choose. To show off how hard you worked, there are eye-catching fancy sandwiches to adorn such variegated platters. In addition to the tea-table roll-ups and cornucopias, try these easy dainties.

FOLD-UPS

12 slices whole wheat bread
3 tablespoons soft butter
3 cups egg spread, chicken spread, or ham spread
(see pages 158–160)

Cut the crusts from the bread. Butter one side of each piece and spread with filling not quite to the edge. Fold in the opposite corners and fasten with toothpicks.

12 sandwiches.

Equally decorative are open-faced dainties. They look so pretty, and they have the practical advantage that the guest knows at a glance what he is getting.

OPEN-FACED CHICKEN SANDWICHES DE LUXE

Very thin white bread
1/4 cup soft butter
1 2 3/4-ounce can Pâté de foie gras
About 1/2 pound thin slices cooked chicken

Cut off the crusts from the bread and spread with soft butter and foie gras. Top with the slices of chicken. Serve open or cover and cut each sandwich into 3 or 4 pieces.

About 30 small sandwiches.

CAMEMBERT AND CHUTNEY SANDWICHES

6 ounces Camembert cheese
2 to 4 tablespoons heavy cream
1 teaspoon curry powder
1/4 cup finely chopped chutney
4 slices toast or 16 small toast rounds

The cheese should be at room temperature. Mash it with a fork and add 2 tablespoons of cream, blending until smooth. Add the curry and chutney. If too thick to spread easily, blend in the remaining cream. Spread on toast or toast rounds. Cut the toast into quarters or fingers.

12 to 16 sandwiches.

CHEDDAR CHEESE ROUNDS

3/4 pound cheddar cheese
2 chopped hard-cooked eggs
1/4 cup chopped pecans
1/4 cup chopped dill pickle
1 teaspoon Worcestershire sauce
30 rounds of toast or rye or pumpernickel
Soft butter (optional)

Grate the cheese coarsely and mix with the eggs, nuts, pickle, and Worcestershire sauce. Shape into a roll the same circumference as the rounds. Wrap in waxed paper and chill. Slice and place 1 slice on each round, buttered or not as you wish.

30 sandwiches.

SWISS CHEESE ON PUMPERNICKEL SANDWICHES

3/4 pound Swiss cheese, grated
1/4 cup soft butter
1 teaspoon prepared mustard
Few drops Worcestershire sauce
About 2 tablespoons mayonnaise or cream (optional)
8 thin slices pumpernickel bread

Combine the cheese with butter, mustard, and Worcestershire sauce. If the mixture is too thick to spread, add a little mayonnaise or cream. Spread onto the pumpernickel. Cut off crusts and cut into 4 pieces each.

32 sandwiches.

MUSHROOM CANAPÉ SANDWICHES

1/2 pound mushrooms, chopped
2 tablespoons minced chives or scallions
2 tablespoons minced parsley
2 tablespoons butter
2 tablespoons mayonnaise
6 to 8 slices bread or toast
Chopped parsley

Heat the mushrooms, chives or scallions, and parsley in butter. Remove from heat and add mayonnaise. Adjust seasoning. Spread on bread or toast, quarter it, and sprinkle with parsley. Serve face up.

24 to 32 sandwiches.

cocktail parties

When cocktail party time comes, many of the sandwiches in the reception section, are appropriate,
especially if the spread is highly flavored. No need
to get fancy. A man with a glass in his hand doesn't
care if he is nibbling a ribbon, a cornucopia, or a
pinwheel. He will appreciate much more a simple
tasty morsel topping a bite-sized sliver of well-
flavored bread or crunchy thin toast. He calls it a
canapé.

TOMATO EGG ANCHOVY CANAPÉS

4 small tomatoes, sliced
24 buttered toast rounds
2 tablespoons mayonnaise
4 hard-cooked eggs, sliced
1 can (2 ounces) rolled anchovy fillets

Put a thin slice of tomato on each toast round. Top
with a bit of mayonnaise. Add a slice of egg and top
with an anchovy.

24 canapés.

SARDINE CANAPÉS

20 finger-sized slices toast
1 can (3 3/4-ounces) Norwegian sardines
1/2 lemon

Place a sardine on each toast finger and sprinkle with a few drops of lemon juice.

20 sandwiches.

DEVILED HAM CANAPÉS

1 (5-ounce) can deviled ham
1 (4-ounce) package cream cheese
2 tablespoons mayonnaise
1 tablespoon minced pimiento
15 toast rounds or bread rounds or triangles
2 tablespoons capers

Mix the ham, cheese, and mayonnaise. Stir in the pimiento and spread mixture on toast or bread. Garnish with capers.

15 canapés.

ROQUEFORT CANAPÉS

1/3 cup Roquefort or blue cheese
1/3 cup unsalted butter
1 tablespoon Worcestershire sauce
12 toast rounds or 3 slices toast or 3 slices bread

The cheese and butter should be at room temperature. Mix them with the Worcestershire sauce until thoroughly blended. Spread on toast rounds, toast, or bread. Quarter the toast or bread. Refrigerate for about 1 hour to harden the butter and cheese.

12 canapés.

MUSHROOM CANAPÉS

1 (8-ounce) package cream cheese
1/4 pound mushrooms
1 tablespoon cream
1 teaspoon onion juice
Pinch oregano
8 slices thin white bread

The cheese should be at room temperature. Chop the mushrooms. Mix the cheese thoroughly with the cream, onion juice, and oregano. Stir in the mushrooms and spread on small pieces of trimmed bread. Cut in quarters.

32 canapés.

CREAM CHEESE AND ANCHOVY CANAPÉS

1 (8-ounce) package Philadelphia cream cheese
3 ounces anchovy paste
4 slices bread or toast
1 hard-cooked egg, grated

Mix the cheese and anchovy paste. Trim crusts and cut the bread or toast into 4 pieces each. Spread with the cheese-anchovy mixture and garnish with grated egg.

16 canapés.

Worth the last-minute effort to run them under the broiler are a few choice hot canapés. Choose cheese. It profits by toasting, and it can be prepared ahead, sliced or in a snappily seasoned spread. Everybody likes cheese with drinks.

HOT CHEESE PUFFS

1 cup grated cheddar cheese
1/4 cup mayonnaise
1 teaspoon prepared mustard
2 medium egg whites, beaten stiff
8 slices toast

Mix the cheese, mayonnaise, and mustard. Fold in the egg whites. Trim the edges from the toast and spread with the mixture. Cut into 4 pieces each. Broil under low heat for 4 to 5 minutes until puffy and browned.

32 canapés.

HAM AND CHEESE PUFFS

Soft butter
6 slices bread
6 slices ham
1/8 teaspoon freshly ground pepper
Pinch salt
2 egg whites
1 cup grated American cheese
Dash cayenne

Butter one side of the bread, cover with the ham, and sprinkle with pepper. Cut in quarters. Add salt to the egg whites and beat until stiff. Fold in the cheese and cayenne. Place the bread with ham on a baking sheet. Put a small spoonful of the cheese egg-white mixture on each and broil at 375° for 8 minutes until puffed up and slightly browned.

24 canapés.

TOASTED CHEESE ROUNDS

1 egg white, beaten stiff
1/2 cup grated sharp cheese
1/2 teaspoon salt
Pinch pepper
1/8 teaspoon paprika
1 tablespoon Worcestershire sauce
24 bread rounds

Combine the egg white and cheese with salt, pepper, paprika, and Worcestershire sauce. Toast the bread rounds on one side. Spread the cheese mixture on the untoasted side and put under the broiler for 5 to 7 minutes until lightly browned and puffy.

24 canapés.

HOT CHEESE FINGERS

1 tablespoon butter
1 tablespoon flour
1/3 cup milk
1 cup grated cheddar cheese
1/2 teaspoon salt
1 egg
8 slices toast, cut into 24 finger-shaped pieces

Melt the butter, stir in the flour, and add the milk slowly while stirring. Add the cheese and salt and cook in a double boiler until the cheese is melted. Remove from heat. Stir in the slightly beaten egg yolk and fold in the beaten egg white. Pile on the toast fingers and broil until puffy and brown.

24 canapés.

All hot canapés are appreciated, so why not swank with at least one at every cocktail party? Keep them hot and keep them coming. Hamburgers in miniature, served on melba toast rounds, are certain to please. Hot stuffed mushroom canapés too are sure-fire successes.

HOT HAM CANAPÉS

8 slices rye or white bread
1 1/2 cups ground ham
1/3 cup grated cheddar cheese
1 tablespoon prepared mustard
2 tablespoons mayonnaise

Trim the edges from the bread. Toast it and cut into 4 squares or triangles. Mix the remaining ingredients and spread on the toast. Broil under low heat for 3 minutes.

32 canapés.

SAUSAGES IN BLANKETS

12 cocktail-size (about 1 pound) frankfurters or small link sausage
Water
12 small finger rolls
Soft butter
Prepared mustard (optional)

Sauté the sausages in a little water in a skillet. Roll them around to brown evenly. Pork sausages may be pricked with a fork, covered with water, and simmered 3 minutes. Pour off the water and brown 3 minutes longer. Warm the rolls. Split lengthwise without cutting all the way through. Spread with a little butter. Place a hot sausage in each and serve at once. You may add a little prepared mustard to the butter if you use frankfurters.

12 sandwiches.

STUFFED MUSHROOM CANAPÉS

16 medium-sized mushrooms
1/4 cup minced onion
1/4 cup butter
2 tablespoons cream
1 teaspoon Worcestershire sauce
1/2 teaspoon salt
1/4 teaspoon pepper
16 toast rounds

Pull the stems out of the mushrooms. Wipe the caps with a damp cloth. Chop the stems. Sauté the onion in 2 tablespoons butter for 2 minutes, add the mushroom stems, and cook 2 minutes more. Stir in the cream, Worcestershire sauce, salt, and pepper. Meanwhile, warm the mushroom caps in 2 tablespoons butter in a skillet or in the oven—it takes only a few minutes to warm them. Place a mushroom cap on each round of toast and fill it with the stuffing. Serve warm or cold.

16 canapés.

STUFFED MUSHROOM CANAPÉS II

1 pound medium-sized mushrooms
2 onions, minced
1/4 cup butter
2 tablespoons water
3 tablespoons half-and-half
3 tablespoons minced ham or crisp crumbled bacon
40 toast rounds

Remove the stems from the mushrooms and chop them fine. Wipe the tops with a damp cloth; do not submerge them in water. Cook the onion in 2 tablespoons butter for 2 minutes. Add mushrooms stems and cook 2 minutes more. Add the water and after 2 minutes the cream. Add the ham or bacon and remove from heat. Meanwhile sauté the mushroom caps in the remaining butter for 1 minute face down, turn, and cook 1 minute face up. Place the mushroom caps on rounds of toast and fill each with a spoonful of the stem mixture. Serve hot, warm, or cold.

40 canapés.

"after" parties

There's still another kind of party to which sandwiches are invited more often than not. It's an "after" party. After swim, after skating, après ski, after the game on TV or on the field, or after the card game, the theater, the concert—who isn't hungry? Enjoyment whets appetite. The group comes from its fun sharp-set and ready for casual good things to eat—and isn't that a definition of a sandwich?

In Copenhagen the jolly Danes find their fun in the pleasure garden called Tivoli. There they can enjoy the simple gaiety of the old-time pantomime theater, or take in a ballet, or a band playing under the trees, or a classical concert, or just stroll in the walks, where a thousand lamps light up as darkness falls. Before they part, they will drop in at one of half a dozen cozy eating places round about, and call for smörrebröd.

Smörrebröd (literally "smear bread") is a sandwich, but such a sandwich as the gambling Earl of Sandwich never dreamed of. This enticing concoction is begun by spreading a morsel of bread with a smear of smör, which is sweet Danish butter. Upon this base is erected a neat construction of good things, contrasting in savor and texture, till it is almost as high as it is wide. The Danes take knife and fork to it, demolish it in three bites, and call for another.

At Oskar Davidsen's famous restaurant, a hungry Dane could call for another ninety-nine times, and not repeat once. The Davidsen menu comes by the yard.

A smörrebröd layout makes an ideal "after" repast for a party of hungry merrymakers anywhere. Call it a Sandwich Soiree. The table makes such a handsome and appetizing appearance; and yet the hostess needn't miss any of the foregoing entertainment for last-minute fussing. If the filled platters are given the plastic and damp towels treatment, they can be whisked to the previously prepared buffet table in jig time when the supper party is about to start.

The possible varieties aren't held to Davidsen's one hundred; the hostess can choose among endless kinds. She is not even confined to Danish specialties. The Norwegians and Swedes yield to no one in the matter of piling up good things on a basis of bread. The following Scandinavian pileups would look festive on the platters and complement one another on the individual plate and palate.

DANISH CHEESE AND TOMATO SANDWICHES

6 slices Danish rye bread
3 tablespoons soft butter
6 slices cheese
Prepared mustard
6 slices sweet onion
12 slices salami or liver sausage
6 slices tomato
12 anchovy fillets

Spread the bread with butter and cover with cheese. Spread with a little mustard and add the onion. Cover with salami or liver sausage. Place a slice of tomato on top of each and garnish with anchovy fillets.

6 sandwiches.

SWEDISH SALMON SANDWICHES

6 slices white bread
2 tablespoons soft butter
6 pieces smoked salmon
Few drops lemon juice
3 tablespoons capers
3 hard-cooked eggs, cut in wedges
6 teaspoons mayonnaise
Paprika
3 tablespoons caviar (optional)
3 teaspoons minced chives

Spread the bread lightly with butter and cover with the salmon, cut to fit. Add a few drops of lemon juice and the capers. Decorate with egg wedges and top each wedge with a bit of mayonnaise and a sprinkling of paprika. Pile the caviar, red or black, in the center and sprinkle chives over all.

6 sandwiches.

NORWEGIAN HERRING SANDWICHES WITH EGG

6 slices white bread
2 tablespoons soft butter
4 hard-cooked eggs, sliced
6 herring fillets or 12 smaller pieces
2 tablespoons chopped watercress or parsley

Spread the bread evenly with butter. Cover with slices of egg and top with herring. Garnish with chopped watercress or parsley.

6 sandwiches.

SCANDINAVIAN FISH SANDWICHES

6 pieces of fillets of sole
6 tablespoons butter
Salt
Pepper
6 slices white bread
3 cucumbers, sliced
6 lemon wedges
1 tablespoon minced parsley

Sauté the fish in 3 tablespoons butter until browned on both sides. Sprinkle with salt and pepper. Spread the bread with remaining butter. Place a fish fillet on each piece of bread. Garnish with cucumbers and place a lemon wedge on each. Sprinkle with parsley. This sandwich is particularly good served while the fish is warm.

6 sandwiches.

TUNA SANDWICHES

6 slices whole wheat or light rye bread
3 tablespoons soft butter
6 slices Swiss cheese
1 (6 1/2-ounce) can tuna
1/4 cup chopped green pepper
1/4 cup mayonnaise
2 tablespoons minced fresh dill or 2 teaspoons dried

Spread the bread with butter and cover with Swiss cheese. Flake the tuna and combine with green pepper and mayonnaise. Pile onto the cheese and sprinkle with dill. Top with a bit of mayonnaise if you wish.

6 sandwiches.

BEEF AND POTATO SALAD SANDWICHES

6 slices bread
3 tablespoons soft butter
6 slices rare roast beef
3 cups potato salad
6 tablespoons minced pickle

Spread the bread evenly with butter and place a slice of beef on each piece. Pile the potato salad in the center of each and sprinkle the pickle over the top or around the edges.

6 sandwiches.

CHEESE AND HAM SANDWICHES

6 slices bread
3 tablespoons soft butter
6 slices cheese
3 teaspoons prepared mustard
6 slices ham
6 tablespoons potato salad
3 teaspoons minced scallions or chives
6 teaspoons mayonnaise or boiled dressing

Spread the bread with butter. Cover with slices of cheese and spread with mustard. In the center of each piece, place a slice of ham, rolled or folded up. Surround with potato salad and sprinkle the scallions or chives over all. Put bits of dressing here and there on the salad.

6 sandwiches.

HAM, HERRING, AND BEET SANDWICHES

6 slices bread
2 tablespoons soft butter
6 slices ham
6 pieces herring in sour cream or wine sauce
3 cups diced beets
1 hard-cooked egg, grated
1 tablespoon minced parsley

Spread the bread with butter and cover with the slices of ham. Put the herring in the center and surround with beets. Garnish with egg and parsley.

6 sandwiches.

LIVER SAUSAGE AND SHRIMP SANDWICHES

4 slices white bread
2 tablespoons soft butter
4 slices liver sausage
4 thin slices sweet onion
1 teaspoon salt
1 tablespoon minced parsley
1/2 cup cooked baby shrimp
Lemon juice

Spread the bread evenly with butter. Put a slice of liver sausage on each. Cover with a slice of onion and sprinkle it with salt and parsley. Pile the shrimp high in the center of each sandwich and sprinkle with lemon juice.

4 sandwiches.

HAM AND BABY SHRIMP SANDWICHES

4 slices white bread
2 tablespoons soft butter
4 slices ham
Lettuce
1 cup cooked baby shrimp
2 tablespoons minced pickle
1 tablespoon mayonnaise

Spread the bread evenly with butter and cover each piece with a slice of ham, cut to fit. Add lettuce leaves to cover and pile the shrimp in the center. Edge with the pickle and put a bit of mayonnaise on top of the shrimp.

4 sandwiches.

The "after" table needs one more touch to round out the picture: a bowl of soup. In summer, what could be more refreshing than a cold fruit soup in the Scandinavian manner, ladled from the chilled tureen? Or there's piquant gazpacho, or rosy red borsch, or creamy vichyssoise, or many another bright soup to cool and refresh a summertime gathering.

In winter, a steaming tureen of hot soup is a positive necessity. Rising warm and fragrant, the good aroma of French onion soup, Italian minestrone, or New England fish chowder beckons the hungry. A flavorsome cupful will warm the cockles of the heart and make the smörrebröd slide down in a glow, while the guests enjoy that best of parties, a Soup and Sandwich Soiree.

Index

SPECIAL OFFER-

SIX GREAT INTERNATIONAL COOKBOOKS

Regular $6⁷⁵ Value

Now Only $3⁵⁰

Plus 4 carton end flaps from any 2 cartons of L&M, Lark, Chesterfield or Eve Cigarettes

Here's what you get:

- **THE FANNIE FARMER COOKBOOK** • **THE COMPLETE BOOK OF ORIEN-TAL COOKING** • **THE SPANISH COOKBOOK** • **THE ART OF ITALIAN COOKING**
- **THE ART OF JEWISH COOKING** • **THE ART OF FRENCH COOKING**

Hundreds of interesting and exciting recipes from favorite cuisines. Easy to read, understand and prepare.

Add zest to your everyday cooking and a new dimension to entertaining.

This handsome set comes complete with decorative bookcase.

A $6.75 Value...Yours for Only $3.50

Mail to: L&M Cookbook Offer, P.O. Box 60-1937, Minneapolis, Minn. 55460

Gentlemen:

Please send me the set of Six Great International Cookbooks. I am enclosing $3.50 (Check or money order) Plus 4 carton end flaps from any 2 cartons of L&M, Lark, Chesterfield or Eve Cigarettes.

Name_____

Address_____

City_____ State_____ Zip_____

Please Allow 4-6 weeks for delivery. For persons 21 years or older. Offer void where prohibited, licensed, taxed or restricted by law. This offer expires March 31, 1974.

CONTENTS

THE ART OF SALAD MAKING

* To locate recipes designated with an asterisk and/or initial Capital Letters consult the Index.

Chapter One

SALAD ON THE MENU

My father was by profession a judge of the State Supreme Court, and by avocation a judge of good food. When he came home from the courthouse, he would doff his high silk hat, and his otter-collared greatcoat, and come to the nursery to continue my education in the things that mattered.

The way any other parent might take a child on his knee and nourish the growing mind by reading aloud from improving works, my father would take me on his broad lap and nourish me with choice tidbits, a succulent snail, an oyster Rockefeller, or an artichoke heart, improving my mind the while with a grave and expert discourse on gustatory lore. Escoffier was always more real to me than Brer Rabbit. In such sessions he taught me to appreciate the place of salad on the menu long before my time. At an age when other American moppets were protesting, in the classic phrase, "I say it's spinach . . ." I was reaching eagerly for my broccoli vinaigrette. I was already turning up my nose at a meal without salad in the saladless age of Yankee gustatory innocence, many years ago.

I have been spreading the gospel of salad ever since. Like the apostles of old, I have had my moments of

peril, and my almost-martyrdoms, while as a food lecturer I spread the good word.

There was the fatal day when I journeyed to Philadelphia to preach the art of the salad. A group had sum-
moned me to take part in their series in which cookbook
authors demonstrated their techniques. With a stack of
copies of my *Weekend Chef* under my arm, I journeyed
into the wilderness. The blizzard howled, the temperature dropped with a thud, as I struggled through the
storm to the auditorium and began operations.

I was delighted to find that the last word in equipment had already been installed for my demonstration.
I was equally delighted to find two very pretty young
ladies ready to carry out my behests. They stood at attention like magicians' assistants, one at the sink, one at the
stove, as the crowded audience threw back their furs and
rustled into silence, and the lecture started.

"Ladies," I said, "I will demonstrate the important
art—and it is an art—of washing and drying salad greens.
First we half-fill the sink with cold water—"

Assistant No. 1 turned on the spigot.

Nothing happened.

What can be wrong?

The pipes have burst!

Five minutes later, like Rebecca at the well, we were
washing the greens in a pail of water.

"Thus we see," I advised solemnly, "that even if you
live on the Main Line, it is good to have running water
laid on in your kitchens.

"Now for a cooked dressing. Please turn on the gas
under the double boiler."

Assistant No. 2 turned the control.

Nothing happened.

What can be wrong?

The gas line is frozen!

Five minutes later, I was compounding a sour cream dressing for the cole slaw. It was delicious.

"French dressing," I announced. "In these days of educated machines, nothing is easier than to buzz a dressing in a blender."

Assistant No. 1 manned the blender.

"Salt and pepper," I ordered. She put it in.

"Sugar—paprika—tarragon—"

She pinched and sprinkled.

"Vinegar—oil—

"Cover the blender, and buzz."

My acolyte buzzed gently. The audience could see the appetizing mixture creaming against the glass.

"And now I'll taste it."

The assistant switched off the blender, uncapped it, and handed me a spoon.

"Mm—more tarragon? Yes, I think so, a dash."

She added a dash of tarragon.

"And now—blend once more—and *voilà!*" I said grandly, with a cordon bleu flourish.

The zealous assistant switched on the blender full speed—and the dressing, as the saying goes, hit the fan.

Out flew a fountain, ceiling high, and settled down again on everything, on my carefully coiffed head, on the young assistant's bubble hairdo, on shoulders and table and blender and salad bowl. Never had a food lecturer and her food been so marinated.

Not counting on such blind obedience, I had omitted to instruct my sorcerer's apprentice to re-cover the blender.

"Ladies," I added hastily, mopping dressing from my hair, my shoulders, and my shoes, "one more word about blending a dressing—always cover the blender!"

That tore it. The audience howled.

"And remember," I concluded, wiping off my eyelashes, "that salad is nature's gift to menu making!"

I have never given another demonstration to prove so graphically that you have to cover the blender; but every time I demonstrate the art of salad making, I prove that salads are the most versatile of foods. On your table they can do anything.

Take the standard menu of soup, meat-and-vegetable, and dessert. You can't have the dessert first or the soup last (unless you're Chinese), but salad can substitute for any of these courses in any position. It can also augment any course. In America, many a salad makes the whole meal.

In the restaurants of European countries, the salads are often listed with the first course, the *antipasto*, the *Vorspeise*, the *hors d'oeuvres*. There salad does on a plate what the aperitif does in a glass: it whets, not satiates, the appetite.

That is why the menu-maker chooses a light salad to begin the meal: an aspic, seafood, fruit, something green, anything slight and piquant. This salad is only the overture. The opus is to follow.

Perhaps, instead, you choose to serve your salad with or immediately following the main course, as a grace note to the opus. For a grace note, there is nothing like a green or tossed salad.

Such a salad can be served right on the dinner plate, where it exchanges its good flavors with the juice from the roast beef, or the wine sauce from the chicken casserole.

A stuffed tomato or artichoke or other sculpture, topped with mayonnaise or vinaigrette, goes better on a salad plate by itself, and may be served following the main course rather than along with it.

The green salad, with or without cheese and crackers, is equally delightful as a course by itself following the main dish.

Any salad served in mid-meal, in association with the

main course, must be considered as part of that course, and carefully chosen to go with it, considering texture and taste as well as color. I'll have more to say about this point as we go along.

Then there is the dessert salad, which crowns the meal with something light and refreshing, whether it is sweet or not. For this purpose, mousses and aspics are ideal; but the greatest of all is blended fruits. Here is your chance to balance your whole meal, to tie it up and pull it together in a memorable finale. As you rise from the table, the beautiful dessert is the latest impression of your eye and the taste you carry in your mouth.

Sometimes a salad can be so good, and so substantial, that you want to give it your entire attention. Many salads take the whole spotlight for luncheon or supper, or as the main meal on a very hot day. An ideal choice is a bountiful chef's salad, an American term loosely used for a salad of greens and vegetables with a generous scattering of smoked or other meat, chicken, fish or shellfish, and slivered cheese. Equally suited to absorb the whole attention would be a shrimp, crab, or lobster salad, a roast beef salad, or a chicken salad, still the queen of them all.

There is also the huge platter salad, which looks so good, and suits itself so well to every taste, as each one helps himself to exactly the right amount of exactly the things he likes best, such as: sliced or slivered meat, flaked or salted fish, cooked or raw vegetables, and assorted greens.

As you put together your handsome platter salad, and present it to the admiring eyes and the appreciative palates of your family and guests, you realize anew that the salad maker is an artist. Every salad you serve is a picture you have painted, a sculpture you have modeled, a drama you have created.

Warning to food artists: Don't get carried away! Don't

be over dramatic or over colorful, the platter must look appetizing and the salad taste good.

The hostess who gets carried away is a dreadful menace, and most of all to the cookbook writer. The food expert can't win. Half the world won't invite you to eat because you scare them. The other half has to show off.

"You write cookbooks, so you must taste my marshmallow surprise with pink dressing—my tomato and raisin treat—my banana special—"

No escape. She served the banana special. When I saw it I thought it was an oversized caterpillar; but it turned out to be a whole banana drenched in honey and rolled—believe it or not—in cornflakes.

"You *must* have the recipe." She had it ready for me. I'm afraid I lost it.

Food, then, is made to eat, not to look at. But appearance contributes to taste, and precedes it. Every good thing you put into your mouth, you have looked at first, and at sight of the artistry of its presentation and the harmony of its color and form, you have already begun to enjoy it. This is especially true of your salad course.

The beauty of a well-constructed salad is more than skin deep: it is a promise of the taste sensation to come. The eye reacts to color before the palate experiences flavor; and rightly so, because color goes hand in hand with taste.

When you vary the flavor of a dish, you are likely to find you have changed the color as well. The natural rich yellow of that mayonnaise looks appetizing on the red and white of cold lobster; and it tastes right too. Herb mayonnaise goes better with cold salmon; and it takes on a fresh green color which strikes a high note against the frosty pink of the chilled fish. Tomatoed mayonnaise dressing is subtle enough to enhance without overpowering the delicate flavor of crab meat. It

pleases the eye equally with the accent of pink dressing against white meat edged with red.

With a platter of cold seafood, the salad artist may offer three shades of dressing at once, in a triple dish, or in three little saucers. The three bright colors, yellow, green, and frosty pink, make a pleasing combination to lift the spirits and whet the appetite.

It is important to remember the principle of contrast in choosing and decorating your salad vegetables. They should contrast with one another, and with the rest of the menu, both to refresh the eye, and because the color contrast ensures flavor variety also.

There's no use making your guests see red by surrounding a Westphalian ham with consommé Madrilene, buttered beets, tomato aspic, and watermelon. Nor need you give them creeping anemia with a repast of cream of celery soup, breast of chicken, mashed potatoes, hearts of palm salad, and vanilla ice cream. With your chicken you could just as well serve the bright tomato aspic, and keep the subtle pastel hearts of palm to adorn the ham.

In short, when you are fitting a salad into the menu, you are decorating the exterior as well as the interior. You are painting a picture with your palette of eatables as well as tickling the palates of the eaters. You are calling upon your artistry of eye and nose and taste buds to appeal to the same senses in others.

The following favorite menus of mine are for guidance only, suggesting what can be done by the salad course to add sparkle and life to the meal, to provide the taste touch, to add the refining and decorating supplement to the bill of fare. They prove that a meal becomes a dinner, a lunch becomes a luncheon, when the right salad is included. Salads do honor to the guests. Mix and match your own as your inventiveness indicates.

MENUS

Use the following menus as guides,
it's fun to plan your own.

LUNCHEON MENUS

Baked Macaroni and Cheese
Green Salad, Chicken Liver Dressing
Frozen Fruit Salad

ॐ

Broiled Fish
Stuffed Tomatoes
Ice Cream Cake

ॐ

Chicken Broth
Tomato Aspic with Seafood
English Muffins
Pears and Cheese

ॐ

Baked Grapefruit
Caesar Salad

French Rolls
Spanish Cream

ॐ

Cold Roast Beef
Hearts of Palm Salad
Melba Toast
Hot Baked Pears

ॐ

Clam Broth
Chef's Salad
French Bread
Crème Caramel

ॐ

Platter Salad
Hot Rolls
Apple Pie

ॐ

Consommé
Gazpacho Salad
Hot Biscuits
Chocolate Roll

ॐ

Shrimp, Crab, or Lobster Salad
Toasted Crackers

Raspberry Sherbet
Pound Cake

❧

Mushroom Soup
Fruit Salad
Crackers
Irish Coffee Ice Cream

❧

Fruit Cup
Broiled Sweetbreads
Tossed Green Salad
Chocolate Roll

❧

Tomato Juice
Eggs Benedict
Spinach Salad
Strawberry Shortcake

❧

Oyster Soup
Artichokes Vinaigrette
Strawberry Tart

DINNER MENUS

Oyster Cocktail
Roast Turkey
Glazed Onions   Mashed Potatoes

Cole Slaw with Grapes
Pumpkin Pie

ॐ

Lobster Cocktail
Roast Pheasant
Fois Gras Toast   Pilaf   Braised Endive
Grapefruit and Orange Salad
Vanilla Soufflé

ॐ

Smoked Salmon with Capers
Pot Roast
Potato Pancakes, Applesauce
Cooked Vegetable Salad
Lemon Sherbet

ॐ

Turtle Soup
Roast Beef
Cauliflower   Roast Potatoes
Tomato Salad
Crème Brûlée

ॐ

Melon Prosciutto
Baked Fish
New Potatoes   Green Beans with Almonds
Cucumber Salad
Chocolate Mousse

ॐ

Pea Soup
Fried Chicken
Spoon Bread   Asparagus
Water Cress Salad
Chocolate Cake

❧

Fruit Salad
Baked Ham
Asparagus in Mustard Sauce   Sweet Potatoes
Cole Slaw
Cheese Cake

❧

Tomato Aspic with Vegetables
Chicken Fricassee
Dumplings   Green Beans
Hot Fruit Compote   Cookies

❧

Crab Meat Cocktail
Broiled Steak
French Fried Potatoes   Mushrooms
Avocado Salad
Strawberry Pie

❧

Melon
Roast Pork
Brussels Sprouts   Baked Onions

Waldorf Salad
Coffee Ice Cream

❦

Seafood Salad
Roast Leg of Lamb
Puree of Peas   Roasted Potatoes
Green Salad, Anchovy Dressing
Meringue Ring with Fruit

Chapter Two

AMERICA IS THE SALAD BOWL
OF THE WORLD

On many occasions those two great American institutions meet—the salad luncheon and the literary lion.

I remember once when I was the lion, with a corsage on my shoulder, *The Ladies' Home Journal Cookbook* at my elbow, and chicken salad on my plate. I was glad to oblige the large group of good ladies by eating their chicken salad and telling them about my book.

When the affair ended, the chairman surprised me by producing a check. Out of the corner of my eye I could see that the amount was negligible. I waved it away with a grand gesture.

"Oh, I'm here to promote my book, I couldn't take money!"

"No? Thank you very much. May we put it in our special fund?"

"Of course. What is your special fund for?"

"For getting better speakers next year."

This put me off lecturing free at American literary luncheons; but nothing has ever put me off the American salad.

Salad is rapidly becoming the American national dish. American salads are second to none, from the substantial

meal salad to the light tossed green salad. More and more calorie-conscious, the American housewife increasingly favors salad, the dieter's chosen food.

Americans abroad get homesick for their salads. Marketing for salad greens in foreign lands is likely to be a disappointment except at exactly the right time and place. You get the fresh ingredients only at the peak of the salad-growing season, and the best of these are found only in the regions where they grow. In many countries it is not advisable for Americans to eat raw vegetables. At home, shopping for salad is an adventure all year round. American expatriates begin to dream of their own supermarkets, colorfully stacked with salad ingredients of every description. We are indeed fortunate that nature—and the hybridizers—have been so generous in the many types of greens that are available to the salad maker.

Imagine one country offering such a variety of good things in salads: Florida citrus, Maine lobster, Colorado celery, Pacific Coast crab, Pennsylvania Dutch wilted greens, Hawaiian fruit-filled pineapple, California avocados on the half shell, Kentucky Bibb lettuce tossed in an herbed dressing.

The American green salad goes with everything. It is delicious made of soft Boston head lettuce, or bronze or other leaf lettuce. A contrast in texture and color adds interest, as when a crisp lettuce like iceberg, and dark green water cress or spinach are mixed. Endive or escarole adds a bitter tang as well as a changed texture.

LETTUCES AND SALAD GREENS

Greens are called by various names in different places, some alternate names are given in parentheses.

BIBB (Limestone) Miniature fragile heads, each leaf yellow to green, grows only in limestone soil—delicious, and not easily available, about the best lettuce in the world.

BOSTON (Butter, Simpson) Sometimes erroneously called Bibb. A round loosely packed head, tender leaves, delicious and mild.

BRONZE (Red) A garden lettuce similar in texture and taste to leaf lettuce, leaves edged with bronze.

CABBAGE A firmly packed head of thick, heavy, pale green or purple-red leaves.

CHICORY (Curly Endive) Feathery leaves that spread out, yellow at center, pale to darker green outside, crisp with a slightly bitter taste, mixes well with other greens.

DANDELION Thin, long, arrowlike, dark green leaves, tart flavor.

ENDIVE (Belgian Endive) Is a long, narrow, very pale yellow, firm head made of tightly packed, long, pointed, waxy leaves. Unusual tangy flavor.

ESCAROLE Flat spread-out heads, yellow center to dark green edges, leaves are curly, firm, and rough-textured with a distinctive bitter taste.

FIELD LETTUCE (Lamb's Tongue) Very small spears on delicate stems. Soft, delightful, not always available. Always worth buying.

ICEBERG (Head) A round firm head lettuce, keeps well —is crisp, watery, and not flavorful.

LEAF LETTUCE (Garden Lettuce) Soft long leaves with crumpled edges, tends to form heads, tender, fragile, and good. Does not keep or ship well. There are a number of varieties of leaf lettuce.

OAK LEAF (Salad Bowl, Australian) Soft oak-leaf shape, suedelike, pale to medium green leaves. A slightly tangy flavor.

ROMAINE A long narrow head, oval leaves dark green outside, yellow at the heart—firm, crisp, and juicy, a tasty lettuce that keeps well.

SPINACH Dark green leaves, some crinkly, on stems; use young spinach leaves only. A special flavor and good color contrast with other greens.

WATER CRESS Small stalks with numerous small, round, dark green petals; sold tied in bunches, strong lively taste, not bitter, an excellent addition to the salad bowl.

Salad greens must be washed. Firm lettuces may best be cleaned by cutting out the stem. Cut it out about an inch deep, not just off. Let cold water run briskly into this hole. To drip dry, turn the head right side up on the drainboard. Remove outside wilted leaves, pull the head apart, pat dry with a towel, and put in the refrigerator to crisp. Romaine lettuce, escarole, and other clusters of firm leaves may be pulled apart first, then washed, patted dry, and crisped in the refrigerator. Boston, field, and other soft lettuces are too delicate to be patted dry. After floating them in water, spread them out on a dish towel, brown paper, or paper toweling to dry in the air.

A French salad basket, in spite of its looks, isn't a birdcage. It's a wire gadget that gives a sporting touch to cleaning greens. Fill it, hang it on the faucet, and let the

water stream through. Then, as you whirl the contraption wildly around your head you work off your aggressions and sprinkle the kitchen as you dry the lettuce. Your daily dozen done, let the greens stand in the basket until toss-time comes.

Wet lettuce tends to dilute the salad dressing. Sometimes you may choose to have your dressing thinned, in which case don't worry about drying the greens completely. On most occasions, lettuce shouldn't be wet. You don't want your potato salad to go swimming in the lettuce cup, and you never want your mayonnaise diluted.

If you are making a tossed salad, now is the time to prepare the greens into bite-size pieces. Take the washed lettuce, and tear it; be sure to tear, not cut. Only torn lettuce coats itself completely when turned in the dressing. Dry the pieces in a towel, and put towel and contents in the refrigerator to crisp. If your towel overflows, use a pillow case. It is so easy to dump the crisped green bites out of the moist cloth directly into your salad bowl. No fuss, no muss! It will keep fresh and crisp all day, so prepare it ahead of time.

In food photography the salad bowl is always heaped high to make a pretty picture. I defy anybody to toss that salad, or even to serve it, without sprinkling herbage all over the scenery. That doesn't mean that you can't make a pretty picture of your salad. You can and must. For any salad whose ingredients you wish to show off choose a low broad salad bowl or a deep platter. For a green salad to be tossed, use a deep bowl.

A wooden bowl for salad is the tradition, and if you really keep it clean, there is nothing against wood; but from time to time it must be scrubbed and set in the sun, to purge it of the stale garlic and rancid oil that lurk in the grain. For daily care, a swipe with a paper towel will do. Glass, plastic, or ceramic bowls are easy to

take care of and lovely to look at. For a handsome salad, the prettier the container the better. Select one of generous size to toss your salad in, or you will find you have tossed it right onto the kitchen floor or the dining room table.

Finally, consider garlic. Wherever crushed garlic is called for, use a garlic press. In making salad dressing, you may crush the garlic with a fork, but remove it before serving.

GREEN AND MIXED
TOSSED SALADS

TOSSED GREEN SALAD

1 quart torn assorted salad greens
2 teaspoons minced parsley
⅓ cup French Dressing*
2–3 tablespoons grated Parmesan cheese (optional)

Put the greens in a bowl. Mix the parsley into the French Dressing. Pour over the greens and toss. Top with cheese if you wish.

(4 SERVINGS)

MIXED GREEN SALAD

1 head romaine
1 head chicory or escarole
4–5 heads Belgian endive
2 tablespoons minced chives or scallions
¼ cup minced parsley
½–¾ cup French Dressing*
¼ cup grated Cheddar cheese or Parmesan cheese
  (optional)

Wash and dry the greens thoroughly. Break the romaine and chicory or escarole into bite-size pieces and cut the endive. Put the greens in a bowl and sprinkle with chives and parsley. When ready to serve, pour the dress-

ing over and toss thoroughly. Don't use too much dressing, just enough to coat the lettuce. Sprinkle with cheese if you wish.

(8 SERVINGS)

MIXED GREEN SALAD WITH RADISHES

1 head lettuce
1 bunch radishes
4 tomatoes
2 hard boiled eggs
2 tablespoons chopped chives
¼ cup French Dressing*

Wash and dry the lettuce and break into bite-size pieces. Slice the radishes thin. Peel and slice the tomatoes and chop the eggs, keeping yolks and whites separate. Put the lettuce in a salad bowl and add the radishes and tomatoes. Top with the chopped or grated egg, put yolk in the center and white around the edge. Sprinkle with chives. Pour the dressing over and toss at the table.

(6 SERVINGS)

GREENS WITH ONIONS

1 pound spinach
1 head lettuce
1 (3½ ounce) can French fried onions
½ cup French Dressing*

Wash the spinach thoroughly and pick it over. Dry thoroughly and break into bite-size pieces. Break the lettuce also, and toss together. Heat the onions and put over the top, and pour the dressing over all.

(6 SERVINGS)

ENDIVE SALAD

1 pound Belgian endive
Few leaves soft lettuce (optional)
¼ cup French Dressing*
1 hard boiled egg, chopped or grated (garnish)

Wash the endive, remove any wilted leaves. Cut each head into quarters lengthwise and place on the greens. Serve with the dressing poured over and garnish if you wish with the egg.

(4 SERVINGS)

BELGIAN ENDIVE SALAD

1 pound Belgian endive
10 anchovies
½ cup chopped water cress
¼ cup French Dressing*

Wash the endive, trim the root ends. Pull off a few outside leaves and put into a salad bowl. Cut centers in quarters lengthwise. Add to the bowl. Cut up 6 of the anchovies and mix with water cress and French Dressing. Pour over the salad and garnish with remaining anchovies rolled.

(4 SERVINGS)

ROMAINE SALAD BOWL

2 heads romaine
2 bunches leaf lettuce
2 large tomatoes, peeled, cut in wedges
1 cucumber, sliced
1 avocado, peeled, sliced
6 scallions, chopped
⅓ cup French Dressing*
½ teaspoon dry tarragon or chervil

Tear the romaine and lettuce into bite-size pieces into a salad bowl. Add the tomatoes, cucumber, avocado, and scallions, and toss with French Dressing, and tarragon or chervil.

(6 SERVINGS)

FIELD SALAD

½ pound field lettuce
1 can tiny whole beets (optional)
¼ cup French Dressing*

Wash and dry the salad gently. Field salad is not too easy to come by and is delicious alone or in a mixed salad. Add the beets if you wish and toss with the French Dressing.

(4 SERVINGS)

MUSHROOM TOSSED GREENS

1 head romaine
1 head leaf lettuce
½ pound Belgian endive (optional)
½ pound mushrooms
½ cup Lemon French Dressing*

Wash and dry all the greens. Break them up and put in a bowl. Wipe the mushrooms and trim the end of the stems—if they are discolored, peel them. Slice them thin, stem and all. Put on top of the greens. Pour the dressing over and toss.

(6 SERVINGS)

SPINACH SALAD

1 pound spinach
1 teaspoon salt
1 tablespoon sugar
½ teaspoon paprika
½ teaspoon dry mustard
1 teaspoon Worcestershire sauce
2 tablespoons lemon juice
¼ cup catsup
1 cup oil
2 tablespoons vinegar

Wash the spinach in several waters, and remove hard stems. Cut the spinach into strips, dry, and chill. Make the dressing by mixing the salt, sugar, paprika, and mustard with Worcestershire sauce, lemon juice, and catsup. Slowly add the oil and vinegar alternately while beating in an electric mixer or with a rotary hand mixer. The dressing should be thick. Stir in a lump of ice to ensure the thickness. Serve over the spinach.

(4 SERVINGS)

SPINACH AND BACON SALAD

2 pounds spinach
3 hard boiled eggs, chopped
8 slices crisp cooked bacon, crumbled
⅓ cup Yogurt Dressing* or French Dressing*

Wash spinach thoroughly, dry, and break into bite-size pieces into a salad bowl. Sprinkle with the chopped eggs and bacon. Toss with Yogurt Dressing or French Dressing.

(6 SERVINGS)

PENNSYLVANIA DUTCH WILTED LETTUCE

4 slices bacon
⅓ cup sugar
½ teaspoon salt
½ cup vinegar
2 hard boiled eggs
Soft lettuce and/or young dandelion greens

Dice the bacon and fry until crisp. Remove and set aside. Add the sugar, salt, and vinegar to the bacon drippings and add ¼ cup water. When this comes to a boil, pour over the greens, which have been broken into pieces, and toss. Sprinkle coarsely chopped eggs and diced or crumbled bacon over the top and toss.

(4 SERVINGS)

PLATTER SALADS

Every salad on a platter is a thing of beauty. It is "a joy forever" to dieters, pickers, and omnivorous eaters alike, because the various ingredients are presented attractively arranged for the guest to choose what he enjoys, what he needs, or—alas—what he is allowed to eat.

Here is where you can let your creativity run rampant, designing an abstraction on a platter, massing color and form with piles of cucumbers, string beans, or beets, ranks of asparagus or hearts of palm, chubby stuffed tomatoes, and stuffed artichokes rising over all.

Did you ever try making a miniature smorgasbord spread on a platter? Add to your handsome vegetable assortment several fish items, such as herring in sour cream or wine sauce, anchovies, sardines, or flaked cooked fish, as well as cold cuts and perhaps a chicken salad. This impressive presentation looks as if you had spent all day working your fingers to the bone, but really there is nothing easier than to assemble these delicious ingredients into a dainty dish to set before a guest. It is necessary to arrange the various items with space or a little lettuce between so they will not run or merge into each other. Watch the color scheme too, not potato salad right next to a white fish nor tomatoes or beets next to a red meat. This kind of a salad is especially suitable for a supper following an evening event, because it can be put together early, and produced still in its prime when the party is ready for it.

VEGETABLE SALAD PLATTER

1 large head Boston lettuce
½ pound zucchini, sliced
2 kohlrabi or white turnips, sliced very thin
1 head cauliflower, pulled into sprigs
1 head celery, sliced
4 scallions, chopped
1 bunch carrots, cut into strips
1 box cherry tomatoes or 3 tomatoes cut into wedges
2 green peppers, sliced
1 bunch water cress or parsley
½ cup French Dressing* or Vinaigrette*

Wash, dry, and pull the lettuce apart, do not break it up. Line the platter with lettuce, cup face up. Prepare all of the vegetables. To assemble the salad, arrange the vegetables on the lettuce in piles by color—putting contrasting ones next to each other, placing the white cauliflower and pale greens to offset the bright carrots and tomatoes. Use the water cress or parsley when you need to fill in a spot of darker green, and around the edge here and there. Pour the dressing over at the last minute.

(8 SERVINGS)

SALAD PLATTER

½ pound cold sliced ham
½ cup diced celery
1 cup seedless white grapes
¼ cup French Dressing*
4 tomatoes, peeled and quartered
1 teaspoon basil
½ teaspoon sugar

Arrange the ham on sides of the platter in slices or roll-ups. Mix the celery with grapes and moisten with a little dressing. Sprinkle the tomatoes with basil and sugar. Make separate piles of the tomatoes and the grapes mixed with celery. Sprinkle a little dressing over all.

(4 SERVINGS)

CHEF'S SALADS

All of these mixed salads go equally well before, with, or after the main course. By adding to a tossed green salad julienne strips of meat, cheese, and/or fish, you can make it into a meal as the very popular "Chef's Salad."

Anything goes in a chef's salad. You may be using up what's in the refrigerator, the last few slices of cheese, the steak left from dinner or the bacon from breakfast. You may be planning a high-style luncheon party. The classic version of the chef's *chef d'oeuvre* would be a bowlful of green salad generously heaped with shredded ham, chicken, and Swiss cheese. Other smoked and fresh meats, other firm cheeses, a few croutons, would blend together equally well. Shrimp on top makes a different salad and a different chef out of you.

BASIC CHEF'S SALAD

1 head lettuce
Escarole, endive, garden lettuce, water cress, or young spinach
2 tomatoes, peeled and cubed
1 cucumber, peeled and cubed
3 scallions, minced
½ pound ham, tongue, and/or chicken, cut into julienne strips
¼ pound Swiss or Cheddar cheese, cut into julienne strips
1 can anchovies, drained
¾ cup French Dressing*

Tear up the lettuce and use an equal amount of other greens, one or a mixture. Put into a large shallow salad bowl. Add the tomatoes, cucumber, and scallions. Scatter the meat, cheese, and anchovies on top and pour the dressing over. Toss at table.

(6 SERVINGS)

CHEF'S SALAD BOWL

2 heads Boston lettuce
1 cup julienne strips cooked chicken
1 cup sliced radishes
1 cup julienne strips baked ham
1 cup julienne strips Swiss cheese
1 cucumber
½ bunch water cress
2 tomatoes
¼ cup French Dressing*

Tear up the lettuce and put into a salad bowl. Add chicken, sliced radishes, ham strips, cheese, and peeled and sliced cucumber. Place peeled tomato wedges around the rim and tuck in the water cress. Add French Dressing. Toss at table.

(6 SERVINGS)

CHEF'S SALAD

1 head soft lettuce
1 cup julienne strips cooked chicken
½ cup julienne strips celery
1 cup julienne strips Swiss cheese
2 tomatoes, peeled and quartered
1 (4 ounce) can artichoke hearts
2 hard boiled eggs, quartered
¼ cup Thousand Island Dressing*
¼ cup French Dressing*

Tear the lettuce into bite-size pieces and toss with the remaining ingredients except the eggs. Garnish with eggs and pour over a mixture of the two dressings. Toss at table. You may prefer to arrange the ingredients in piles on the greens and toss all at table.

(4 SERVINGS)

SHRIMP CHEF'S SALAD

1 quart mixed greens, torn into small pieces
½ pound cooked shrimp
2 tablespoons capers
¼ cup Lemon French Dressing*
Curry powder (optional)

Put the chilled greens in a bowl. If the shrimp are small, leave them whole; if medium, slice them through the center lengthwise; if large, slice them through the center and then cut across, making each shrimp into four pieces. Place on top of greens and sprinkle with capers. Pour over the dressing, to which you have added a little curry powder, if you wish.

(4 SERVINGS)

SALMON CHEF'S SALAD

1 (7¾ ounce) can salmon
1 cucumber, peeled and diced
1 large tomato, peeled and chopped
3 tablespoons French Dressing*
1 teaspoon lemon juice
3 tablespoons sour cream
1 tablespoon chopped fresh dill or 1 teaspoon dry

Flake the salmon and combine with cucumber and tomato. Mix the French Dressing with lemon juice, sour cream, and dill, and blend with the salmon mixture.

(4 SERVINGS)

DEVILED EGG CHEF'S SALAD

6 hard boiled eggs
¼ teaspoon minced chives or 1 teaspoon minced scallions
2 tablespoons butter or oil
2 tablespoons Mayonnaise*
⅛ teaspoon curry powder
½ teaspoon salt
¼ teaspoon pepper
1 head soft lettuce
1 head chicory, romaine, or leaf lettuce
3–4 tomatoes
2 cucumbers
1 cup shredded salami, baloney, or other sausage
1 can anchovies
½ cup Garlic French Dressing*

Cut the eggs in half and remove yolks. Sauté the chives or scallions in the butter or oil for 2 minutes, then add to the mashed egg yolks with the Mayonnaise, curry, salt, and pepper. Fill the egg whites with the yolk mixture. Tear the greens and put into a salad bowl. Peel and slice tomatoes and cucumbers and arrange the vegetables on the lettuce. Add salami or other sausage. Add the oil as well as the anchovies. Toss with the dressing. Then add the stuffed eggs around the edge of the salad.

(6–8 SERVINGS)

Salad-happy Californians dreamed up Caesar Salad, and it has caught the public fancy. Here is my special version of this magnificent salad bowl.

CAESAR SALAD

1 clove garlic, crushed
¾ cup olive or salad oil
2 quarts salad greens: head lettuce, water cress, leaf lettuce, endive, etc.
1 teaspoon Worcestershire sauce
1 teaspoon salt
¼ teaspoon freshly ground pepper
1 egg, coddled
¼ cup lemon juice
3 ounces Roquefort cheese, crumbled
2 cups croutons, toasted or fried

Add the garlic to the ¾ cup of salad oil or olive oil and let stand several hours. Tear the salad greens into bite-size pieces using assorted greens. Put into a large bowl with the oil and the seasonings. Open the egg (cooked for 1 minute only) onto the greens. Sprinkle with the lemon juice and toss until all greens are coated with the oil and seasonings. Add cheese and toss again. Top with croutons.

(6 SERVINGS)

CALIFORNIA CAESAR SALAD

1 head lettuce
1 head romaine
2 eggs, coddled
6 anchovies, chopped
½ teaspoon freshly ground pepper
1 tablespoon Worcestershire sauce
½ teaspoon prepared mustard
¼ cup grated Parmesan cheese
½ cup French Dressing*
1 cup garlic croutons

Wash the lettuce and dry thoroughly. Break up into a large bowl. Open the eggs (cooked 1 minute only) into a bowl and add remaining ingredients except croutons. Mix thoroughly and pour over the greens. Add croutons and toss.

(8 SERVINGS)

VEGETABLE SALADS

Cooked vegetable salad is an ideal buffet dish, because it needs no cutting on the plate, and can be eaten unimpeded from the lap. Having no juice to slop around, it goes well with other comestibles on your one plate. It can be made ready ahead, and waits without wilting. Substantial and colorful, it fills the place of both a vegetable and a salad.

COOKED VEGETABLE SALAD

1 package frozen peas
1 package frozen cut green beans
1 package frozen baby limas
1 package frozen corn
1 cup diced cooked celery
1½ cups diced cooked carrots
½ cup French Dressing* or ½ cup Mayonnaise*
¼ cup cream (optional)

Cook the vegetables according to package instructions, drain and chill. Mix together with the celery and carrots, which have been chilled. Toss gently with French Dressing—don't use too much, the salad should not be wet, just moistened. If you use Mayonnaise, thin with cream or juice from the vegetables.

(8–10 SERVINGS)

35

THREE OR FOUR BEAN SALAD

1 pound green beans or 1 box frozen
1 pound wax beans or 1 box frozen
1 box frozen small limas
1 (1-pound) can kidney beans
3 scallions, chopped
1 clove garlic, crushed
½ cup French Dressing*
Salad greens (optional)

Cut and cook the green and wax beans if using fresh. If frozen buy cut or French cut and cook all the package beans according to directions. Toss all of the beans together with the scallions. Mix garlic with the dressing, and pour over. Toss again. Serve on greens if you wish.

(8 SERVINGS)

BEAN AND ASPARAGUS SALAD WITH GRAPES

½ pound green beans, or 1 box whole frozen beans
1 pound asparagus, or 2 boxes frozen, or 1 can white, drained
¾–1 pound white grapes
1 head iceberg, Boston, or leaf lettuce
Juice 1 lemon
2 tablespoons oil
½ cup heavy cream
½ teaspoon salt
⅛ teaspoon pepper
¼ teaspoon sugar

Cook the beans in salted water until just tender; rinse them at once in cold water so they will not be overdone. If using fresh asparagus, tie it in 4–5 bunches, removing about half of each stem, and cook in a quart of salted water. Remove from water as soon as it is almost tender.

If using frozen, follow package directions, cooking a little less than prescribed. Refrigerate the vegetables. Pull the grapes off the stems. Break the greens into bite-size pieces in a salad bowl. Place the asparagus and beans on the greens. Garnish with grapes. Pour over the dressing made by mixing all remaining ingredients together thoroughly.

(4–6 SERVINGS)

ASPARAGUS VINAIGRETTE

2½ pounds fresh asparagus, or 2 cans large white
  asparagus
*¾ cup Vinaigrette**
Greens (optional)

Cook the asparagus, being careful not to overcook. Drain and cool. Marinate in the dressing for about an hour. If you use canned asparagus, drain thoroughly. Serve on lettuce if you wish.

(6 SERVINGS)

BEETROOT SALAD

4–6 large beets, cooked
1 onion, sliced thin
*½ cup Mayonnaise**
2 teaspoons tarragon vinegar
¼ cup heavy cream, whipped

Slice the beets, and add the onion, and mix in a salad bowl. Mix the Mayonnaise with the vinegar, and fold in the whipped cream. Pour the sauce over the salad. Serve cold.

(6 SERVINGS)

ROMAINE AND BEET SALAD

1 head romaine lettuce
2 cups julienne of beets
3 ounces Roquefort or blue cheese (optional)
1/4 cup French Dressing*

Pull off most of the large leaves of the romaine and break them into bite-size pieces. Pull inside leaves apart leaving them whole. Put the torn-up pieces in a bowl and mix with the beets. Garnish with the center leaves, sprinkle with crumbled cheese if you wish. Add the French Dressing.

(4 SERVINGS)

BEET AND FRUIT SALAD

1/2 pound sliced cooked beets
1 cup cubed pineapple
1 apple, peeled, cored, and sliced
Sections of 2 oranges
2 bananas, sliced
1/2 cup Lemon French Dressing*
1/2 cup coarsely chopped peanuts

Mix the beets with the fruit, working quickly so that the apples and bananas will not darken. Pour the Lemon French Dressing over and sprinkle peanuts over the top.

(6 SERVINGS)

CAULIFLOWER SALAD

1 large head cauliflower
Salad greens
2 tomatoes
1 green pepper
1/2 cup Mayonnaise*
1 tablespoon lemon juice
1-2 tablespoons minced chives and/or parsley

Cook the cauliflower in salted water until it starts to get tender, about 10–15 minutes. Do not overcook or it will be mushy and will fall apart. Drain and chill. Place on some salad greens on a deep platter or shallow salad bowl. Peel and slice or cut the tomatoes in eighths and put around the cauliflower. Cut the green pepper into strips and put around the salad. Mix the Mayonnaise with lemon juice. Spread a thin layer on the cauliflower and a little on the tomatoes. Sprinkle chives and/or parsley over all.

(6 SERVINGS)

CAULIFLOWER AND AVOCADO SALAD

1 large head cauliflower
¼ cup vinegar
6 tablespoons oil
1½ teaspoons salt
¼ teaspoon pepper
3 avocados
½ cup coarsely ground almonds
1 small onion, minced
Dash of nutmeg
Tomato wedges, radishes, olives (garnish)

Cook the cauliflower in salted water until tender. Mix half of the oil and vinegar with 1 teaspoon salt and the pepper and pour over the cauliflower while it is still warm. Chill. Peel and mash the avocados and mix with remaining oil, vinegar, salt, almonds, and onion. Add nutmeg and any remaining marinade from the cauliflower. Put the cold cauliflower on a round plate. Pour the avocado sauce over. Garnish if you wish with tomato wedges, and/or radishes, and olives.

(6 SERVINGS)

CELERY VICTOR

8 celery hearts or 4 heads pascal celery
Beef broth, consommé, or bouillon cubes
Water cress or salad greens
1 cup French Dressing* or Vinaigrette*

Cook the celery in broth, consommé, or water with bouillon cubes until just tender. If using large stalks, remove outside leaves and cut the head in half before cooking. Let celery cool in the broth. Be sure to remove from heat before the celery is done as it will continue to cook in the hot broth. Chill. Serve on a bed of water cress or salad greens and spoon the dressing over.

(8 SERVINGS)

CELERY ROOT SALAD

1 pound celery root
½ cup French Dressing*

Scrub the roots. Boil in salted water until tender. Plunge into very cold water and then peel and slice very thin into a bowl. Pour the French Dressing over and let marinate for a couple of hours.

(6 SERVINGS)

CHICK PEA SALAD

2 cups drained canned garbanzo peas
½ pound cream cheese, diced
2 onions, sliced thin
½ cup olive oil
¼ cup lemon juice
1 teaspoon salt
¼ teaspoon pepper
½ teaspoon ground coriander
Salad greens

Combine the peas, cheese, and onions. Mix the rest of the ingredients, except greens, and pour over the pea mixture. Let stand several hours before serving. Toss, and serve on lettuce or other greens.

(4 SERVINGS)

WINTER SALAD

2 large Bermuda or Spanish onions
1 cup milk
1 head celery or 3 celery hearts
2 large cooked beets
2 hard boiled eggs
1 teaspoon mustard
1 teaspoon salt
¼ teaspoon pepper
½ teaspoon sugar
1 teaspoon anchovy paste (optional)
¼ cup olive oil
2 tablespoons wine vinegar

Boil the onions in half milk and half water until tender. Drain and chill. Slice the celery and beets, and chill while making the dressing. Chop the eggs and mix with mustard, salt, pepper, and sugar. Add the anchovy paste if you wish. Stir in the oil, blending well, and then the vinegar. Mix the sliced onions with celery and beets, and pour the dressing over. Let stand several hours in the refrigerator.

(6 SERVINGS)

French or globe artichokes are an artistic addition to a meal as well as a taste delight. These artichokes must be cooked, drained, and chilled. Trim the stem so the artichoke will sit flat on a plate. Cut the leaves across the top or trim each leaf with scissors if you wish. Boil in a

large pot of water with 1 tablespoon salt and 1 tablespoon vinegar to the quart. The artichoke is done when a leaf pulls out easily—30–45 minutes depending upon size. Drain upside down.

You can buy tiny artichoke hearts in cans or in jars or frozen. Any variety is a good addition to a mixed salad. The best of the canned artichokes are the *fonds* or bottoms. They're expensive, but oh so good!

ARTICHOKES

4 artichokes*
½–1 cup Vinaigrette* or ⅓ cup Mayonnaise*
1–1½ tablespoons prepared mustard or 1 cube butter, melted

Cook the Artichokes. Chill and serve on a plate and pass the Vinaigrette or Mayonnaise mixed with mustard, or serve hot with hot drawn butter.

(4 Servings)

ARTICHOKES IN MUSTARD SAUCE

12 tiny artichokes
2 cloves garlic
Juice 1 lemon
½ cup French Dressing*
¼ cup prepared brown mustard

Pull off the outside leaves of the artichokes and clip the tips of the rest of the leaves if you wish. Boil in salt water with the garlic and lemon juice until tender. You may test it by pulling out a leaf. If it pulls out easily, the artichokes are done. Drain upside down. Marinate for several hours in the dressing made by blending the French Dressing and mustard.

(6 Servings)

RAW VEGETABLE SALADS

There are many vegetables which, though usually served cooked, are great raw, such as mushrooms, zucchini, carrots, cauliflower, and asparagus. They are available for salads in addition to the ones often eaten raw, such as celery, radishes, onions, fennel, cucumbers, and avocados.

AVOCADOS

2 avocados
Juice ½ lemon
¼ cup Lemon French Dressing*
Lettuce

Cut the avocados in half and remove pits. Sprinkle edges with lemon juice to prevent discoloration. Fill center with Lemon French Dressing and serve on a bed of lettuce.

(4 SERVINGS)

AVOCADO SALAD

2 cups peeled diced avocado
2 hard boiled eggs, coarsely chopped
3 medium tomatoes, peeled and diced
1 teaspoon grated onion
1 teaspoon lemon juice
¼ teaspoon salt
Dash of freshly ground pepper
½ teaspoon sugar
About ¼ cup French Dressing* or Lemon French
  Dressing*
Lettuce

Combine the avocado, eggs, tomatoes, onion, and seasonings. Add enough French Dressing to moisten and toss
until well blended. Serve on lettuce.

(6 SERVINGS)

FILLED AVOCADO SALAD

½ cup oil
¼ cup wine vinegar
1 teaspoon salt
¼ teaspoon freshly ground pepper
½ teaspoon paprika
3 scallions
2 tomatoes
1 clove garlic, crushed
3 avocados

Mix the oil, vinegar, salt, pepper, and paprika. Chop
the scallions, peel and chop the tomatoes, and mix
together with the garlic. Add to the dressing. Cut the

avocados in half lengthwise and remove pits. Fill centers at once with the dressing mixture.

(6 SERVINGS)

AVOCADO CITRUS SALAD

1 head lettuce
2 avocados
1 cup grapefruit sections
1 cup orange sections
⅓ cup Lemon French Dressing*

Line a salad bowl with lettuce. Tear the remaining lettuce into bite-size pieces. Peel and slice the avocados into the bowl. Add the Lemon French Dressing and toss together lightly.

(6 SERVINGS)

CUCUMBERS IN SOUR CREAM

3–4 cucumbers
2 tablespoons salt
1–1½ cups sour cream
1 tablespoon sugar
3 tablespoons vinegar
½ teaspoon freshly ground pepper
1 tablespoon minced dill or chives (optional)

Slice the cucumbers thin. Sprinkle generously with salt and let stand for at least a couple of hours. Rinse in cold water and squeeze out the moisture. Mix rest of ingredients, and fold the cucumbers into the sauce. Chill.

(6 SERVINGS)

SHREDDED CUCUMBER SALAD

2 large cucumbers
2 tablespoons salt
1 tablespoon peanut oil
1 tablespoon soy sauce
1 tablespoon sesame oil
1 teaspoon MSG
1 clove garlic, crushed
1/2 teaspoon sugar
1/4 teaspoon pepper

Peel and shred the cucumbers and sprinkle with salt. Let stand in the refrigerator for several hours. Rinse in a sieve under cold running water. Drain thoroughly, and squeeze out moisture. Mix all of the remaining ingredients together, and pour over the cucumbers.

(4 SERVINGS)

GRATED CUCUMBER SALAD

2 cucumbers, grated
2 tablespoons grated onion
1 teaspoon salt
1/4 teaspoon pepper
1 cup yogurt

Drain the grated cucumbers. Combine all of the ingredients.

(4 SERVINGS)

STUFFED CUCUMBER SALAD

3 cucumbers, cut in half lengthwise
6 tablespoons cottage cheese
2 tablespoons minced celery
2 tablespoons minced green onion
1 teaspoon salt
*2 tablespoons Mayonnaise**
Chives (garnish)

Scrape the seeds from the center of the cucumber, and mix with the remaining ingredients, except chives. Taste for seasoning and refill the cucumbers. Serve on the half shell chilled or put halves together and chill for several hours and then cut into thick slices. Sprinkle with chives.

(6 SERVINGS)

HAWAIIAN CUCUMBER SHOYU SALAD

¼ pound very fresh white fish, raw
⅓ cup vinegar
1 teaspoon minced ginger
2 tablespoons sugar
½ teaspoon salt
2 cucumbers, sliced
1½ tablespoons Shoyu, or soy sauce

Cut the fish in very thin pieces. Mix the vinegar, ginger, sugar, and salt, and pour over the fish. Let stand half an hour. Add cucumbers, which have been let stand in salt, rinsed, and drained. Add Shoyu sauce or soy sauce, and mix gently.

(4 SERVINGS)

COLE SLAW

½ teaspoon salt
½ teaspoon onion salt
¼ teaspoon pepper
1 tablespoon sugar
1 teaspoon mustard
1 teaspoon celery seed or ½ teaspoon celery salt
3 tablespoons wine vinegar
½ cup olive oil
4 cups shredded cabbage
1 sweet bell pepper, red or green, chopped
1 tablespoon minced parsley

Blend all of the seasonings with the vinegar and oil in a large bowl. Add cabbage and the red or green pepper and mix thoroughly. Just before serving, sprinkle with the minced parsley.

(6–8 SERVINGS)

SOUR CREAM COLE SLAW

1 small head cabbage
1 cup sour cream
1 tablespoon vinegar
1 tablespoon sugar
1 teaspoon salt
½ teaspoon pepper
½ teaspoon prepared mustard (optional)

Shred the cabbage fine. Mix the sour cream with vinegar, sugar, salt, and pepper. Add mustard if you wish. Fold into the cabbage, mixing thoroughly. Let stand a few hours before serving.

(4 SERVINGS)

FINOCCHIO SALAD

1 head soft lettuce
3 cups diced finocchio
1 clove garlic, crushed, or ½ teaspoon garlic salt or
    powder
4 tomatoes
¼ cup French Dressing*

Wash and tear the lettuce into bite-size pieces, dry and chill. Soak the finocchio in ice water with garlic. When ready to put the salad together, drain the finocchio, peel and quarter the tomatoes, and arrange both on salad greens in a bowl. Pour the dressing over.

(8 SERVINGS)

LEEK SALAD

3 or 4 young tender leeks
2–3 tomatoes, peeled
½ teaspoon dry tarragon or 1 teaspoon fresh
1 teaspoon dry basil or 1 tablespoon fresh
Soft lettuce or romaine
¼ cup garlic croutons
¼ cup French Dressing*

The number of leeks and tomatoes depends upon their size. Cut the leeks into pieces about ½ inch long. Cut the tomatoes into sections and mix the two gently. Sprinkle with the herbs. Line a salad bowl with soft lettuce or romaine. Add croutons to the leeks and fold in the French Dressing. Put into the greens and serve at once.

(6 SERVINGS)

MUSHROOM CELERY SALAD

¾ pound mushrooms
1 head celery
½ cup olive oil
⅛ cup lemon juice
1 teaspoon salt
¼ teaspoon pepper
Bibb or Boston lettuce

Wipe the mushrooms and remove stems (use stems for
soup or sauce, do not throw away). If the mushrooms
are not pure white, peel the caps. Slice thin across the
head making half oval slices. Wash the celery, pull the
stalk apart, and cut across making slices the width of the
mushrooms. They will be similar in shape. Mix together.
Blend the oil, lemon juice, salt, and pepper, and toss
gently into the salad. Chill and serve on the lettuce.

(6 SERVINGS)

HEARTS OF PALM SALAD

1 (14 ounce) can hearts of palm
Shredded lettuce
¼ cup Lemon French Dressing*
Freshly ground pepper

Cut the larger pieces of palm in half or quarters lengthwise. Place on the lettuce and add the dressing. Dust top
with a little pepper.

(6–8 SERVINGS)

PALM AND TOMATO SALAD

1 head chicory lettuce, shredded
1 (14 ounce) can hearts of palm
2 tomatoes
½ cup French Dressing*
1 teaspoon lemon juice

Put the crisp lettuce on a platter or individual plates. Put the pieces of palm on the lettuce and garnish with tomatoes. Pour over the dressing, which has been mixed with lemon juice.

(8 SERVINGS)

TOMATO SALAD

4 large tomatoes
1 teaspoon thyme
½ teaspoon salt
¼ teaspoon sugar
½ teaspoon pepper
2 tablespoons olive oil
2 tablespoons minced chives or scallions (optional)

Peel and slice the tomatoes and arrange them in overlapping rows around a serving dish. Sprinkle with thyme, salt, sugar, and olive oil, and let stand for an hour or two. You may add the chives or scallions if you wish. You may cut the tomatoes in eighths if you prefer.

(8 SERVINGS)

TOMATO AND AVOCADO SALAD

3 tomatoes, peeled, cut in wedges
1 large avocado, peeled, sliced
½ cup French Dressing*
1 head lettuce
2 tablespoons grated cheese

Marinate the tomatoes and avocado in the French Dressing in the refrigerator. Tear the lettuce into bite-size pieces into the salad bowl. Add the marinated tomatoes and avocado. Sprinkle with the cheese and toss lightly.

(6 SERVINGS)

STUFFED TOMATOES

4 large tomatoes
1 cup diced celery
1–2 tablespoons minced chives or scallions
2 teaspoons minced fresh dill or ½ teaspoon dried
or same quantity sweet basil
¾ cup Mayonnaise*
Lettuce

Cut the top off of the tomatoes and scoop out pulp and seeds. Mix the pulp, not much juice, with celery, chives or scallions, and dill or basil. Stir in the ½ cup Mayonnaise. If too thick, add a little of the tomato juice. Adjust seasoning to taste, adding salt, pepper, or lemon juice to taste. Refill tomatoes with the mixture. Chill, and serve on lettuce leaves. Top each with a generous dab of Mayonnaise.

(4 SERVINGS)

HAWAIIAN STUFFED TOMATO SALAD

6 tomatoes
1½ cups shredded pineapple
½ cup chopped roasted peanuts
2 tablespoons Lemon French Dressing*
1 teaspoon salt
Lettuce

Peel the tomatoes and cut slice from top, and remove seeds and pulp. Chill the tomatoes. Combine tomato pulp, pineapple, peanuts, Lemon French Dressing, and salt. Fill tomatoes with the mixture, and serve on lettuce leaves.

(6 SERVINGS)

ZUCCHINI SALAD WITH VEGETABLES

8 zucchini
2 tomatoes, peeled and coarsely chopped
1 green pepper, chopped
1 onion, chopped fine
1 teaspoon sugar
1 teaspoon salt
½ teaspoon pepper
¼ teaspoon paprika
2–4 tablespoons Mayonnaise* or French Dressing*
Lettuce

Cut the zucchini in thin slices, do not peel. Mix with all of the other ingredients. Add the dressing a tablespoon at a time. You do not want the salad to be too moist. Serve on lettuce.

(8 SERVINGS)

ZUCCHINI SALAD

6 small zucchini
1 tablespoon salt
Lettuce
¼ cup French Dressing*

Cook the zucchini with skin left on in salt water until almost tender, about 5 minutes. When cool, slice thin lengthwise in about ⅓ inch slices within 1 inch of the

bottom and not through the skin. Spread gently apart fan shape. Put on lettuce and pour the dressing over.

(6 SERVINGS)

Potato salad is the king of the heavy salads in many lands: *Kartoffelsalat* in Germany, *Papas a la Huancaina* in Peru, *Salatt El Bataater* in Lebanon, and what would we do without our potato salad with the cold ham at supper? Under any name, this dish is best made of new potatoes, if available; they're less mushy. You may vary potato salad tremendously by making it with French Dressing, Cooked Dressing, Sour Cream Dressing, or with Mayonnaise.

POTATO SALAD

2 pounds potatoes, boiled in jackets
6 tablespoons olive oil
6 tablespoons wine vinegar
½ cup beef broth
1 teaspoon salt
¼ teaspoon pepper
1 small onion, minced, or 2 tablespoons minced scallions
1 tablespoon minced parsley

Peel and slice the potatoes while warm. Pour a mixture of oil, vinegar, and broth over the potatoes while they are still warm. Let stand for 1 hour. Mix the salt, pepper, onions, and parsley, and fold into salad.

(4–6 SERVINGS)

POTATO SALAD WITH MAYONNAISE

2 pounds potatoes, boiled in jackets
1 onion, sliced thin
3 tablespoons minced parsley
1 cup Mayonnaise*

Peel and slice the potatoes. Mix gently with the onion. Add 2 tablespoons of parsley to the Mayonnaise, and fold it into the potato salad. Garnish the top with remaining minced parsley.

(4–6 SERVINGS)

POULTRY AND MEAT SALADS

Meat salads often make the meal. They are delightful as a luncheon or supper dish, especially in hot weather. Served in small portions they are used as an appetizer salad. Leftovers come into the salad bowl with success. Turkey, chicken, ham, beef, veal, or what you have, combined with something crisp and a tangy dressing make a tasty salad.

CHICKEN SALAD WITH ALMONDS

2 cups diced cooked chicken
1 cup chopped celery
¾ cup sliced toasted almonds
1 tablespoon minced parsley
1 cup Mayonnaise*
¼ cup chicken stock
Lettuce

Mix the chicken, celery, almonds, and parsley. Combine the Mayonnaise and chicken stock, and stir into the salad. Serve on lettuce.

(4 SERVINGS)

CHICKEN SALAD WITH CREAM DRESSING

1 quart cut up cooked chicken
1½ cups chopped celery
2 cups Mayonnaise*
½ cup strong chicken broth
½ cup heavy cream, whipped
2–3 tablespoons sliced truffles (optional)
Greens
Tomato wedges, hard boiled eggs, olives (optional
    garnishes)

Cut the chicken into large bite-size pieces, preferably
about 1 inch long. Mix with celery and Mayonnaise.
Combine broth and cream, and stir into the salad
mixture. Fold in truffles if you wish. Serve on crisp greens.
You may garnish with tomato wedges, hard boiled eggs,
and/or olives.

(6 SERVINGS)

CHICKEN AND CORN SALAD

3 cups diced cooked chicken
2 cups cooked, canned, or frozen corn
4 tomatoes, peeled and cubed
2 green peppers, chopped
2 cups Mayonnaise*
Lettuce

Mix the chicken and corn with the tomatoes and
peppers. Stir in 1½ cups of Mayonnaise, and adjust the
seasoning to taste. Serve on a bed of lettuce, and
decorate with remaining Mayonnaise.

(8 SERVINGS)

CHICKEN SALAD MOLD

2 cups diced cooked chicken
1 cup chopped celery
1 cup white grapes, cut in halves
2 tablespoons minced parsley
1 teaspoon salt
1/4 teaspoon white pepper
1 1/2 tablespoons gelatin
1/2 cup hot chicken stock
1 cup Mayonnaise*
2 tablespoons heavy cream

Mix the chicken, celery, grapes, and parsley. Season with salt and pepper. Soften the gelatin in 1/4 cup cold water, and dissolve in the hot chicken stock, and stir into the salad. Combine the Mayonnaise with cream, and fold in. Put into a wet mold or in 6 individual molds.

(6 SERVINGS)

CHICKEN LIVER SALAD

1/2 pound chicken livers
2 tablespoons butter
1/2 teaspoon salt
1/4 teaspoon freshly ground pepper
1 head lettuce
1/2 bunch curly endive (optional)
4 scallions, chopped
1/4 cup crumbled Roquefort or blue cheese
2 hard boiled eggs, chopped
1/3 cup French Dressing*

Sauté the chicken livers in the butter with salt and pepper until lightly browned. Chill. Drain and cut into small pieces. Tear the lettuce into bite-size pieces. Add

the chicken livers, scallions, cheese, and eggs. Toss with French Dressing.

(6 SERVINGS)

TURKEY SALAD

3 cups bite-size pieces roast turkey
2 cups diced celery
2 cups white seedless grapes (optional)
½ cup sliced blanched almonds (optional)
1 tablespoon grated onion
¼ cup strong turkey broth, if available
¼ cup French Dressing* (optional)
¾ cup Mayonnaise*
Greens
2 hard boiled eggs (optional)

Mix the turkey and celery and add if you wish the grapes and/or nuts. Mix the onion with strong turkey broth, or French Dressing, and the Mayonnaise. Toss the salad with the dressing and refrigerate for several hours. Serve on a bed of greens and garnish with a few nuts and grapes or sliced or quartered eggs.

(8 SERVINGS)

SUNSET SALAD

1½ cups young cabbage, shredded
1½ cups julienne strips smoked cooked tongue
1½ cups julienne strips cooked chicken
½ cup Lorenzo Dressing*

Mix the cabbage, tongue, and chicken. You should have about the same quantity of each. Top with the dressing and toss lightly but thoroughly.

(4 SERVINGS)

COBB SALAD

1 head soft lettuce
1/2 bunch water cress
2 large tomatoes, peeled and diced
2 cups diced cooked chicken
2 avocados, peeled and diced
4 slices bacon cooked
2 tablespoons chopped scallions
4 ounces Roquefort cheese
2 hard boiled eggs, minced or grated
Minced parsley or chives (garnish)
*1/2 cup French Dressing**

Use lettuce such as Boston, leaf, or chicory. Wash, dry thoroughly, and shred. Cut up the water cress. Line a flat salad bowl with greens. Put the tomatoes, chicken, and avocados in three separate strips across the bowl. Crumble crisp bacon over the salad. Add the scallions, the grated or crumbled Roquefort cheese, and eggs; top with minced parsley or chives. Add the dressing and toss at table.

(6 SERVINGS)

SWEETBREAD SALAD

4 pairs sweetbreads
1 tablespoon lemon juice
1 tablespoon salt
1/2 envelope gelatin
1/4 cup white wine
*1 cup Mayonnaise**
1 tablespoon minced parsley
1 teaspoon minced chives (optional)
Salad greens

Cook the sweetbreads in water to cover to which you have added the lemon juice and salt. Simmer for 15–20 minutes. Drain and put in ice water for an hour or more. Sprinkle the gelatin on ¼ cup cold water and dissolve over heat. When cool, add the white wine and fold into the Mayonnaise. Add the parsley, and chives if you wish. Mix well. Cut the sweetbreads into small bite-size pieces removing any membrane. Pour the Mayonnaise over the sweetbreads. Chill for several hours. Serve on lettuce.

(6 SERVINGS)

BEEF SALAD

2 cups diced cooked roast beef
1 cup diced celery
1 tablespoon chopped chives or scallions
½ cup Mayonnaise*
1 tablespoon vinegar
1 teaspoon prepared mustard
Lettuce
1 teaspoon minced parsley

Mix the beef, celery, and chives. Combine the Mayonnaise with vinegar and mustard and toss into the salad. Serve on lettuce and sprinkle with parsley.

(4 SERVINGS)

HAM SALAD

2 cups ham, julienne strips or diced
1 cup celery, diced or julienne strips
2 small sweet pickles, chopped
2 hard boiled eggs, quartered
1 tablespoon prepared mustard
1 teaspoon pickle juice
⅓ cup Mayonnaise*
Greens

Combine the ham with celery, pickles, and eggs. Mix the mustard and pickle juice into the Mayonnaise. Toss all together. Serve on a bed of greens.

(4 SERVINGS)

FISH SALADS

The meat salad is not the only salad that makes a meal. Many another salad meal comes out of the sea. A fish salad is delicious for luncheon, supper, or an evening party, and substantial enough to rest on its own laurels (or a bed of lettuce). In addition to the usual—but delicious—salads of shrimp, crab, lobster, tuna, or salmon, fisherman's luck brings up the more exotic salad of mussels, or the marine mélange that makes a bouillabaisse salad. Like the typical Marseilles mixed fish bouillabaisse, this salad includes several kinds of fish and shellfish, presenting a handsome picture on the individual flat soup plate, or ranged on a deep platter in all the glory of its different colors, white fish, the pink of salmon, the red of shellfish, and the golden aura of saffron or curry.

BOUILLABAISSE SALAD

½ *pound each of two white fish such as cod and halibut*
½ *pound salmon*
½ *pound scallions (optional)*
½ *pound crabmeat*
½ *pound lobster meat*
½ *pound cooked shrimp*
1 *pound mussels or 12 oysters and/or clams (optional)*
Greens, water cress or parsley (garnish)
2–3 *lemons*
*Lemon French Dressing**

Poach the fish and scallions gently in a little salted water or preferably court bouillon for about 5 minutes. Reserve liquid and chill fish. When cold break the fish into large bite-size pieces. If using mussels steam in ¼ cup water or white wine until the shells open; debeard and chill. Oysters and clams may be used raw. You do not have to have all of the different shellfishes; if lobster is not available or is terribly expensive double the quantity of shrimp or salmon; use your judgment and your fish monger to plan an effective, pretty salad. This salad is best assembled and served in individual flat soup plates, but you may use a large deep platter if you prefer. Place the white fish to offset the pink. Use firm lettuce leaves under the fish or garnish with water cress or parsley. Put a lemon wedge on each serving. Pass the dressing to which you have added 3 or 4 tablespoons of boiled-down liquid from the fish.

(8 SERVINGS)

FISH SALAD

2 *pounds cooked fish, haddock, turbot, halibut, or*
   cod
1 *pound potatoes, cooked in their jackets*
4 *tomatoes*
1 *onion, sliced thin*
2 *tablespoons minced parsley*
½ *cup French Dressing**
1 *tablespoon minced chives*
1 *tablespoon capers (optional)*

Cook and bone the fish, and break into small bite-size pieces. Peel and slice the potatoes and tomatoes. Put alternate layers of fish, potatoes, tomatoes, onions, and a sprinkling of parsley in a bowl. Spoon a tablespoon or two of dressing on the layers. Top with remaining parsley and chives and dressing, and capers, if you wish. Let stand at least an hour in refrigerator.

(6 SERVINGS)

CRAB SALAD

2 *cups crabmeat (1 pound)*
1½ *cups diced celery*
2 *teaspoons lemon juice*
1 *teaspoon Worcestershire sauce*
¾ *cup Mayonnaise**
4 *large lettuce leaves*
2 *tomatoes*
2 *hard boiled eggs (garnish)*

Use lump crabmeat or legs. Treat it gently so it doesn't get mashed. Mix with celery. Add lemon juice and Worcestershire sauce to the Mayonnaise, and fold into the crab. Serve on lettuce leaves and garnish with sections of tomato and hard boiled eggs.

(4 SERVINGS)

CRABMEAT SALAD WITH THOUSAND ISLAND DRESSING

1 pound crabmeat
Boston lettuce or other greens
2 tomatoes, and/or 1 avocado
Blanched almonds and/or capers
½–¾ cup Thousand Island Dressing*

Pick over the crabmeat trying not to break up the lumps. Put onto the greens in a bowl or individual plates. Garnish with sliced tomatoes and/or avocado, peeled and sliced. If you use the latter, sprinkle with lemon juice to prevent discoloration. Garnish with almonds and/or capers. Serve with Thousand Island Dressing or you may use a Caper Mayonnaise* or Mayonnaise with a half teaspoon of dill added.

(4 SERVINGS)

CRAB SALAD IN AVOCADOS

Make like Shrimp in Avocados*, substituting crabmeat for the shrimp.

BASIC LOBSTER SALAD

1 pound cooked lobster meat
4 tablespoons olive oil
1 tablespoon wine vinegar
1 tablespoon lemon juice
½ teaspoon salt
¼ teaspoon white pepper
Lettuce cups or leaves
1 lemon (garnish)

Cut the lobster into large bite-size pieces. Mix the oil, vinegar, lemon juice, salt, and pepper. Shake to blend

thoroughly. Put the lobster on lettuce and pour the dressing over. Garnish with lemon wedges.

(4 SERVINGS)

LOBSTER SALAD

1 pound cooked lobster meat
Juice ½ lemon
2 tablespoons sherry or white wine
⅔ cup diced celery
¼ cup Mayonnaise*
¼ cup heavy cream, whipped
Salad greens

Cut the lobster meat into bite-size pieces and moisten with lemon juice and wine. Let stand for about an hour. Add the celery. Mix the Mayonnaise with cream and fold into the salad. Blend thoroughly. Serve on greens.

(6 SERVINGS)

LOBSTER SALAD WITH MAYONNAISE

3 cups cut up cooked lobster meat
3 hard boiled eggs, chopped
½ cup diced celery
¼ cup minced parsley
1 tablespoon lemon juice
1 teaspoon Worcestershire sauce
1 teaspoon dry mustard
1 cup Mayonnaise*
Lettuce

Cut the lobster meat into large bite-size pieces. Put the eggs into a bowl, add celery and parsley, and stir. Add lemon juice, Worcestershire sauce, and mustard to the

Mayonnaise. Pour this over the eggs, add the lobster, and mix well. Serve on lettuce leaves.

(6 SERVINGS)

LOBSTER SALAD IN AVOCADOS

Make like Shrimp in Avocados*, substituting lobster meat for the shrimp.

TO COOK SHRIMP

Start shrimp in cold water to cover, and when the water comes to a boil, remove from heat and let them cool in the water. If the shrimp are quite large let them boil for 3 or 4 minutes. Do not overcook or the shrimp will be dry. For more flavorful shrimp add the juice of one lemon and a teaspoon of freshly ground pepper for each quart of water, or cook the shrimp in any Court Bouillon*.

SHRIMP SALAD

1 pound small cooked shrimp
Juice ½ lemon
1 cup diced celery
1 cup chopped water cress or lettuce
*3 tablespoons Mayonnaise**
1 tablespoon heavy cream
¼ teaspoon curry powder

Peel and devein the shrimp and sprinkle with lemon juice, and chill. Mix the shrimp with celery and water cress or lettuce. Mix the Mayonnaise with cream and curry powder to taste; add a teaspoon or two of the

water the shrimp was cooked in. Moisten the salad carefully with the dressing.

(4 SERVINGS)

SHRIMP SALAD VINAIGRETTE

2 pounds cooked shrimp or 3 cups canned or frozen
1 cup Vinaigrette*
½ teaspoon curry (optional)
Lettuce

If the shrimp are large, cut in half lengthwise; if very large, cut once more across. If using canned or frozen shrimp, drain them. Put into a bowl and pour the Vinaigrette over. Add curry to the Vinaigrette if you wish. Let stand in refrigerator for at least two hours. Serve on lettuce leaves.

(6 SERVINGS)

SHRIMP WITH RED WINE

4 hard boiled egg yolks
1 teaspoon dry mustard
1 teaspoon anchovy paste
1 cup Mayonnaise*
½ cup red wine (claret type)
1 pound cooked shrimp
1 cup diced celery
2 tablespoons minced parsley
Lettuce

Mash the egg yolks with mustard and anchovy paste. Stir into the Mayonnaise. Add the wine and blend well. Fold in the shrimp, celery, and parsley. Chill. Serve in lettuce cups.

(6 SERVINGS)

SHRIMP IN AVOCADOS

3 avocados
1 lemon
1 pound cooked small shrimp
3 stalks celery, chopped
½ teaspoon celery salt
¾ cup Lemon French Dressing*
Lettuce

Cut the avocados in half lengthwise and remove pits, do not peel. Sprinkle avocados with lemon juice to prevent discoloration. Mix the shrimp, celery, and celery salt. Add ½ cup of the dressing. Put the avocados on lettuce leaves, fill with the shrimp mixture, and spoon the remaining dressing over.

(6 SERVINGS)

SOLE IN MARINADE

1 pound fillet of sole
¼ cup lemon juice
1½ cups olive oil
¾ teaspoon salt
⅛ teaspoon pepper

Cut the fish into strips about ½ inch wide and 1½ inches long. Place in a bowl and cover with lemon juice. Refrigerate for an hour or two turning the fish once or twice to coat all sides with the lemon juice. The lemon juice "cooks" the fish! Sprinkle with olive oil to which you have added the salt and pepper.

(4 SERVINGS)

COD OR FLOUNDER SALAD

2 cups flaked cooked fish
1 cup chopped celery
1 small onion, minced
1 cup diced cooked potatoes
8 sardines, drained and sliced
½ teaspoon salt
¼ teaspoon pepper
1 cup Mayonnaise*
1 tablespoon lemon juice
½ teaspoon dry thyme or dill
Lettuce
1 (½ ounce) can anchovy fillets
Celery leaves

Mix the fish gently with the vegetables and sardines. Sprinkle with salt and pepper. Mix the Mayonnaise with lemon juice and herbs. Toss the fish mixture very gently into the dressing. Serve on lettuce and decorate with anchovies and a few celery leaves.

(6 SERVINGS)

CANNED SALMON SALAD

1 cup diced cucumbers
1 cup diced celery
1 teaspoon minced onion
1 teaspoon minced parsley
1 (pound) can red salmon, drained
½ teaspoon salt
⅛ teaspoon pepper
2 teaspoons lemon juice
1 cup Mayonnaise*
Salad greens

Flake the salmon. Add the cucumbers, celery, onion, and parsley. Add the salt, pepper, and lemon juice to the Mayonnaise, and fold gently into the salmon mixture. Serve on greens.

(6 SERVINGS)

TUNA SALAD

2 (7 ounce) cans tuna
2 cups diced celery
2 teaspoons minced parsley (optional)
1 cup Mayonnaise*
Lettuce (optional)

Flake the tuna with the celery and parsley. Fold the Mayonnaise gently into the salad. Serve on lettuce if you wish.

(8 SERVINGS)

TUNA CHEESE SALAD

1 (7 ounce) can tuna
1 cup cubed Cheddar cheese
1 head lettuce, shredded
⅔ cup Mayonnaise*
Leaf lettuce

Drain, flake the tuna, combine with cheese and lettuce. Add the Mayonnaise, and toss. Serve in a bowl lined with lettuce.

(4 SERVINGS)

NICOISE SALAD

1 head Boston lettuce
½–¾ cup French Dressing*
2 cups French cut green beans, cooked
2 cups diced cooked potatoes
1 cup canned tuna
2–3 tomatoes, peeled and quartered
2 hard boiled eggs, quartered
6 anchovies, cut in half
*1 tablespoon minced fresh tarragon, chervil, or
  parsley*

Clean the lettuce and break into pieces, dry and put
into a salad bowl. Sprinkle with a few tablespoons of
the dressing. Arrange the beans, potatoes, and tuna on
top of the greens, and place the tomatoes here and
there around the edge. Decorate with eggs and anchovies. Pour over the remaining dressing and sprinkle with
fresh tarragon, chervil, or parsley.

(6 SERVINGS)

MUSSELS REMOULADE

2 cups mussels, cooked or canned or frozen
¾ cup white wine or vermouth
Sprigs parsley
2 shallots or 3 scallions or 1 onion
½ cup Mayonnaise*
½ teaspoon anchovy paste
1 teaspoon minced pickles
½ teaspoon blended salad herbs
½–1 teaspoon capers

If you steam fresh mussels, you will need about 4 pounds. Scrub thoroughly and put in a large pot with the wine or vermouth, a few sprigs of parsley, and minced shallots, scallions, or onions. Cover tight, steam until the mussels open, about 5 minutes. Remove from shells. Reduce some of the liquid and use 2–3 tablespoons in the Mayonnaise. If using canned or frozen mussels add 2–3 tablespoons liquid in the Mayonnaise. Mix Mayonnaise with remaining ingredients and toss the mussels gently with the sauce.

(4 SERVINGS)

MUSSEL AND POTATO SALAD

4 pounds fresh mussels
1 onion
1 carrot
2 stalks celery
¾ cup white wine
5 medium potatoes, boiled in jackets
1 teaspoon tarragon or chervil
1 cup Mayonnaise*

Scrub and debeard the mussels and put them into a large pot with the onion, carrot, celery, and white wine. Steam until the shells open, about 5 minutes. Peel and slice the potatoes while hot. Sprinkle with ½ cup liquid from the mussels. Put alternate layers of mussels, reserving a few for garnish, and potatoes in a salad bowl. Mix the tarragon or chervil with the Mayonnaise. Spoon a little Mayonnaise on each layer. Cover with Mayonnaise and decorate with a few mussels.

(6 SERVINGS)

PASTA SALADS

Pasta makes a good, hearty salad, and can be served on any occasion when you might choose to serve a hot pasta. Macaroni salad teams well with cold cuts. In salad bowl or casserole, macaroni and cheese go well together.

MACARONI CHEDDAR SALAD BOWL

2 cups cooked small elbow macaroni
2 tablespoons chopped onion
2 tablespoons chopped pimento
2 tablespoons chopped green pepper or dill pickles
½ cup diced celery
½ cup French Dressing*
¼ cup Mayonnaise*
1 cup shredded Cheddar cheese
1 teaspoon salt
¼ teaspoon pepper
Lettuce

Combine the macaroni, onion, pimento, green pepper or pickles, and celery, and let stand in the French Dressing for an hour or more. Add the Mayonnaise and cheese. Season with salt and pepper, and toss. Serve in a salad bowl lined with crisp lettuce.

(6 SERVINGS)

MACARONI SALAD PLATTER

1 (8 ounce) package small elbow macaroni
¼ cup French Dressing*
1 pound fresh peas shelled or 1 package frozen
1 can whole kernel corn or 1 package frozen
½ cup Mayonnaise*
½ cup sour cream
1 tablespoon prepared mustard
Lettuce

Cook the macaroni following package instructions. Drain. Put into a large bowl. Sprinkle with the French Dressing and toss. Stir in the peas and corn. If you use frozen, cook ahead and drain. Mix the Mayonnaise, sour cream, and mustard, and fold in the macaroni. Spoon into a 6 cup bowl or mold, and pack down with back of a spoon. Chill. Unmold onto lettuce.

(6 SERVINGS)

MACARONI SALAD

1 pound small elbow or bow macaroni
1 cup chopped celery
½ cup chopped sweet onion
1 small green pepper, chopped
1 cup Boiled Dressing*
¼ teaspoon oregano
1–2 teaspoons minced parsley
Lettuce
2 tomatoes (optional)

Cook the macaroni following package instructions. Drain and chill. Mix with the celery, onion, and pepper. Toss with the dressing and with oregano and parsley. Serve on lettuce with peeled tomato wedges or slices if you wish.

(6–8 SERVINGS)

RICE SALAD

2 cups cooked rice
3 tomatoes, peeled and sliced
2 green peppers, cut into strips
½ teaspoon salt
¼ teaspoon pepper
2 tablespoons oil
1 tablespoon vinegar
1 teaspoon prepared mustard
Minced parsley (garnish)

Put the rice, tomatoes, and green pepper in a bowl. Mix the salt and pepper with oil, vinegar, and mustard. Pour into the salad and stir gently. Sprinkle with a little parsley if you wish.

(4–6 SERVINGS)

MOLDED SALADS

Aspics are the jewels of the salad family. They go well by themselves, or served first, filled with something light, or eaten last, molded or filled with fruit, or providing the main course at luncheon or supper, surrounding something substantial. A tomato aspic typically comes first, a fruit concoction last.

An aspic is a set piece, interesting in its form as well as in its glowing color. You deliberately select the mold that will do the most for the dish, deep enough to bring out the inner gleam of the aspic, and perhaps faceted to make it sparkle like a gemstone; or you can use any bowl to produce a cabochon jewel; or small molds out of custard cups can march around the filling in a circle. Mousses don't glow; they are opaque but are equally decorative and delicious.

An unusual aspic can bring variety to the meat course. Tired of cranberry sauce? Why not try Cranberry Mold with your turkey? Why not serve Prune Aspic with duck, Asparagus Mousse with ham, and Cucumber Aspic with fish?

All molded salads add glamor to a meal. They are a little trouble but it is time spent ahead. They must be made several hours before they are served. If you make this kind of salad, you will be free at the last minute.

To unmold an aspic or mousse run the tip of a small knife around the edge of the bowl, invert over a platter—if the salad doesn't pop out, try to pry it gently with a fork or put a warm cloth over the bottom of the mold for a few moments, or dip the mold in hot water.

BASIC TOMATO ASPIC

3½ tablespoons gelatin
3 cups tomato juice
1 cup consommé
¼ cup sugar
½ teaspoon salt
2–3 tablespoons vinegar

Sprinkle the gelatin on 1 cup of the cold tomato juice. Heat the remaining 2 cups of tomato juice with the consommé, sugar, salt, and vinegar, and pour onto the gelatin. Stir to dissolve. Pour into a large mold or 6 to 8 individual cups. Chill until set.

(6–8 Servings)

HERBED TOMATO ASPIC

¼ cup chopped celery
⅛ cup chopped onion
1 teaspoon salt
⅛ teaspoon freshly ground pepper
1 tablespoon sugar
½ teaspoon basil
1 tablespoon vinegar
1 bay leaf, crushed
2 cups tomato juice
2 tablespoons gelatin
1 cup Mayonnaise*

Cook the celery and onion with the seasonings in tomato juice until they are very soft. Strain. Mix the gelatin in ½ cup cold water, and add to the hot tomato mixture. Stir to dissolve. Pour into a ring mold if you're filling it with seafood or other salad. Serve with Mayonnaise.

(8 Servings)

TOMATO ASPIC

3 cups tomato juice
1/2 teaspoon celery salt
1 tablespoon prepared mustard
1/2 teaspoon onion salt
1/2 teaspoon salt
1/8 teaspoon pepper
2 envelopes unflavored gelatin
Salad greens
1 cup Mayonnaise* or Herb Mayonnaise*

Heat the tomato juice in a pot with celery salt, mustard, onion salt, salt, and pepper. Simmer 3–4 minutes. Add the gelatin (it has been softened in 1 cup cold water). Stir to dissolve and remove from heat. Pour into a wet ring mold. Chill. Serve on crisp greens. You may fill the center with seafood, artichoke hearts, mixed vegetable salad, or almost anything. Serve with Mayonnaise or Herb Mayonnaise.

(8 SERVINGS)

VEGETABLES IN ASPIC

1 envelope gelatin
1 chicken bouillon cube or 3/4 cup broth
1/2 cup tomato juice
12 cooked asparagus tips
1 cup cooked peas
Lettuce
3/4 cup Mayonnaise* or French Dressing*

Soften the gelatin in 1/4 cup cold water. Heat the bouillon cube in 3/4 cup water and pour over the gelatin to dissolve. Add tomato juice. Pour into a mold to

depth of 1/4″ only. When set, arrange the asparagus tips. Chill. Chill remaining gelatin until syrupy, fold in the peas and add to mold. Chill. Serve on lettuce with Mayonnaise or French Dressing.

(6 SERVINGS)

VEGETABLE ASPIC

- *1 envelope gelatin*
- *1 cup hot chicken or beef broth*
- *1 tablespoon lemon juice*
- *1/2 teaspoon salt*
- *1/4 teaspoon pepper*
- *1 cup mixed chopped vegetables, carrots, cucumbers, celery*
- *1 tablespoon minced scallions*
- *1 teaspoon minced parsley*

Soften the gelatin in 1/4 cup cold water and add 1/4 cup hot broth; stir to dissolve. Add remaining broth, lemon juice, salt, and pepper. Chill until the mixture begins to get thick. Mix in the vegetables, scallions, and parsley. Pour into a mold and chill.

(4 SERVINGS)

CUCUMBER ASPIC

- *1 package lemon gelatin*
- *1 envelope unflavored gelatin*
- *1/4 teaspoon salt*
- *2 cucumbers, peeled*
- *1 tablespoon lemon juice*
- *1 teaspoon chopped onion*
- *3/4 cup Mayonnaise**

Mix the lemon gelatin and the unflavored gelatin with salt and 1 cup boiling water. Stir to dissolve the gelatin. Put the cut-up cucumber in a blender with lemon juice and onion. Buzz until mushy and add to the gelatin. Pour into a mold and chill until firm. Serve with Mayonnaise. Especially good with fish.

(4 SERVINGS)

HAM ASPIC

1 envelope gelatin
1½ pounds cooked ham, ground
1 teaspoon lemon juice
1 cup minced celery
1 onion, grated
1 cup tomato juice
Lettuce

Soften the gelatin in ½ cup hot water and pour over the ham. Add remaining ingredients and pour into a mold. Chill until set. Unmold onto shredded lettuce.

(6 SERVINGS)

PRUNE ASPIC

2 envelopes gelatin
2 cups prune juice
2 cups pitted coarsely chopped cooked prunes
2 tablespoons lemon juice
1 teaspoon grated lemon rind

Dissolve the gelatin in ½ cup water, and stir in the heated prune juice to dissolve the gelatin. Let thicken slightly, then stir in the prunes, lemon juice, and rind. Pour into a mold and chill.

Especially good with meat such as veal, ham, or roast pork.

(8 SERVINGS)

TONGUE IN ASPIC

1 envelope gelatin
2 (10½ ounce) cans beef bouillon
Salt and pepper
1½ pounds cooked smoked tongue, sliced very thin
1 (1 pound) can tiny peas
Water cress and/or greens

Soften the gelatin in ⅓ cup hot water. Add the bouillon and season to taste with a little salt and pepper. Coat the bottom of a ring mold with aspic and chill. Dip the tongue slices into the remaining aspic and line the mold with overlapping slices and chill again. Add the peas and pour in remaining aspic. Chill until set. Unmold on round platter and fill center and garnish sides with water cress. If water cress is not available, use other greens.

(6 SERVINGS)

ASPARAGUS MOUSSE

1 envelope gelatin
1 tablespoon vinegar
1 tablespoon lemon juice
1 teaspoon salt
⅛ teaspoon pepper
Dash paprika
3 cups cooked, diced asparagus
1 tablespoon minced pimento
1 teaspoon minced onion

Dissolve gelatin in a little cold water. Reserve 1 cup of water asparagus was cooked in. Boil down to about ½ cup and add hot. Stir to dissolve. Add all seasonings and chill until syrupy. Fold in the asparagus, pimento, and onions. Pour into a mold and chill.

(6–8 SERVINGS)

SALMON MOUSSE

1 envelope gelatin
¼ cup vinegar
1 teaspoon dry mustard
½ teaspoon salt
1 small onion, chopped
1 (1 pound) can salmon
½ cup chopped celery
Few sprigs parsley
½ cup heavy cream, whipped

Soften the gleatin in ½ cup hot water and put in blender with vinegar, mustard, salt, and onion. Blend for a minute, then add the salmon, juice and all, and the celery and parsley. Blend until smooth—about a minute. Combine with the whipped cream and pour into a mold and chill.

(6 SERVINGS)

TUNA MOUSSE

Make exactly as you do the Salmon Mousse, substituting tuna for the salmon.

ROQUEFORT MOUSSE

1 envelope gelatin
1 teaspoon salt
1/4 teaspoon pepper
1/4 pound Roquefort or blue cheese
2 tablespoons minced scallions or chives
1/2 cup minced celery
1 cup heavy cream, whipped
Salad greens
1 cup French Dressing*

Soften gelatin in 1/4 cup cold water. Add 1 cup boiling water and stir to dissolve. Add salt and pepper and chill until syrupy. Mash the cheese and mix with scallions or chives, and celery. Fold the cheese mixture into whipped cream and add to the gelatin. Pour into a wet ring, or other mold, and chill. Serve on salad greens with French Dressing.

(6 SERVINGS)

LIGHT LEMON ROQUEFORT MOLD

1 package lemon gelatin
2 tablespoons vinegar
3 ounces Roquefort cheese
3 ounces cream cheese
1/2 cup heavy cream, whipped

Dissolve the gelatin in 3/4 cup of boiling water. Add the vinegar. Mix the cheeses together until smooth, and add to the gelatin. Fold in the whipped cream, and turn into a wet ring mold or other mold. Chill.

(6 SERVINGS)

CRANBERRY MOLD

2 envelopes gelatin
¾ cup sugar
1 tablespoon lemon juice
Juice 1 orange
1 cup raw ground cranberries
Ground rind 1 orange
1 tablespoon grated lemon rind
½ cup crushed pineapple
1 cup chopped celery

Dissolve the gelatin in ½ cup water. Add hot juice from the pineapple, and stir to dissolve. Add sugar, lemon and orange juices. Chill until thickened. Stir in the remaining ingredients, and pour into a ring or other mold.

Good with turkey or chicken.

(6 SERVINGS)

PINEAPPLE CHEESE MOUSSE

2 envelopes unflavored gelatin
1 can crushed pineapple
3 tablespoons lemon juice
⅓ cup sugar
Pinch salt
⅓ pound Cheddar cheese, shredded
1 cup heavy cream, whipped

Soften the gelatin in ½ cup cold water. Add the heated pineapple and stir to dissolve the gelatin. Remove at once from heat. Add lemon juice, sugar, and salt. Chill until syrupy. Fold in the cheese and cream. Pour into a mold and chill until firm.

(6 SERVINGS)

GRAPEFRUIT AVOCADO MOLD

1 package lime gelatin
1 envelope unflavored gelatin
½ cup grapefruit juice
2 grapefruit
1 large avocado
1 teaspoon lime or lemon juice
½ cup chopped celery

Soften the gelatin in ¼ cup cold water, add 2 cups boiling water and stir to dissolve. Add the grapefruit juice. Chill until syrupy. Peel and section the grapefruit. Peel and slice the avocado and sprinkle with a little lime or lemon juice. Mix the grapefruit, avocado and celery into the gelatin. Pour into a mold and chill. Unmold on a platter to serve.

(6 SERVINGS)

FRUIT SALADS

Fruit salads, chilled or frozen, take their place beside the aspics and mousses. An infinite variety of fruit salads, all delicious, may be presented in a wide choice of ways. Take a pineapple, for instance, split it lengthwise, plumes and all, and scoop out the meat. Now freeze the shell. After a couple of hours, it comes out of your freezer like a solid ceramic bowl realistically modeled in the fruit shape. Frozen hard, it will not drip nor wilt, and besides it keeps the contents well chilled. The contents will be the pineapple bits, sugared and chilled and combined with any suitable fruit, best of all strawberries; use a fruit French Dressing. For a children's party, make an orange basket by cutting a large orange in half and scooping out the fruit, pulp, and core. Scallop the edge with a scissors or sharp knife. Fill the shell with citrus or mixed fruit salad or sugared grapes. You can freeze the shells for a colder salad.

SUNBURST SALAD

2 cups grapefruit sections
2 cups orange sections
Lettuce
1 (3 ounce) package cream cheese
2 tablespoons heavy cream
1/4 cup French Dressing* or Lemon French Dressing*

For each serving arrange the fruit sections, petal fashion, on lettuce. In the center place cream cheese slightly softened with cream and whipped until fluffy. Serve with French Dressing or Lemon French Dressing.

(6 SERVINGS)

ORANGE AND WATER CRESS SALAD

4 oranges
1 stalk celery
¼ teaspoon sugar
*¼ cup Lemon French Dressing**
1 bunch water cress

Section the oranges and shred the celery. Add sugar to the Lemon French Dressing. Pour it over a mixture of the orange and celery. Pile this on water cress which has been put into a salad bowl.

(6 SERVINGS)

ORANGE AND CELERY SALAD

6 oranges
¾ cup chopped celery
*¼ cup Fruit French Dressing**
Salad greens
Chopped mint (optional)

Section the oranges and combine with celery, and dressing, and let stand a few hours to marinate. Serve on crisp greens, and sprinkle with mint if you wish.

(6 SERVINGS)

ORANGE ONION SALAD

6 oranges
1 large sweet onion, sliced thin
½ cup French Dressing*
Few strips of pimento
Greens

Peel and slice the oranges and combine with the onion. Marinate for about an hour in the French Dressing. Garnish with pimento and serve on crisp salad greens.

(6 SERVINGS)

ORANGE AND OLIVE SALAD

4 blood oranges, peeled and sliced thin
2 sweet onions, sliced thin
½ pound black olives
2 tablespoons olive oil
Pinch salt
½ teaspoon sugar

Mix the oranges and onions. Add the pitted olives, cut in half. Pour the oil, to which you have added a pinch of salt and sugar, over the salad.

(4 SERVINGS)

GRAPEFRUIT AND AVOCADO SALAD

2 avocados
2 tablespoons lemon juice
2 grapefruit, sectioned
1 bunch water cress
1 (3 ounce) package cream cheese (optional)
½ cup Lemon French Dressing*

Cut the avocados in half lengthwise, peel, and slice. Dip in lemon juice to prevent darkening. Place alternate sections of grapefruit and sliced avocado, petal fashion, on the water cress. Roll the cream cheese into balls, and place balls around the salad if you wish. Serve with Lemon French Dressing.

(4 SERVINGS)

GRAPEFRUIT, PERSIMMON, AND AVOCADO SALAD

2 avocados
1–2 tablespoons lemon juice
French Dressing* or Lemon French Dressing*
2 grapefruit
2 persimmons
Boston or Bibb lettuce

Peel and cut the avocados into thick slices and sprinkle with a little lemon juice. Section the grapefruit, being careful to avoid the membrane. Cut the persimmons into eighths. Arrange the soft lettuce on a plate and alternate pieces of avocado, grapefruit, and the persimmons. Top with the dressing mixed with a tablespoon or two of juice from the grapefruit.

(8 SERVINGS)

CHERRY SALAD

½ pint small curd cottage cheese
1–2 tablespoons cream
⅛ teaspoon salt
1 pound fresh large black Bing cherries
Lettuce
1 cup Fruit French Dressing*

Soften the cheese with cream and add the salt. Remove the pits from the cherries and fill with the cheese, letting some cheese stick out from the opening of the cherries. Arrange the filled cherries on lettuce and pass the Fruit French Dressing.

(6 SERVINGS)

CHERRIES AND CREAM CHEESE

1 (3 ounce) package cream cheese
3 tablespoons heavy cream
1 pound fresh cherries or 1 large can Bing cherries, pitted
Salad greens
*½ cup Mayonnaise**

Soften the cheese with 1 tablespoon cream, and fill the cherries with this mixture. Serve on salad greens. Thin the Mayonnaise with the remaining cream, and serve with the salad.

(4–6 SERVINGS)

SPICY PEACH OR PEAR SALAD

⅓ cup vinegar
1 stick cinnamon
⅓ cup sugar
6 whole cloves
6 halves of cooked or canned peaches or pears
½ cup cream cheese or cottage cheese
*3 tablespoons Mayonnaise**

Add ¼ cup water to the vinegar in a sauce pan. Put in the cinnamon, sugar, and cloves, and simmer 5 minutes. Pour over the fruit and chill. Drain and put the fruit

hollow side up on lettuce. Fill centers with cream cheese or cottage cheese mixed with the Mayonnaise.

(6 SERVINGS)

PEACH AND CHEESE SALAD

1 (¼ pound) package small curd cottage cheese
1 tablespoon cream
8 canned peach halves
Lettuce
Paprika
¼ cup chopped nuts (optional)
1–1½ cups Boiled Dressing* or Sour Cream Dressing*

Soften the cheese with cream and a tablespoon or two of juice from the peaches. Fill the peach halves with this. Place on lettuce cups or shredded lettuce and sprinkle with a little paprika and chopped nuts, if you wish. Pass Boiled Dressing or Sour Cream Dressing.

(4–8 SERVINGS)

PEAR AND CHEESE SALAD

Make exactly like the Peach and Cheese Salad, substituting canned or fresh pears for peaches.

WALDORF SALAD

2 cups diced apples
1 cup diced celery
½ cup Mayonnaise*
Broken or coarsely chopped walnuts
Lettuce

Mix the apple, celery, and Mayonnaise. Toss until both are well coated with Mayonnaise. Serve in a chilled bowl, top with walnuts, and put a border of lettuce around.

(4 SERVINGS)

PEAR WALDORF SALAD

Substitute cut up fresh pears for the apples in Waldorf Salad.

APPLE AND CELERY SALAD

½ cup diced apple
½ cup diced celery
¼ cup Mayonnaise*
1 head lettuce
6 slices bacon

Mix the apple, celery, and Mayonnaise. Break the lettuce into bite-size pieces. If using firm lettuce such as iceberg, shred it. Cook the bacon and dice it or cut into thin strips. Toss all together or put half the lettuce in a bowl, add bacon to remaining lettuce, and toss with the apple and celery.

(6 SERVINGS)

CRANBERRY ORANGE SALAD

1 pound raw cranberries
2 small oranges
1 cup sugar
Lettuce (optional)
10 small marshmallows (optional)

Put the cranberries and cut up oranges, peel and all, through a meat grinder. Stir in the sugar. Serve on lettuce. If you wish, cut up the marshmallows with wet scissors and add to the salad.

(6–8 SERVINGS)

CRANBERRY-ORANGE MOLD

    2 cups cranberry juice cocktail
    2 packages orange flavored gelatin
    1 cup orange juice
    4 oranges, peeled and sectioned
    1 cup coarsely chopped walnuts

Heat cranberry juice and pour over the gelatin, which has been softened with 1/4 cup water. Chill until syrupy, about 45 minutes. Pour half the gelatin into a mold. Let refrigerate 30 minutes. Add orange juice and sections, walnuts and remaining gelatin. Chill until firm. To unmold, run a knife around the edge, invert over a plate, and hold a hot cloth over the mold for a few moments. A good dessert aspic.

(8 SERVINGS)

GRAPE ALMOND SALAD

    Soft lettuce, preferably bronze or other garden
       lettuce
    2 cups seedless or seeded grapes
    3/4 cup toasted almonds
    1/2 cup Lemon French Dressing*
    1/4 teaspoon ground coriander or curry

Break up the lettuce into a dessert or salad bowl. Cover with grapes and sprinkle with almonds. Pour the

dressing mixed with coriander or curry over the salad and toss at table.

(6 SERVINGS)

PLUM SALAD

3 pounds fresh plums
Lettuce, shredded
½ cup Mayonnaise*
1 tablespoon minced fresh tarragon or 1 teaspoon dried
1 tablespoon sugar
1 tablespoon tarragon vinegar
½ cup heavy cream, whipped

Cut the plums in slices or wedges. Arrange on individual plates or in a salad bowl, on shredded lettuce. Mix the Mayonnaise with tarragon, sugar, tarragon vinegar, and whipped cream. Pour over the plums. You may make this with canned plums draining off most of the liquid.

(6 SERVINGS)

DESSERT SALADS

Here is summertime magnificence. Melon makes a magnificent salad served first or for a meal ending. Chunks, slices, cubes, or balls of melon may be served alone, with other fruits, or combined with each other. Spanish melon, cantaloupe, Persian, honeydew, casaba, or cranshaw if used in combinations should be chosen for contrasting color flesh. Melon should be served cold and may be marinated in wine, French dressing, or sprinkled with a little rum or sherry. Fruits, hot or cold, with or without a liqueur or wine, are delicious desserts.

HONEYDEW RING FRUIT SALAD

1 large honeydew melon, peeled
Lettuce
2 cups cantaloupe balls
2 cups fresh raspberries (optional)
2 cups seedless grapes
Sprigs of mint
¾ cup French Dressing*

Slice the melon into 6 thick rings, removing seeds. Put rings on lettuce, and fill the centers with cantaloupe balls, raspberries if available, and grapes. Garnish with mint. Serve with French Dressing.

(6 SERVINGS)

DOUBLE MELON SALAD

1 cantaloupe, peeled
Leaf lettuce
2 cups watermelon balls
1½ cups honeydew melon balls
Sprigs of mint (garnish)
¾ cup Sherry Mayonnaise*

Slice the cantaloupe into rings about an inch thick and remove seeds. Place on lettuce on salad plates. Fill each ring with watermelon and honeydew balls. Garnish with sprigs of mint, if you wish. Serve with Sherry Mayonnaise.

(4 SERVINGS)

WATERMELON BOWL SALAD

Designed to impress people at your next patio party, this watermelon half is filled with chilled melon balls, pineapple slices, and blueberries. It's also distinctive as a buffet centerpiece. Remember, choose a handsome melon.

½ watermelon
2 cups cantaloupe balls
2 cups pineapple chunks
1 cup blueberries
Greens
1 cup Lemon French Dressing*
2 tablespoons honey (optional)

With a ball cutter, remove the center from half of a short thick watermelon. Scrape out remaining flesh, and put shell in deep freezer. Toss together the watermelon and cantaloupe balls, pineapple chunks, and blueberries. Chill. Place the watermelon bowl on greens on

a platter, and fill it with the mixed fruit. Serve with Lemon French Dressing, add honey to the dressing, if you wish.

(6 SERVINGS)

APRICOTS WITH LIQUEUR

12 very ripe fresh apricots
3 ounces Grand Marnier, Cointreau, or Curaçao

Plunge the apricots into boiling water for a moment and they will peel easily. Slice them into a bowl and pour over the liqueur of your choice. This salad may be made with drained canned apricots.

(4 SERVINGS)

FRUIT AS FINGER FOOD

Cut fruit, such as pineapple, apple, pear, or melon, into sticks, thick or thin, or cut into wedges. Arrange assortment on a platter and pass sauce for dunking the fruit.

FRUIT PLATTER

1 melon
2 apples or pears
4 peaches or apricots
4 slices pineapple
2 bananas
1½ cups Fruit French Dressing*

Choose a ripe cantaloupe or small honeydew. Peel and cut into spears or wedges. Core and cut the apples or pears into eighths, the peaches or apricots into quarters, the pineapple into wedges, and the bananas into slices.

The banana will discolor, so add it last. Serve the dressing in little bowls or sauce dishes so that each can dunk his fruit into the dressing.

(8 SERVINGS)

CALIFORNIA FRUIT SALAD

2 grapefruit, sectioned
4 oranges, sectioned
3 peaches fresh or canned, cut up
1 cup seedless or seeded grapes
1 cup cut up pineapple
1 cup diced melon
½ cup Fruit Mayonnaise*
2 tablespoons orange juice
1 teaspoon lemon juice
½ cup sweetened whipped cream

Mix the fruits together in a chilled bowl, preferably glass. Mix the Mayonnaise with orange juice, lemon juice, and the whipped cream, and serve with the salad or toss into the salad.

(6–8 SERVINGS)

WHITE WINE FRUIT MOLD

2 packages lemon gelatin
¾ cup white wine (sauterne type)
2–2½ cups cut up mixed fruit (peaches, pears, apricots, plums, bananas, seedless grapes, and/or cherries)
1 teaspoon lemon juice
½ cup nuts (walnuts, pecans, or almonds) (optional)

Soften the gelatin in 1¼ cup boiling water. Add wine and cool. Add fruit, lemon juice, and nuts if you wish. Pour into a mold and chill. If you use canned fruits, be sure to drain and use ½ cup juice in place of ½ cup of the water. Use a mixture of the suggested fruits.

(6 SERVINGS)

PORT APPLESAUCE MOLD

1 envelope unflavored gelatin or 1 package lemon
    or raspberry flavored gelatin
½ cup port wine
1 teaspoon lemon juice
1 tablespoon grated orange peel
1 (1 pound 1 ounce) can applesauce
½ cup whipped cream or sour cream (garnish)

Soften the gelatin in ½ cup of water. Add the hot wine and stir until gelatin is dissolved. Add lemon juice, orange peel, and hot applesauce. Pour into an oiled mold. Chill until firm. Turn out on a plate. Good with roast pork or duck. If serving as a dessert, garnish with slightly sweetened whipped or sour cream.

(6 SERVINGS)

HOT PEAR DESSERT

6 canned pears
Apple and/or mint jelly
Coarsely chopped candied ginger and/or orange
    peel
2 tablespoons rum

Lay pear halves on a piece of foil. Fill the centers with jelly and crystallized ginger or orange peel. Sprinkle

with rum and wrap carefully cut side up in foil. Bake 10–15 minutes in 450° oven.

(6 SERVINGS)

BROILED GRAPEFRUIT

2 large grapefruit
4 tablespoons rum
4 tablespoons warm honey
Mace

Cut the grapefruit in half, cut out the core and loosen each section from the skin with a sharp pointed knife or grapefruit knife. Do not cut the membrane between the sections, run the knife around each section not around the outside. Mix the rum and honey, and pour over the grapefruit. Sprinkle with a pinch of mace. Broil for 10 minutes to brown top; or wrap in aluminum foil, cut side up, and broil 15–20 minutes. Unwrap to serve.

(4 SERVINGS)

PINEAPPLE SLICES FLAMBE

1 pineapple
¼–½ cup brown sugar
¼ pound butter
¼ cup rum

Cut the pineapple into ½ inch slices and place on a baking sheet. Sprinkle with brown sugar, and dot with butter. Broil until the sugar and butter melt and are light brown. Immediately transfer to a fireproof dish. Pour the heated rum over and ignite.

(4–6 SERVINGS)

FROZEN FRUIT SALAD

½ cup cherries, pitted and cut in half
½ cup pears, diced
½ cup peaches, diced
½ cup pineapple, diced
2 tablespoons powdered sugar
½ cup Mayonnaise*
1 teaspoon lemon juice
1 cup heavy cream, whipped
½ cup Mayonnaise* (optional)

Mix the fruits and drain reserving ½ cup of the juice from the fruit. Mix the sugar, Mayonnaise, and lemon juice. Fold in the fruit and whipped cream. Put into a wet mold and freeze. Serve with Mayonnaise if you wish.

(6 SERVINGS)

EASY FROZEN FRUIT SALAD

1 envelope gelatin
2 tablespoons lemon juice
½ cup Mayonnaise*
1 (1 pound 13 ounce) can fruit cocktail
1 cup heavy cream, whipped

Soften the gelatin in ¼ cup hot water. Combine with lemon juice, Mayonnaise, and ¼ cup juice from the fruit. Pour in the drained fruit and fold in the cream. Freeze until almost firm. The fruit should not be frozen too hard.

(8 SERVINGS)

FROZEN PINEAPPLE SALAD

1½ cups crushed drained pineapple
¼ cup maraschino cherries
6 marshmallows, cut up
2 tablespoons sugar
1 (8 ounce) package cream cheese
3 tablespoons Mayonnaise*
1 cup heavy cream, whipped
Lettuce (optional)

Mix the pineapple, cherries, and marshmallows, and add sugar. Soften the cheese with the Mayonnaise. When smooth, fold in the whipped cream. Add the fruit. Pour into a mold, bowl, or refrigerator tray, and freeze until firm. Serve on lettuce, if you wish.

(8 SERVINGS)

Chapter Three

SALAD DAYS AROUND THE GLOBE

"*Et ensuite, de la salade, madame, naturellement,*" ruled the *maître d'hôtel* at a Michelin three-star restaurant, creating a menu. "*Mais oui!*" I cried.

"*Und Dazu, Kartoffelsalat, natürlich,*" urged the *Kellner* in the Rathskeller. "*Natürlich!*" I agreed.

"*Borani Esfanaj!*" cried the Iranian waiter in a flood of voluble Persian. Of course I nodded, even if I didn't understand him. I soon found that the spinach salad he suggested, blended with yogurt and garlic, made the perfect complement to the skewered broiled lamb; just as the German potato salad pointed up the *Nierenbraten,* and the French tarragon-flavored greens set off the rich *coq au vin.*

I first encountered foreign salads tagging along with my father on his gastronomic tours of Europe, trundling from repast to repast in the high Peugeot touring car. Often the repast was a luncheon alfresco by the roadside. Majestic in his voluminous dun-colored duster, his high silk hat laid aside in favor of a hound's-tooth-check motoring cap, Father would descend from the high step, hand down my mother, and direct operations. The chauffeur spread the white damask cloth, my mother unpacked the replete hamper, and my sister

and I watched impatiently. Out of the hampers would come wine and wineglasses, a long crusty French loaf, a fat sausage, native cheese, and some madeleines.

Because Father thought no meal was complete without its green course, there might be radishes and sweet butter, or fennel, or sometimes a white asparagus. It was best of all when Father spied lamb's-tongues or dandelion in the field or water cress in the stream. Then an expedition was organized, with Father in command and Carol and my sister Rhoda as skirmishers. We liked the water cress best because it gave us an excuse to get wet; and good eating it was too, crisp and pungent from the cold, tumbling water, with no dressing at all.

Even when we didn't pick it fresh for him, Father never failed to call for salad whenever he lunched or dined. Still under his influence decades later, I keep on trotting around the world, sampling the best salad specialties of every country I visit, East or West. On foreign tables, I have found, salads are seldom the star performer; but each country has its own typical favorites. The variety is great, from green Chinese salad to the green and red of Sweet Pepper Salad to White Hearts of Palm Salad to Greek *Taramasalata*, a blending of pink roe, to pepper-red Mexican *Ceviche*, made with raw fish and—it sometimes seems—GUNPOWDER.

Every foreign menu is a new adventure, and sometimes a heroic one.

In Hong Kong as I prepared to dine out with Maple Quong, the Hurok of Hong Kong, I was glad to think about dining out Chinese style. Chinese style, as I understood it, decrees that the soup ends the meal.

Twelve of us sat down to the table, with a silent servitor in white standing behind every chair. As course followed course, they were ready to furnish fresh plates and hot towels. One new sensation succeeded another:

the chicken breasts with black mushrooms were sensational, the minced quail was even better, the pork with crisp Chinese vegetables and fresh water chestnuts was as good as a salad. After I had done honor to six such dishes centering the table in turn, I was glad to see the bowl of soup appear.

It was shark fin soup, and the best soup I ever tasted. My host seeing how fast my bowlful was disappearing, courteously ladled me a refill. I had just a small cranny left to stow it in. Knowing this was the end, I stowed it.

Imagine my surprise, when vinegared vegetables appeared "to clear our palates," and the whole thing started over!

What did this mean?

"It is the custom," explained my dinner partner, "to salute the honored guest at a formal dinner, by counting one course for each guest, and one over."

Of course the honored guest had to pay tribute to every one of the thirteen courses by eating it. I was never more convinced that "a little learning is a dangerous thing."

Thus I arrived in Bangkok pretty wary of Oriental feasting.

"Madam's plane was late," fretted the desk clerk. "You must make haste to be ready. The car will call in five minutes to take you to a luncheon with the Princess Chumbhot."

"I can't possibly make it!"

The clerk's mouth and eyes opened wide.

"You will be ready," he said with finality. "You will not keep the princess waiting."

I was ready.

I wouldn't have missed it. The princess welcomed me to a classic Siamese house soaring on stilts, and sat me down to a classic Siamese meal which did *not* conclude with soup. I enjoyed every bite.

"And tomorrow night," proposed the princess, "I will take you and your escort to a formal dinner at my cousin's, Prince Pandit, in honor of Marlon Brando and the cast of *The Ugly American!*"

"A formal dinner!" I said wistfully. "How can you wedge in two crashers at a formal sit-down dinner?"

"Easily," said the princess, "since I am lending my cousin twenty-five of my best servants and all of my tablecloths."

I went. There were 270 guests seated. As I added 270 + 2 and figured out 272 courses, I was glad this was Thailand and not China.

FRENCH SALADS

In France, everybody likes to serve salad before or after the main course, because the salad vinegar interferes with the important wines of the meal. French salads go well on the *hors d'oeuvre* plate, or at the end of the main course, accompanied or followed by cheese.

FRENCH GREEN SALAD

2 heads Boston or other soft lettuce
¼ cup French Dressing*

Wash the lettuce and pull the leaves apart. Spread out to dry thoroughly. Break up only the larger outside leaves. Put into a salad bowl. Add the dressing and toss gently.

(4–6 SERVINGS)

FRENCH MIXED GREEN SALAD

1 head romaine
1 head Boston lettuce
1 chapon—being a crust of French bread with a clove of garlic inserted into it
½ teaspoon salt
¼ teaspoon freshly ground pepper
⅓ cup French Dressing*
3 hard boiled egg yolks

Wash, dry, and tear up the greens. Rub bowl with the chapon and leave it in the bowl. Add the greens and salt and pepper. Just before serving, add the French Dressing and toss. Sprinkle with grated hard cooked egg yolks.

(6 SERVINGS)

FRENCH WATER CRESS SALAD

1 bunch water cress
½ teaspoon salt
Freshly ground pepper
3 tablespoons olive oil
1 tablespoon lemon juice or wine vinegar (optional)

Wash the water cress thoroughly in several changes of water. Dry and refrigerate. When ready to serve, cut off tough stem ends and toss with salt, pepper, and oil. You may add lemon juice or vinegar if you wish. If serving good wine, omit the lemon or vinegar.

(4 SERVINGS)

PARISIAN SALAD

1–1½ cups strips of cooked beef or veal
1 cup sliced cooked potatoes
1 onion, parboiled and sliced thin
2 tomatoes, peeled and sliced
Soft lettuce
½ cup French Dressing*
1 tablespoon minced parsley

Mix the beef with potatoes, onion, and tomatoes. Put onto lettuce leaves and break a few leaves into small

pieces and add to the salad. Pour the dressing over and
sprinkle with parsley. Toss at the table.

(4–6 SERVINGS)

FRENCH BEAN AND TOMATO SALAD
SALADE DE HARICOTS VERTS ET TOMATES

1 pound French cut beans or 2 boxes frozen
1 teaspoon salt
2 large tomatoes
½ cup French Dressing*

Cook the beans in salted water until just tender. Rinse
at once in cold water. Drain and chill. If using frozen
beans, cook according to instructions. Put the beans in
a bowl with the peeled, quartered tomatoes and pour
the French Dressing over. Toss gently.

(6 SERVINGS)

FRENCH TOMATO SALAD

6 tomatoes
4 tablespoons oil
1 tablespoon vinegar
1 teaspoon salt
Freshly ground pepper
½ teaspoon sugar
2 tablespoons minced parsley
2 shallots, minced

Peel the tomatoes and slice thin. Place the tomatoes on
a cold platter so they overlap a little. Mix the remaining ingredients thoroughly. Pour the dressing over.

(6 SERVINGS)

ITALIAN SALADS

The Italian salad, like the Italian genius, is spicy, original, and varied. Tossed salads are piquant with fresh herbs flavoring fragrant greens and raw mushrooms. For an *antipasto,* raw vegetables which have been soaked with garlic in salted ice water are dipped by each diner in seasoned olive oil. Celery, fennel, radishes, baby artichokes, strips of green pepper, and tiny carrots emerge fresh and crunchy from their garlic-flavored bath.

ITALIAN SALAD BOWL

2 heads soft lettuce
1 small iceberg lettuce
½ bunch curly endive
1 cup julienne strips salami
¼ cup French Dressing*
Pinch oregano
1 clove garlic, crushed

Tear the greens into bite-size pieces, and put into a salad bowl with the salami. Toss lightly with the French Dressing, oregano, and garlic.

(6 SERVINGS)

ITALIAN TOMATO SALAD

6 large tomatoes
1 tablespoon oregano, or 1 teaspoon dried
½ teaspoon salt
¼ teaspoon pepper
2 tablespoons olive oil

Peel and slice the tomatoes and arrange on a platter. Sprinkle with oregano, salt and pepper. Dribble the oil over and let stand a number of hours.

(6 SERVINGS)

ITALIAN SEAFOOD SALAD
INSALATA DI FRUTTI DI MARE

1 cup cleaned small clams
1 cup lobster meat
1 cup crabmeat
1 cup small shrimp
1 cup mussels (if available)
½ cup white wine
1 cup cut up squid (optional)
1 cup diced celery

Clams, lobster meat, crab, and shrimp; these are probably all available at your fish market. If you use mussels, steam 2 pounds with 2 pounds of clams in ½ cup of water and white wine. Remove from shell and set aside. Let the broth settle and pour off the top being careful to avoid sand. Cook the cut up lobster and crab in this broth for 20 minutes. If the shrimp are not cooked, they should also be cooked in the broth, but take only 5 minutes after the broth comes to a boil. Mix all of the seafood together with the celery. If the shrimp are large, cut them in half. You need about 4 cups of seafood for 6 people as a luncheon or main course dish.

There must be a variety of fish to give different flavor and texture.

(6 SERVINGS)

SEAFOOD SAUCE

½ cup olive oil
1 teaspoon salt
¼ teaspoon white pepper
¼ teaspoon mustard
¼ teaspoon paprika
⅛ cup wine vinegar
Juice 1 lemon
1 tablespoon minced anchovies

Blend all of the ingredients together. Pour over the fish salad and let stand for an hour in the refrigerator.

SALAD WITH MUSHROOMS
INSALATA DI OVOLI

1 cup very thinly sliced mushrooms
⅓ cup julienne carrots
⅓ cup julienne celery
½ cup thinly sliced Swiss cheese
¼ cup oil
⅛ cup vinegar
1 teaspoon salt
¼ teaspoon pepper

Do not wash the mushrooms; if they are sandy, wipe them with a damp cloth and cut them as thin as possible. Cut the carrots into matchstick pieces and the Swiss cheese the same size. Mix the oil, vinegar, salt, and pepper, and pour the mixture over the mushrooms, carrots, celery, and cheese. Toss gently. Chill.

(4 SERVINGS)

SICILIAN SALAD

1 large head lettuce
1 (2¼ ounce) can pitted ripe olives
2 oranges, peeled and sliced thin
¼ cup oil
¼ cup orange juice
1 tablespoon lemon or lime juice
1 teaspoon salt
¼ teaspoon paprika

Break the lettuce into bite-size pieces. Put into a deep platter or shallow salad bowl. Scatter olives and oranges over the greens. Make a dressing with remaining ingredients and pour over the salad.

(4 SERVINGS)

SALAD OF RAW MUSHROOMS
INSALATA DI FUNGI CRUDI

¾ pound mushrooms
½ cup olive oil
Juice 1 large lemon
½ teaspoon salt
¼ teaspoon white pepper
Soft salad greens

Slice the heads of the mushrooms very thin. Mix the oil, lemon juice, salt, and pepper, and pour over the mushrooms. Toss gently and let stand ½ hour. Serve on greens. Wild mushrooms are particularly good served this way.

(4–6 SERVINGS)

ITALIAN BROCCOLI SALAD VINAIGRETTE

1 bunch broccoli
1 teaspoon salt
1 cup Vinaigrette*
Lettuce or water cress
2 hard boiled eggs (optional)

Trim the ends of the broccoli and peel the stems if they are tough. Cook in about an inch of salted water until barely tender, about 10–12 minutes. Drain and pour the dressing over while the broccoli is hot. Chill and serve on lettuce or water cress. Garnish with egg slices or wedges if you wish.

(4 SERVINGS)

SWISS SALADS

Crossing the Alps into Switzerland, the vertical country of goat-herds, yodeling, and goats cropping edelweiss, salad gains a new dimension. One would expect the Swiss to use Swiss cheese in salad; and so they do.

SWISS SALAD

½ *pound Swiss cheese*
1 *head lettuce*
½ *pound spinach, or chicory, or 1 bunch water cress*
¼ *cup Mayonnaise**
1 *tablespoon prepared mustard*
½ *teaspoon paprika*
2 *tablespoons oil*
1 *tablespoon wine vinegar*

Cut the cheese in julienne strips. Break the greens into bite-size pieces and mix with the cheese. Blend the Mayonnaise with mustard, paprika, oil, and vinegar. Pour over the salad and toss.

(6–8 SERVINGS)

SWISS CHEESE AND ANCHOVY SALAD

1 head soft lettuce
1 cup Swiss cheese, cut in sticks
1 (3 ounce) can anchovy fillets
1 bunch water cress (optional)
¼ cup French Dressing*

Break lettuce into small pieces. Put in bowl and top with cheese and anchovies. Place water cress around the salad if you wish. Pour on the French Dressing and toss at table.

(6 SERVINGS)

SWISS LETTUCE AND LEEK SALAD

1 head lettuce
3 leeks
3 slices bacon
2–3 tablespoons vinegar
¼ teaspoon salt

Shred the lettuce, and chop the leeks. Mix together. Fry the bacon and crumble it over the salad. Add vinegar and salt to the bacon drippings, and pour warm over the salad.

(4 SERVINGS)

GERMAN SALADS

The Germans, like the Swiss, like their salads solid.
Their potato salads are famous. They have a way with
cabbage salads. Such salads come to the table on equal
terms and at the same time with the good roast meat.

GERMAN POTATO SALAD WITH
SOUR CREAM DRESSING
KARTOFFELSALAT

2 *pounds potatoes, boiled in jackets*
¼ *cup vinegar*
1 *tablespoon sugar*
1 *teaspoon salt*
¼ *teaspoon pepper*
⅛ *teaspoon paprika*
1 *pint sour cream*

Peel and slice potatoes while warm. Mix remaining
ingredients and pour over potatoes; stir gently.

(4–6 SERVINGS)

GERMAN HOT POTATO SALAD

2 pounds potatoes, boiled in jackets
6 slices bacon, diced
1 large onion, minced
½ cup vinegar
½ cup beef or chicken broth
1 teaspoon salt
¼ teaspoon pepper
1 teaspoon sugar
2 egg yolks

Peel the potatoes while warm, and slice thin. While the potatoes are cooking, fry the bacon, and when almost crisp add onions. Cook 2 minutes and add the vinegar, broth, and seasonings. Simmer a minute or 2. Remove from heat, and stir into the egg yolks which have been beaten with 2 tablespoons of water. Pour over the potatoes, and mix gently.

(6 Servings)

AUSTRIAN POTATO APPLE SALAD

3 tablespoons olive oil
3 tablespoons vinegar
½ teaspoon salt
⅛ teaspoon pepper
1 pound potatoes, boiled in jackets
1 pound apples
2 hard boiled eggs
2 cooked beets diced (garnish)

Peel and dice the potatoes. Core, peel, and dice the apples. Make the dressing by mixing oil, vinegar, salt, and pepper. Pour this over a mixture of the potatoes and apples, and garnish with sliced eggs and/or beets.

(6 Servings)

AUSTRIAN RED AND WHITE CABBAGE SALAD

1 small head white cabbage, shredded
1 small head red cabbage, shredded
2 apples, peeled, cored, and diced
2 tablespoons vinegar
1 teaspoon sugar
½ cup French Dressing*

Mix the red and white cabbage together. Add the apples, vinegar, and sugar, and toss lightly. Then toss in the French Dressing.

(6 SERVINGS)

GERMAN COLE SLAW

1 large head cabbage, shredded
1 onion, minced
1 green pepper, diced
2 egg yolks
1 teaspoon salt
¼ teaspoon pepper
⅛ teaspoon dry mustard
1 cup olive oil
3 tablespoons vinegar
1 cup sour cream

Scald the cabbage and squeeze dry. Add the onions and peppers and mix. Put the egg yolks in a bowl with salt and pepper and mustard and add the oil a few drops at a time at first and then in a slow stream beating steadily. Add a little vinegar from time to time. Pour this mixture over the cabbage and then fold in the sour cream.

(6 SERVINGS)

GERMAN KNOB CELERY SALAD

2 pounds celery root
2 teaspoons salt
1/2 cup olive oil
1/2 cup vinegar
1/4 teaspoon pepper
1 tablespoon sugar
1 cup broth
1/2 teaspoon mustard

Cut the celery into julienne strips and boil in water with 2 teaspoons salt for 5 minutes. Drain and cool. Mix all of the other ingredients. Warm them and pour over the celery root. Chill.

(6 SERVINGS)

GERMAN CUCUMBER SALAD
GURKENSALAT

2 large cucumbers, peeled and sliced thin
2 tablespoons salt
3 tablespoons sour cream
1 tablespoon vinegar or lemon juice
1/4 teaspoon sugar
Pinch paprika

Put the cucumbers in a bowl and sprinkle generously with salt. Let stand at least 3 hours. Drain off the water, rinse, and squeeze out any remaining moisture. Put in a bowl and cover with a dressing made by mixing the sour cream, vinegar or lemon juice, and sugar. Sprinkle with paprika.

(4 SERVINGS)

GERMAN CHICKEN SALAD

½ pound mushrooms, sliced
1–2 tablespoons butter
4–5 cups diced cooked chicken
1½ cups chopped celery
1 cup Mayonnaise*
1 cup heavy cream, whipped
Lettuce
Capers (optional)

Sauté the mushrooms in butter for 2–3 minutes and cool. Mix the chicken, mushrooms, and celery with the Mayonnaise. Let this mixture stand for several hours in the refrigerator. Fold in the cream just before serving. Serve on a bed of lettuce and garnish with capers, if you wish.

(6–8 Servings)

SCANDINAVIAN SALADS

Herring swims into the salad bowl in Scandinavia. In every guise this favorite fish appears on the smorgasbord table. No spread is complete without a shoal of herring flanked by dilled cucumbers, pickled beets, and lively meat and fish salads.

HERRING SALAD
HERRINGSALAT

2 salt herrings
1 dill pickle
1 cucumber
4 apples
6 tablespoons oil
½ cup white wine
¼ cup vinegar
1 onion, minced
⅛ teaspoon salt
⅛ teaspoon pepper
⅛ teaspoon sugar
1 teaspoon dry mustard

Fillet the herring, and dice. Add the pickle and cucumber both diced, and the apples peeled, cored, and diced. Make a dressing out of the oil, white wine, vinegar, and onion. Season with salt, pepper, sugar, and mustard, and pour over the salad.

(6 SERVINGS)

NORWEGIAN HERRING SALAD

1 salt herring
1 cup diced pickled beets
⅓ cup diced sweet pickles
¼ cup chopped onion
1 cup diced boiled potatoes
2 small apples
2 tablespoons sugar
¼ cup vinegar
¼ cup heavy cream, whipped (optional)

Clean the herring and soak at least overnight in cold water. Skin the fish and cut into dice. Add the beets, pickles, onion, potatoes, and apples, which have been cored, peeled, and diced. Toss gently. Mix the sugar and vinegar with 2 tablespoons cold water, and toss into the salad. Add cream, if you wish.

(4 SERVINGS)

SWEDISH MIXED SALAD

1–2 heads lettuce
4 tomatoes
2 bunches radishes
2 hard boiled eggs
1 tablespoon chopped parsley
2 tablespoons chopped chives
¼ cup French Dressing*

Break the lettuce into bite-size pieces. Peel tomatoes, and slice thin. Slice radishes thin. Chop the egg whites and yolks separately. To assemble the salad, put greens in a salad bowl and arrange slices of tomatoes, radishes, and eggs whites, then yolks around the salad. Mix the parsley and chives and put in the center. Just before

ready to serve, pour the dressing over and toss salad at the table.

(8 SERVINGS)

SWEDISH PICKLED BEET MOLD

1 envelope gelatin
Juice ½ lemon
¾ cup sweet pickled beet juice
1 tablespoon horseradish
2 tablespoons vinegar
2 tablespoons grated onion
½ cup diced celery
1 cup chopped pickled beets
½ teaspoon salt
Lettuce
Mayonnaise*

Add 1 cup boiling water to the gelatin and stir to dissolve. Add lemon juice, beet juice, horseradish, vinegar, and onion. Let stand until syrupy, then add the celery and beets, and salt. Turn into a wet or oiled mold. Chill until firm. Turn out on lettuce. Serve with Mayonnaise.

(6 SERVINGS)

SWEDISH FROZEN FRUIT SALAD
FRUKT SALLAD

1 (3 ounce) package cream cheese
1 cup heavy cream
2 tablespoons lemon juice
2 tablespoons sugar
⅛ teaspoon salt
1 can fruit cocktail or 2 cups cut up fruit
Lettuce

Soften the cheese with 2 tablespoons of cream. Whip the remaining cream. Add lemon juice, sugar, and salt to the cheese and fold in the whipped cream. Add the drained fruit and stir gently. Freeze in refrigerator tray or mold or shallow bowl. Cut in slices and serve on lettuce. Let stand in refrigerator for half an hour before serving so the fruit won't be too hard.

(6 SERVINGS)

DANISH POTATO SALAD

4–5 large potatoes, boiled in jackets
4 tablespoons oil
4 tablespoons tarragon vinegar
1 teaspoon salt
1 teaspoon sugar
1 clove garlic, crushed
3 green onions, chopped
6–8 radishes, sliced thin
¼ cup Mayonnaise*
1 tablespoon fresh dill or 1 teaspoon dried
Parsley (garnish)
3 hard cooked eggs (garnish)

Do not overcook the potatoes, peel and cut into ½ inch cubes. Mix oil, vinegar, salt, sugar, and garlic and pour over the potatoes. Chill. When ready to serve, combine the onions and radishes with the potatoes. Mix the Mayonnaise with dill and fold into the salad. Garnish with parsley and hard cooked egg wedges.

(6 SERVINGS)

SCANDINAVIAN EGGS STUFFED
WITH CUCUMBER
AGG OCH GURKSALLAD

6 hard boiled eggs
1 cup minced cucumber
3 tablespoons Mayonnaise*
¼ teaspoon freshly ground pepper
Few drops onion juice or minced onion (optional)
Parsley sprigs (garnish)
Lettuce

Cut the eggs lengthwise and remove yolks. Drain the cucumber and mix with Mayonnaise and pepper. Add a little onion juice or minced onion, if you wish. Fill the egg whites with the cucumber mixture, and grate egg yolks over the top: garnish with parsley and serve on lettuce.

(6 SERVINGS)

SCANDINAVIAN ANCHOVY EGG SALAD

8–10 anchovy fillets
1 large onion, minced
2 tablespoons capers
1 egg

Put the chopped anchovies around the edge of a round plate, place a circle of onion inside, next a ring of capers. Put the raw egg in the center, and the person who serves himself first mixes the salad until well blended.

(3–4 SERVINGS)

SPANISH AND MEXICAN SALADS

Spanish salads like Spanish marriages are arranged with care. Vegetables sprinkled with salt and olive oil are likely to be set out on a flat platter. Graceful, narrow-spouted cruets of oil and vinegar are often ready on the table to bless the happy union.

GAZPACHO SALAD

4 tomatoes, peeled and sliced
2 Italian or 1 Bermuda onion, peeled and sliced thin
2 cucumbers, sliced thin
2 stalks celery, sliced thin
½–¾ cup dry seasoned bread crumbs
½ cup Garlic French Dressing*
Water cress or lettuce (optional)

Place alternate layers of vegetables in a glass bowl. Sprinkle with a few bread crumbs. Chill for at least an hour. Pour the dressing over and toss at table. Serve on water cress or lettuce, if you wish.

(8 SERVINGS)

SPANISH ORANGE SALAD

½ teaspoon salt
¼ teaspoon freshly ground pepper
¼ teaspoon sugar
¼ cup olive oil
2 tablespoons wine vinegar
3 oranges, peeled and sliced
1 onion
Soft greens
Pimento (garnish)

Mix the salt, pepper, and sugar with oil and vinegar. Pour over the sliced oranges and thinly sliced onion, and let stand for at least one hour. You may peel the oranges or not. Add the greens, which have been broken into small pieces. Garnish with julienne strips of pimento.

(6 SERVINGS)

SPANISH OLIVE ANCHOVY SALAD

1 cup pitted olives
4 anchovy fillets
2 tablespoons minced pimento
3 tablespoons olive oil
1 tablespoon wine vinegar
½ teaspoon salt
½ teaspoon mustard
Salad greens

Cut the olives in half. Use green, ripe, or stuffed olives, or a combination. Mince the anchovies and mix with the rest of the ingredients and let stand 2–3 hours. Pour over salad greens, which have been torn into pieces. Toss.

(4 SERVINGS)

"Olé!" cry the hot-blooded Latins south of the border over food that brings tears to American eyes. At a Mexican meal, the cool touch of salad is especially welcome, and fortunately shredded lettuce adorns many a dish.

MEXICAN EGGPLANT SALAD

1 large eggplant
Juice of 1 lemon
1 tablespoon salt
1 clove garlic
¼ cup minced onion
½ cup chopped celery
*⅓ cup French Dressing**
Romaine lettuce
*1 cup Mayonnaise**

Peel the eggplant, dice, and cook in water with lemon juice, salt, and garlic for about 5 minutes until barely tender. Mix with the onions, celery, and French Dressing. Let stand in the refrigerator for a couple of hours to bring out the flavor. Serve on the lettuce with Mayonnaise on the side.

(6 SERVINGS)

MEXICAN PINEAPPLE COCONUT SALAD

1 cup cubed pineapple
1 cup grated coconut
2 cups shredded cabbage
*1 cup Mayonnaise**
1 teaspoon lemon juice
Lettuce

Combine all ingredients, except lettuce, and toss gently. Chill, and serve on a bed of lettuce.

(4 SERVINGS)

CEVICHE

*1 pound halibut or ½ pound any white fish and ½
    pound scallops*
1 cup lemon juice
½ cup chopped onions or scallions
1 cup tomato juice
1 teaspoon salt
½ teaspoon pepper
2 tablespoons Worcestershire sauce
½ (14 ounce) bottle tomato catsup
½ teaspoon Tabasco sauce
½ teaspoon oregano
2 tablespoons chopped parsley

Cut the raw fish into about ½ inch cubes and marinate in the lemon juice for at least one hour. Mix the onions, tomato juice, salt, pepper, Worcestershire sauce, catsup, Tabasco sauce, oregano, and parsley. Pour off excess lemon juice from the fish and fold into the sauce. Adjust seasoning, adding a little of the lemon juice to taste. Let stand several hours or overnight.

(6 SERVINGS)

MEXICAN FRUIT SALAD

4 bananas
4 oranges
1 sweet pepper or pimento
3 tablespoons shredded coconut
¼ cup Fruit French Dressing*
1 teaspoon fresh mint or ¼ teaspoon dried

Cut the bananas once through lengthwise and then once in half making 16 pieces. Arrange the sectioned oranges and strips of pepper or pimento over the bananas. Add the dressing and let stand in refrigerator for about an hour. Sprinkle with mint.

(6–8 Servings)

SOUTH AMERICAN SALADS

Corn, lima beans, avocados, tomatoes, and potatoes were all part of the "wealth of the Indies" which the conquistadors discovered in New Spain. They still enrich South American salads. Potatoes originated in Peru, and are almost a national dish there. They form one of the important ingredients in South American salads.

PERUVIAN POTATO SALAD
PAPAS A LA HUANCAINA

2 pounds small new potatoes, boiled in jackets
½ pound Cheddar cheese, grated
4 yolks of hard boiled eggs
3 mashed chilies or 1 teaspoon chili powder
1 teaspoon salt
¼ teaspoon pepper
¼ cup olive oil
1 cup evaporated milk
½ teaspoon lemon juice
½ cup minced onion
Lettuce (garnish)
Olives (garnish)

Cool and peel the boiled potatoes. Place on the serving platter. Mash the cheese with the egg yolks, add the mashed chilies or chili powder, salt, and pepper, and beat well with a wooden spoon. Add the olive oil little by little, as in making mayonnaise. Add the milk and lemon juice. Add the minced onion, and adjust the seasoning to taste. Cover the potatoes with this sauce, and garnish with lettuce and olives. Serve cold.

(6–8 SERVINGS)

COLOMBIAN VEGETABLE SALAD

3 Spanish style sausages, diced
½ cup cooked green beans
½ cup cooked corn
½ cup cooked lima beans
2 tomatoes, peeled and diced
1 small head lettuce
⅓ cup olive oil
⅓ cup vinegar
3 scallions, chopped
1 tablespoon minced parsley
1 clove garlic, crushed
1 teaspoon salt
¼ teaspoon pepper

Mix the sausage with the vegetables and lettuce torn into small pieces. Mix the rest of the ingredients and pour over. Toss, chill, and serve.

(4–6 SERVINGS)

SOUTH AMERICAN AVOCADO SALAD

1 teaspoon salt
½ teaspoon freshly ground pepper
½ teaspoon sugar
2 tablespoons wine vinegar
¼ cup olive oil
1 clove garlic, minced
1 tablespoon minced chives or scallions
1 tablespoon minced parsley
1 tablespoon onion juice
1 head lettuce, shredded
2 avocados, peeled and diced

Mix the salt, pepper, and sugar. Add vinegar and oil and stir well. Add the garlic, chives, parsley, and onion juice, and mix well. Add the lettuce and fold in the avocado. Do not cut the avocado until the dressing is ready or it will darken.

(6 SERVINGS)

VENEZUELAN AVOCADO AND SPINACH SALAD

½ pound spinach
2 tablespoons oil
2 onions, sliced thin
*½ cup Mayonnaise**
1 large avocado
1 teaspoon lemon juice
2 hard boiled eggs
Lettuce

Put the spinach in a bowl and pour boiling water over it. Leave it for a few minutes only and then drain. Heat the oil, and sauté the onions for a few minutes until transparent but not brown. Put the spinach in a bowl with the onions. Add the Mayonnaise, peeled, diced avocado, lemon juice, and chopped egg. Chop all together until smooth, and serve on a bed of lettuce.

(4 SERVINGS)

BRAZILIAN AVOCADO SALAD

1 large clove garlic, minced
2 tablespoons minced onion
2 tablespoons chopped capers
2 tablespoons minced parsley
2 tablespoons minced chives
½ cup olive oil
3 tablespoons vinegar
1 teaspoon dry tarragon or 2 teaspoons fresh
1 teaspoon salt
¼ teaspoon pepper
1 large avocado
Salad greens

Mix all of the ingredients except the avocado and the greens. Wash and dry the salad greens and tear into pieces. You may use any kind of lettuce, endive, water cress, or a combination. Peel the avocado and slice thin. Combine the avocado and the greens and pour the salad dressing over. Toss gently and let stand for an hour.

(4 SERVINGS)

RUSSIAN SALADS

There is no iron curtain in the salad world. Russian salads and Russian dressing appear all over. The only question is, what goes in it? Everybody has a different idea of *"Russki Salat."*

RUSSIAN SALAD
RUSSKI SALAT

2 cups diced cooked beef, veal, or chicken
½ cup cooked diced beets
½ cup diced pickles
½ cup diced cooked potatoes
1 cucumber, peeled and diced
2 hard boiled eggs, cut up
2 tablespoons chopped olives
1 cup sauerkraut
1 cup kidney beans
½ cup French Dressing*
½ teaspoon mustard

Use as many of the ingredients as possible. Do not omit the beets, pickles, or potatoes. Mix all of the vegetables together with the meat and add the French Dressing, which has been mixed with mustard. Toss thoroughly but gently.

(6–8 SERVINGS)

RUSSIAN HAM SALAD

3 cups diced ham
1 cup diced cooked potatoes
½ cup chopped onions
1 cup diced pickle
1 tablespoon capers
1 teaspoon lemon juice
2 tablespoons caviar
½ cup Mayonnaise*

Mix the ham, potatoes, onion, pickle, and capers. Add the lemon juice and caviar to the Mayonnaise. Fold into the meat and vegetable mixture.

(8 SERVINGS)

RUSSIAN VEGETABLE SALAD

4 carrots, cooked and diced
1 cup cooked diced green beans
1 cup cooked peas
2 medium potatoes, boiled in jackets
½ cup Mayonnaise*
2 tablespoons catsup or chili sauce
2 teaspoons lemon juice
2 tablespoons French Dressing*

Mix the carrots, green beans, and peas in a salad bowl. Peel and dice the potatoes and add to the other vegetables. Mix the Mayonnaise with catsup or chili sauce, lemon juice, and French Dressing. Toss gently into the vegetable mixture.

(6 SERVINGS)

SWEET PEPPER SALAD
SLADKY PEREZS

6 green or sweet red peppers, or 3 green and 3 red
1 teaspoon salt
¼ teaspoon pepper
2 teaspoons sugar
2 teaspoons prepared mustard
1–2 tablespoons vinegar
⅓ cup olive oil

Cut the pepper into eighths or quarters and boil in salted water for about 15 minutes until tender. Chill. Mix the salt, pepper, sugar, and mustard. Stir in 1 tablespoon vinegar and the oil. Add more vinegar to taste. Pour over the peppers and let stand for several hours.

(6–8 SERVINGS)

NEAR EASTERN SALADS

All around the Eastern Mediterranean, salad greens flourish under the sun. Here the olive and the oil of the olive reign supreme, while yogurt and mint add a distinctive fillip. A few ingredients in salads from the Arab world are not always available in supermarkets; however, native stores in almost all cities can supply such things as Greek fish roe or powdered or dried mint.

GREEK SALAD

3 tomatoes, cut up
1 head lettuce, shredded
1 bunch radishes, sliced
1 cucumber, diced
¼ pound Greek cheese
16 pitted ripe olives
¼ cup French Dressing*

Mix the tomatoes, lettuce, radishes, and cucumbers. Add the cheese broken into small pieces and the cut up olives. Toss with the dressing.

(4 Servings)

TARAMASALATA

½ *pound Tarama or ½–¾ pound cod fish roe*
4–5 slices white bread
1–1½ cups olive oil
Juice of 1–2 lemons
Thin toast or lettuce

If using salted Tarama, rinse it in cold water, letting it stand about 15 minutes. Drain through cheese cloth or a fine mesh sieve. If you use fresh roe parboil it in heavily salted water and pull off any membrane. Cut crusts off the bread, wet it, and squeeze dry. Add the bread to the roe in a bowl and mix. Stir steadily while adding the oil in a very slow stream. This is made as you would make Mayonnaise and should be fluffy and light when finished. Add lemon juice to taste. Serve with thin toast or on lettuce leaves.

(8 SERVINGS—12 HORS D'OEUVRE SERVINGS)

TURKISH CUCUMBER SALAD

1 large cucumber, grated
1 cup yogurt
2 tablespoons blanched white raisins
2 tablespoons chopped walnuts
1 small onion, minced
½ teaspoon salt
¼ teaspoon pepper
1 teaspoon chopped mint

Combine all of the ingredients. Chill.

(4 SERVINGS)

ARMENIAN EGGPLANT SALAD

1 eggplant
1 medium onion, chopped
2 tablespoons minced parsley
1 teaspoon salt
½ teaspoon pepper
¼ cup oil
⅓ cup vinegar
Lettuce
Tomatoes (garnish)
Ripe olives (garnish)

Bake, broil, or boil the eggplant until soft. Cool, peel, and chop. Mix the eggplant with onion and parsley. Add salt and pepper, and mixture of the oil and vinegar. Toss. Serve on lettuce and garnish with tomato wedges and pitted ripe olives.

(6 SERVINGS)

ARMENIAN COLE SLAW

1 head cabbage, chopped fine
2 large cooked beets, chopped
1 large green pepper, chopped
1 cup Mayonnaise*
2 tablespoons vinegar
2 tablespoons sugar

Mix the cabbage, beets, and green pepper. Thin the Mayonnaise with vinegar and add the sugar. Mix into the salad, tossing thoroughly.

(6–8 SERVINGS)

MOROCCAN CUCUMBER SALAD

2 large cucumbers
3 tablespoons vinegar
1 clove garlic, crushed
1 tablespoon soy sauce
1 teaspoon sesame oil

Do not peel the cucumbers. Score them lengthwise with the prongs of a fork before slicing thin if you wish. Put the cucumbers in a bowl with vinegar, garlic, and soy sauce, and let stand several hours in the refrigerator. Stir in the sesame oil just before serving.

(4 SERVINGS)

CRACKED WHEAT AND PARSLEY SALAD
TABBOULEH

1 cup burghot (wheat pilaf)
1 bunch green onions, chopped fine
1 teaspoon salt
½ teaspoon pepper
½ cup chopped fresh mint or 2 tablespoons dried
1½ cups chopped parsley
½ cup olive oil
½ cup lemon juice
2–3 large tomatoes, peeled and chopped
Lettuce

Pour 1 cup boiling water over the burghot and let stand until water is absorbed, about half an hour. Squeeze dry between hands. Mix with onions, salt, and pepper, crushing the onions into the burghot. Stir in parsley and mint. Add the oil and lemon juice and taste for seasoning. Stir in half of the tomatoes and put the rest on the platter or put all on the platter. Serve the salad

on lettuce and if you wish to "go native," provide vine or cabbage leaves to use as scoops to eat with.

(6 SERVINGS)

LEBANESE POTATO SALAD

1 pound potatoes, boiled in jackets
¼ cup oil
¼ cup lemon juice or vinegar
1 clove garlic, crushed
1 teaspoon salt
¼ teaspoon pepper
2 tablespoons chopped scallions
2 tablespoons chopped parsley

Peel and slice the boiled potatoes thin. Add a mixture of oil, lemon juice or vinegar, garlic, salt, and pepper while the potatoes are still warm. Add scallions and 1 tablespoon parsley and toss gently. Garnish top with remaining parsley.

(4 SERVINGS)

PERSIAN SPINACH SALAD
BORANI ESFANAJ

1 pound spinach
1 onion, minced
1 tablespoon oil
2 cups yogurt
1 teaspoon salt
¼ teaspoon pepper
2 cloves garlic, crushed
1 teaspoon fresh mint or ½ teaspoon powdered
2 tablespoons chopped walnuts

Cut up the spinach and combine with onion. Cook only in the water which clings to the spinach after washing. Cook 3 minutes. Drain. Add oil and cook 2 more minutes. Remove from heat, cool. Add the yogurt, salt, pepper, and garlic. Top with mint and nuts.

(4 SERVINGS)

PERSIAN CUCUMBER SALAD

> 2 cucumbers, grated
> 2 cups yogurt
> 2 tablespoons white raisins, plumped
> 2 tablespoons chopped walnuts
> 1 onion, minced
> ½ teaspoon salt
> ¼ teaspoon pepper
> ¼ teaspoon powdered mint
> ¼ teaspoon dried marjoram or basil

Mix the drained cucumbers with yogurt and add the remaining ingredients. Chill. Raisins are plumped by bringing just to a boil, or leaving in water for an hour.

(6 SERVINGS)

ORIENTAL SALADS

As I learned the hard way in Hong Kong, the inscrutable Oriental adds his mystery touch of curry, ginger, sesame, or soy to his characteristic bean sprouts, peppers, and greens. From Singapore to Rangoon, from Yokohama to Bombay, the salads are redolent of the East, with their unmistakable flavor, intriguing and delightful.

SINGAPORE CHICKEN SALAD

1 4 pound frying chicken
⅓ cup sherry or saki
⅓ cup soy sauce
1½ teaspoons minced fresh ginger or ½ teaspoon
    powdered
3 tablespoons oil
1 cup bean sprouts
1 cup diced celery
1 tablespoon sesame seeds
2 cups shredded lettuce
½ cup sliced almonds

Cut the chicken off of the bones into bite-size pieces. Marinate in a mixture of sherry or saki, soy sauce, and ginger for several hours. Reserve marinade. Brown the chicken in the oil. Add ⅓ cup of water and the remaining marinade. Cover and simmer for about 15 minutes until the chicken is tender. Cool. Mix the remaining ingredients. Pour over the chicken and mix thoroughly. Adjust the seasoning to taste.

(6 SERVINGS)

INDIAN CUCUMBER SALAD

2 *cucumbers*
2 *tablespoons salt*
1 *tablespoon peanut oil*
1 *tablespoon sesame oil*
1 *tablespoon vinegar*
1 *teaspoon sugar*
1 *teaspoon curry*
1 *tablespoon soy sauce*
1 *clove garlic, crushed*

Shred the peeled cucumbers, and sprinkle with salt. Let stand for several hours. Put in a strainer and let cold water run over them. Drain. Put into a bowl with all of the ingredients and let stand at least 2 hours in refrigerator.

(4 SERVINGS)

BANGKOK SHRIMP SALAD

2 pounds shrimp
1 bay leaf
1 tablespoon salt
½ tablespoon peppercorns
¼ cup minced shallots
2 cloves garlic, crushed or minced
3 tablespoons olive oil
½ cup minced green peppers
1 apple, minced or grated
3 tablespoons chopped peanuts
2 tablespoons soy sauce
1 cup coconut milk or ¾ cup milk and ¼ cup
    moist coconut
Lettuce

Simmer the shrimp in water with the bay leaf, salt, and peppercorns for 5 minutes. Drain, cool, peel, and devein, and cut the shrimp once through lengthwise. If they are large, cut once or twice across. Sauté the shallots and garlic in olive oil until they are transparent but not brown. Cool and mix with the remaining ingredients. Pour this over the shrimp and serve on shredded lettuce.

(6 SERVINGS)

RANGOON SHRIMP SALAD

2 pounds shrimp
1 tablespoon salt
1 tablespoon coarsely ground pepper
1 cup chopped scallions
½ teaspoon dried chili peppers
4 tablespoons lime or lemon juice
1 tablespoon soy sauce

Bring the shrimp to a boil in water with the salt and pepper. Cook for 3 minutes after the water comes to a boil. Cool, peel, and devein the shrimp, and cut into large dice. Mix with the scallions and chili peppers, and sprinkle with the mixture of lime or lemon juice and the soy sauce.

(6 SERVINGS)

CAMBODIAN AVOCADO LITCHI SALAD

6 avocados
¼ cup lemon juice
1 (1 pound 4 ounce) can litchi nuts
¼ cup oil
2 tablespoons soy sauce
2 teaspoons grated fresh ginger
Lettuce (optional)

Cut the avocados in half—do not peel. Sprinkle cut surfaces with 2 tablespoons of lemon juice. Drain the nuts and save the liquid. Put the nuts in a bowl with remaining lemon juice, oil, soy, and ginger. Add 3 tablespoons of liquid to the nuts. Stir and fill the avocados with this mixture. Serve on shredded lettuce, if you wish. When you are in Cambodia, make the salad with fresh ripe litchis!

(12 SERVINGS)

JAPANESE TURNIPS AND CARROTS

4 cups thinly sliced turnips
1 cup thinly sliced carrots
2 tablespoons salt
½ cup vinegar
2 tablespoons sugar
¼ teaspoon Ajinomoto or MSG
½ teaspoon grated fresh ginger (optional)

Sprinkle the turnips and carrots with salt and let stand for an hour. Rinse and press out moisture. Mix the vinegar, sugar, Ajinomoto or MSG, and the ginger, if you wish, and pour over the salad. Chill and serve.

(6 SERVINGS)

JAPANESE MARINATED MUSHROOMS

1 pound small mushrooms
2 tablespoons soy sauce
¼ cup saki or sherry
3 tablespoons vinegar
2 tablespoons minced onion
1 tablespoon sugar
1 tablespoon salt

Remove the stems from the mushrooms, and unless the caps are pure white, peel them. Mix the soy with the wine, vinegar, onion, sugar, and salt, and bring to a boil. Pour hot over the mushrooms. Refrigerate for a day or two turning the mushrooms once or twice.

(8 SERVINGS—12–15 CANAPÉ SERVINGS)

CHINESE ASPARAGUS SALAD

2 pounds asparagus
2 tablespoons soy sauce
1 tablespoon sesame or olive oil
½ teaspoon sugar
Salad greens (optional)

Cut the green part of the asparagus in 1 inch pieces diagonally. Cook in boiling salted water for 3 minutes only. Drain and chill. Mix the soy sauce, oil, and sugar. Marinate the asparagus in this for at least 1 hour in refrigerator. Serve on greens if you wish.

(4 SERVINGS)

CHINESE FISH SALAD

3–4 pounds pike, tuna, or other very fresh fish
2 tablespoons lemon juice
4 carrots, shredded
1 large or 2 small dill pickles, minced
2 tablespoons peanuts, pounded fine
1 teaspoon grated fresh ginger or ½ teaspoon powdered
1 teaspoon salt
1 tablespoon vinegar
¼ cup olive oil or salad oil
1 tablespoon toasted sesame seeds (optional)

Remove any skin and bones from fish and cut in very thin slices. Sprinkle with lemon juice. Add the carrots, pickles, and nuts. Mix in ginger, salt, vinegar, oil, and sesame seeds, if you wish, and pour over the fish. Let stand in refrigerator several hours.

(8 SERVINGS)

CHINESE CUCUMBER SALAD
LIANG PAN HUANG KUA

2 cucumbers
3 tablespoons vinegar
¼ cup light soy sauce
1 tablespoon sugar
1 teaspoon MSG
3 tablespoons sesame seed oil

Slice the unpeeled cucumbers paper thin. Add the other ingredients except the oil. Let marinate for several hours, then add the oil and stir. Chill.

(4 SERVINGS)

CHINESE TUNA SALAD

2 (7 ounce) cans tuna
1 cup chopped scallions
1 cup chopped celery
¼ cup diced green pepper
2 cups bean sprouts
¾ cup Mayonnaise*
2 tablespoons soy sauce
Lettuce

Break up the tuna, and toss gently with the scallions, celery, green pepper, and bean sprouts. If using canned sprouts, drain them. Mix the Mayonnaise and soy sauce, and fold into the salad. Serve on lettuce.

(6 SERVINGS)

CHINESE CHICKEN SALAD

1½ cups coarsely cut celery
3 cups cut up cooked chicken
3 tablespoons olive oil
3 tablespoons soy sauce
¼ teaspoon pepper
Pinch sugar
Lettuce (optional)

Put celery in warm water. Bring to a boil and cook for 3 minutes. Drain and cool. Mix with the chicken. Pour over a mixture of the oil, soy sauce, pepper, and sugar. Serve on lettuce, if you wish.

(6 SERVINGS)

Chapter Four

WHAT THE WELL-DRESSED SALAD WILL WEAR

Variety is the spice of salad making, and is attained most easily by varying the dressing. There are so many kinds and varieties of dressing, and each has its own place in the range of salads.

First off, you ask yourself: What do I want to highlight, the salad or the dressing? If you wish to snap up the taste of simple greens, you may decide to use a high-flavored dressing, like Roquefort. Chicken salad, however, must taste of chicken, so you will probably thin your mayonnaise with strong chicken broth. To potatoes, which are mild, you will add some member of the onion family to give character to the blend.

Dressing a salad, like dressing a pretty girl, is not an exact science; it is an art. Your own imagination is the extra ingredient that makes menu magic.

My imagination and my long experience have gone into the recipes which follow; but your fancy must add to, subtract from, or vary, the listed ingredients. These recipes are here to suggest; you will improvise upon them.

When I say "Season to taste" I always mean "Taste

to season." Don't overpower the blend by tossing in the whole quantity of anything at once. You may like it better with less.

How big is "a pinch?" As big as you like it. It doesn't depend on the size of your fingers; it depends on your palate. As you try these recipes, start with a scanty pinch, and add if you please. Once the seasoning is in, you can't take it out; but you can add more, a bit at a time, *ad infinitum* (but please, never *ad nauseam!*).

It is so satisfying to blend your own dressings with your own individual imagination, that under normal circumstances it is a shame to buy commercial mixtures. Good ingredients which you mix yourself exactly to your own taste give you the best of dressings, and cost less than ready-mixed preparations at the market.

If you are in a hurry, and must use a "boughten" dressing, make haste slowly. Commercial dressings, on supermarket shelves as on restaurant tables, are more over-salted, over-peppered, over-sugared, over-spiced, over-garlicked with stale garlic, than any other product. Choose a dressing that is not flavored to death, and add your own personal taste touch to it. A pinch of curry (*not* a spoonful) will add an elusive tang to any oil and vinegar dressing. A little more curry, or some dill, added to Best Foods (Hellmann's) Mayonnaise, suits the shrimp salad, as *fines herbes* make a green mayonnaise to complement the salmon.

The best mayonnaise is made in your kitchen. It takes so little time, it's easy to make and tastes so good. All you need in addition to the egg yolks, oil, and either lemon juice or vinegar (at room temperature, please) is a fork or whip, a bowl, and a little patience at the beginning. The secret of handmade mayonnaise is the very slow, almost drop by drop, addition of oil to the egg yolks while stirring. After this thickens you can

add the oil in a thin stream, watching to see that it is absorbed into the mixture. A cup of mayonnaise should not take more than ten minutes to make.

Blender mayonnaise is faster—about three minutes total time. Put the whole egg with vinegar or lemon juice into the blender, turn it on at low speed, and pour in the oil in a steady stream.

You can add flavors to the mayonnaise after it is done: minced parsley or chives, curry, herbs, mustard, pepper, paprika, caraway seeds, capers, or whatever.

Mixing a French salad dressing is one of the easiest of the civilized arts. If you use a glass jar with a cover, it is easiest of all. Condiments go in first, salt and pepper and whatever else is to be used. Add a spoonful of water to dissolve the salt. Next add the vinegar, then the oil. Cover the jar and give it a good shake. Presto! Your salad dressing is mixed.

You don't even need to obey the old adage by calling in a miser to add the vinegar, a spendthrift to pour the oil, and a madman to shake up the whole. You can do it all yourself.

The glass jar technique has many advantages over stirring up the ingredients in a bowl. The dressing can be made ahead, and shaken again to attain the proper consistency at the last moment. You can make a superfluity, and what is left for tomorrow can be stored away in the same jar.

A trick to thicken the oil and mellow the vinegar is to add an ice cube to the mixture just before you shake it. Shake it with a flourish, as if you were shaking a cocktail.

The fine art of mixing a salad dressing reaches its apogee when you do it in public. Then it becomes a production. The guests around the table are your audience.

To set the stage, you assemble your properties. You

must have cruets of oil and vinegar to decant with a flourish. If you are using a fancy vinegar, never mind the cruet. Keep it in the original bottle for the guests to admire. At hand you will also have the pepper-grinder, and a saltcellar for pinches or a shaker for sprinkles, together with a little sugar. With these properties at your elbow and no others, you can compound a delicious French dressing.

Now, if you want to gild the lily, you will have to set out a selection of other ingredients, such as mustard, curry, paprika, or Worcestershire sauce, flanked by herbs, dried or fresh, minced scallions or chives, or garlic in a press. The crowning touch is ready in a topping like croutons, minced egg, crumbled bacon, anchovies, or grated cheese.

Don't go overboard in assembling your properties. You are not whipping up short orders. Lay out only the few interesting ingredients you have chosen to blend into your salad dressing.

The properties are assembled. The curtain rises. The mixing magic begins. With a few mystic passes you mix the dressing, with a fork in a handy saucer, or directly over the salad bowl full of greens.

Now comes the grand gesture, the climax of the drama, as you toss and tumble the greens till every mouthful is lightly coated with the good taste of your original dressing creation.

If you want the flourish of tossing at the table, without the delay of measuring and mixing the ingredients for the dressing, you can make your mixture in the kitchen, compounding it in the bottom of the salad bowl. Then cross the salad fork and spoon over it, gently pile the greens above, and chill till the moment arrives for mixing all together at the table. This ensures keeping the greens crisp and dry till tossing time comes.

I remember how Oscar of the Waldorf used to mix

the salad for Father and me, lunching at the table in his private dining room in the hotel. He would compound enough dressing for the three of us, right into the big salad spoon, holding it over the bowl of greens.

He would start with a sprinkle of salt and pepper, adding a little water to dissolve it. Next, in went the vinegar sparingly, the oil generously, overflowing into the salad. Then he would toss. He was always careful not to get his greens too wet with dressing. It was a delight to watch the expansive old gentleman, his fine features gleaming with the joy of an artist, as he poured and mixed, and to anticipate the pleasure of tasting his delicate, subtle concoction.

In a dressing of such elegant simplicity, of course Oscar used only the most precious ingredients: *olive* oil and *wine* vinegar. Olive oil is the most ancient as well as the best of all oils. Perhaps it was known first in Bible lands. The Homeric Greek warriors rubbed themselves down with it. It was the Greeks who introduced it into Italy, where it has lived happily ever after.

Olive oil comes from green olives pressed in a vat. The lightest of the oil, rising to the top, is the best grade, romantically called "virgin." The heavier oil, lying in lower layers, is graded as less desirable. The lightest of all olive oil is produced by the French. Olive oil from Italy, slightly heavier, is imported in abundance.

Don't suppose that olive oil forms the only basis of a good salad dressing. Other very acceptable oils are made from corn, peanuts, cotton-seed, soybeans, and safflower, which produce bland oils of very little flavor. These salad oils are much less expensive than olive oil, and it is good economy to mix olive and salad oil in a dressing if the olive taste is wanted, or to use all salad oil in a high-flavored dressing.

With oil, from ancient times, comes vinegar.

Medieval alchemists conjured with vinegar. Four hundred years ago Sir Thomas Elyot opined in *The Castel of Helth* that "olyves doth corroborate the stomake, being eaten with vinegar"; and not long afterward, King James I of England called for "winiger to his sallet."

Undoubtedly, what they brought to the King's table was the regal distillation, wine vinegar. In most of Europe, vinegar from white or red wine is still the rule. However, in America today cider vinegar, or a white vinegar, is cheaper and very satisfactory for dressing a salad.

More than one vinegar is needed on every kitchen shelf. You will probably stock both wine and cider vinegar. In addition, you may choose an herb vinegar, flavored with some herb like tarragon or basil, or an exotic vinegar such as pear. Varying the vinegar is one good way to change the taste of your salads.

Another easy means to salad variety is found on your shelf of herbs and spices.

HERBS FOR SALADS

Fresh herbs are much the best. When using dried you need about a third as much as the fresh ones.

*BASIL Aromatic and tangy, basil has a special affinity for tomatoes; also use with seafood, cucumbers, beans, potatoes, and greens.

BAY LEAF (*Laurel*) Strong almost bitter taste, used frequently in French cookery; good in marinades and for beets and artichokes.

BORAGE Fresh young leaves are a splendid addition to greens.

BURNET A cucumber-flavored herb, good with vegetables.

CAPERS The salty taste whets the appetite, so use with first-course salads and on poultry, meat, fish, and tomatoes.

DILL Use the feathery leaves and minced tender tips of stems in seafood and with cucumbers, potato salad, and cole slaw.

FENNEL Bulb and some of the feathery foliage will add a licorice flavor. Slice the bulb into mixed and vegetable salads.

LOVAGE This parsley-family herb has a strong celery flavor; use sparingly.

*MARJORAM (*Sweet Marjoram*) A delightful herb which blends well with most salads—poultry, eggs, cole slaw, tomatoes, spinach, and other vegetables.

MINT A lively taste; use sparingly with fruits, cole slaw, carrots, beans, and beets.

NASTURTIUM Flowers as well as leaves add beauty and a spice taste to green and mixed salads.

*ONION FAMILY (*Chives, garlic, onions, leeks, scallions, and shallots*) The most used of all—use in one form or another, always in potato salad and in most salads and salad dressings. Onions and garlic are available as pungent powder, as salt, and minced. Chives are available minced, dried, or frozen.

OREGANO (*Wild Marjoram*) Used in most Italian and Spanish recipes. A potent herb, use carefully with tomatoes, potato salad, spinach, greens, and seafood.

*PARSLEY A universally popular herb. There are two varieties, curly and flat leaf. Use freely in all salads except fruit and desserts.

ROSEMARY A fragrant herb to be used cautiously with greens and vegetables, especially spinach and potatoes. Good in meat salads.

SAVORY (*Summer Savory and Winter Savory*) Sometimes called "the bean herb." Use summer savory in any green and vegetable salads. Winter savory is particularly good with beans and peas.

SORREL This has a slightly sour taste; use young leaves in mixed greens.

*TARRAGON An unusual fascinating flavor, used often in vinegars, good with almost all salads.

THYME Unexpectedly good if used sparingly in vegetable and meat salads.

WOODRUFF Famous as a flavor in May Wine, try it on fruits.

*FINES HERBES Are a combination of parsley, tarragon, chervil, and chives. Don't mix your own; buy a blend from a reputable herb grower.

*BLENDED SALAD HERBS Are a most useful jar on your shelf. A good herb farm is better able to combine these than you are!

* Denotes the most important herbs for salads.

SPICES AND SEEDS FOR SALADS

Keep spices in tightly sealed jars, grind or grate them yourself when possible. Buy small quantities; they lose their flavor.

ALLSPICE The pungent berry of a tree used to flavor vinegar and in cole slaw and spicy fruits.

CARAWAY SEEDS Aromatic seeds for cabbage and potato salads.

CARDAMOM SEEDS Ground or whole, these are delicious in fruit salads.

CAYENNE (*Cayenne pepper*) Powder made from peppers—very useful in salad dressings.

CELERY SEEDS Use this whenever you want a celery flavor; also available as celery salt.

CHILI POWDER Ground from chili peppers. This distinctive flavor adds to vegetable, egg, and seafood salads.

CLOVE This "spice nail" is available whole or ground; it is a most pungent spice—try a little on fruit for a change.

CURRY POWDER A blend of a number of spices which takes its gold color from tumeric. It adds an exotic taste to seafood, poultry, and potato salads. A pinch or two in French dressing or mayonnaise enhances their flavor.

HORSERADISH The young tender leaves add zest to a green salad. Prepared horseradish root is good in dressing for seafood.

*MUSTARD Dry or prepared (wet) must be kept on your shelf; it may be used in almost any salad dressing. An invaluable spice.

NUTMEG This large oval seed is much more pungent when freshly grated than when purchased in powdered form. Try a very little of this warm rather sweet spice on greens, cabbage, or fruit salads.

*PAPRIKA This bright red powder (preferably from Hungary) adds color as well as a pungent flavor. Use in dressings and as a garnish on vegetables and other salads.

*PEPPER Black pepper is used on almost any salad or salad dressing. White pepper, which is the same seed, with the outside coating removed, is slightly milder and preferable for fruit salad and some mayonnaises when you don't want to see black specks. Both peppers are available as peppercorns to be ground in pepper grinders in the kitchen or at table; pepper is also available in fine or coarse grinds.

POPPY SEEDS These tiny seeds add texture as well as taste to cole slaw and fruit salads.

* Denotes the spices most useful in salads.

SALADS

A list of frequently made salads and suggestions for appropriate herbs and spices. Remember minced parsley and minced scallions or chives help most salads except fruit and dessert. Mustard may be used in most salad dressings along with pepper and often paprika.

BEETS Thyme, dill, chervil, bay

COLE SLAW Thyme, marjoram, basil, mint, caraway seeds, poppy seeds, allspice, nutmeg

CUCUMBER Dill, chervil, basil, borage, tarragon, cayenne

EGG Marjoram, dill, *fines herbes,* curry, chili, celery seeds

FISH AND SHELLFISH Dill, basil, oregano, thyme, capers, dry tarragon, curry, chili, celery seeds

FRUIT Mint, woodruff, allspice, clove, nutmeg, poppy seeds, cardamom seeds, cayenne, paprika

GREEN Tarragon, basil, chervil, marjoram, thyme, fennel, blended salad herbs

MEAT Rosemary, thyme, tarragon, curry, chervil, dill, basil, horseradish

POTATO Savory, basil, dill, chervil, rosemary, capers, oregano, caraway seeds, celery seeds, curry, onions in some form

POULTRY Marjoram, tarragon, rosemary, thyme, fennel, capers, curry, poppy seeds

TOMATOES Basil, thyme, oregano, dill, marjoram, tarragon, savory, chervil, capers

VEGETABLES Thyme, marjoram, basil, tarragon, dill, savory, oregano, chervil, fennel, rosemary, lovage, burnet, celery seeds

Unless you are an expert, I would advise using herb blends put up by reputable farms, which really understand which herbs are allies, not enemies, complementing one another instead of warring. For example, a knowing *fines herbes* mixture presents the correct proportions of the right herbs. An Italian blend knows how to give that real Roman flavor. "Mixed salad herbs" taste different under different labels, but each goes well in a salad.

Spices have been and still are worth ten times their weight in gold to the cook. The Queen of Sheba loaded her camels with princely gifts of spices when she paid King Solomon a call. In search of spices, Marco Polo caravaned to China, and Christopher Columbus stumbled across America.

FRENCH DRESSING AND VARIATIONS

On many a fancy Frenchified menu—*not* in France—I have read (trying to keep a straight face) such redundancies as:

> *Fromage de Brie cheese*
> *Coq au vin with wine sauce*
> *Roast beef with au jus*

A Frenchman would be equally mystified by encountering

> *Green salad with French dressing*

What else, he would wonder, would any gourmet in his senses put on a green salad? People from France would blush at the red dressings currently passing for French. If you want a real French French dressing, you had better make it yourself.

BASIC FRENCH DRESSING

⅓ *cup wine or cider vinegar*
¾ *teaspoon salt*
¼ *teaspoon freshly ground pepper*
1 *cup olive oil*

Mix the vinegar, salt, and pepper, and stir well. Add the oil slowly while beating.

(YIELDS 1⅓ CUPS)

FRENCH DRESSING II

¼ *cup wine vinegar*
1 teaspoon salt
⅛ *teaspoon pepper*
½ *teaspoon sugar*
¼ *teaspoon paprika*
½ *teaspoon dry mustard*
1 cup olive oil

Mix the vinegar with seasonings and add the oil slowly while beating; this may be made with salad oil in place of olive oil.

VARIATIONS OF FRENCH DRESSING I OR II

To French Dressing*, add:
   Catsup French—add 1 tablespoon catsup
   Chili Sauce French—add 2 tablespoons chili sauce
   Chutney French—add 2 tablespoons chutney, cut up
   Curry French—add 2 teaspoons curry
   Caper French—add 1 tablespoon capers
   Chive French—add 2 teaspoons minced chives
   Parsley French—add 1–2 tablespoons minced parsley
   Herb French—add 1–2 tablespoons minced fresh tarragon, chervil, basil, and/or chives or ¼–1 teaspoon dried

FRENCH DRESSING III

½–1 teaspoon mustard
2 teaspoons salt
½ teaspoon pepper
½ teaspoon paprika
½ teaspoon sugar
½ teaspoon grated onion or 1 clove garlic (optional)
⅓ cup wine vinegar
1 tablespoon lemon juice (optional)
1 cup oil

Mix the dry ingredients and onion or garlic together. Add the vinegar, lemon juice, and then the oil. Shake well in a jar with an ice cube just before serving. Remove garlic. You may use a combination of olive and other salad oils if you wish.

LEMON FRENCH DRESSING

3 tablespoons lemon juice
½ teaspoon salt
⅛ teaspoon pepper
¼ teaspoon sugar
¼ teaspoon dry mustard (optional)
½ cup olive oil or salad oil

Mix the lemon juice with salt, pepper, sugar, and mustard, if you wish. Then pour the oil in slowly, a teaspoon at a time.

FRUIT FRENCH DRESSING

½ teaspoon salt
2–3 teaspoons sugar
¼ teaspoon dry mustard
¼ teaspoon curry powder
2 tablespoons lemon juice
2 tablespoons grapefruit or orange juice
⅔ cup oil

Mix the dry ingredients. Add fruit juice and mix well.
Pour in the oil slowly while stirring. Good with citrus
and other fruits.

GARLIC FRENCH DRESSING

1 clove garlic, crushed
1 teaspoon salt
½ teaspoon freshly ground pepper
1 cup olive or salad oil
⅓ cup vinegar

Mix the ingredients in a jar and shake thoroughly
before using.

EGG AND OLIVE FRENCH DRESSING

1 cup French Dressing*
2 hard boiled eggs, chopped
1 tablespoon pitted or pimento stuffed olives,
    chopped

Blend all of the ingredients together. Excellent for
mixed greens.

HERB WINE FRENCH DRESSING

½ teaspoon salt
⅛ teaspoon white pepper
1 teaspoon sugar
¼ teaspoon dry mustard
½ cup white wine
1 teaspoon grated onion or 1 tablespoon minced
   shallots
¼ cup white wine vinegar
½ cup oil

Mix the dry ingredients. Stir in the wine, then add the grated onion, vinegar, and oil.

INDIA FRENCH DRESSING

2 tablespoons chutney, chopped
½ teaspoon curry powder
1 cup French Dressing*

Add chutney and curry to the French Dressing, and mix. Good on fruit or meat salads.

MUSTARD FRENCH DRESSING

½–1 cup French Dressing*
2 teaspoons prepared mustard (Dijon)
1 teaspoon grated onion
¼ teaspoon freshly ground pepper

Mix all of the ingredients thoroughly.

SHERRY FRENCH DRESSING

1 teaspoon sugar
½ teaspoon salt
1 egg
¼ cup vinegar
1½ cups oil (½ olive)
½ cup sherry

Mix sugar, salt, and egg. Add the vinegar and then the oil slowly while beating. Add the sherry in a slow stream while stirring. Use part or all of a light French olive oil. Especially for a dessert salad.

CREAMY PINK FRENCH DRESSING

1 cup French Dressing*
¼ cup catsup
1 egg white
1 tablespoon lemon juice

Put all of the ingredients together and beat with a rotary beater until fluffy. Try this for a change on mixed green salads.

WATER CRESS FRENCH DRESSING
LORENZO

1 cup French Dressing*
5 tablespoons water cress, chopped
¼ cup chili sauce
2 teaspoons Worcestershire sauce

Blend together. Use on mixed salads or lettuces.

VINAIGRETTE

1 cup French Dressing*
2 tablespoons minced parsley
2 tablespoons minced pickle
2 tablespoons minced green pepper
2 tablespoons minced chives
1 tablespoon chopped capers (optional)

Combine all of the ingredients and shake to mix thoroughly. Recommended for asparagus.

VINAIGRETTE II

¾ cup olive or salad oil or combination
¼ cup vinegar
1 teaspoon salt
¼ teaspoon pepper
1 teaspoon sugar
⅛ teaspoon paprika
1 teaspoon minced or grated onion
1 tablespoon minced parsley
3 tablespoons chopped dill pickle
1 hard boiled egg, grated

Mix the oil and vinegar with salt, pepper, sugar, and paprika. Beat, and then add the onion, parsley, and pickles while stirring. Stir in the grated egg.

EGG VINAIGRETTE

2 hard boiled eggs
1 egg yolk
½ cup oil
1 teaspoon minced parsley
1 teaspoon minced oregano
1 teaspoon minced chives
1 teaspoon minced thyme
2 tablespoons lemon juice or vinegar
½ teaspoon salt
¼ teaspoon pepper

Mix mashed hard boiled egg yolks with the raw egg. Add oil a teaspoon at a time while beating. Add the rest of the ingredients and mix thoroughly. Stir in the egg white, chopped fine. Use this with an artichoke.

MAYONNAISE AND VARIATIONS

Who's afraid of making mayonnaise? Nothing could be simpler than whipping up a bowlful.

The best mayonnaise is still made in your kitchen, with the yolk of an egg, some oil, a whisk or a fork, and some patience till the oil begins to take hold.

Have your ingredients at room temperature. Put the yolk in a bowl, add salt, a pinch or two of dry mustard if you wish, and then the oil, a very few drops at a time, stirring constantly. As the mixture thickens, you may add more oil in a thin, steady stream, continuing to stir. When the mayonnaise gets quite thick, thin it with a little lemon juice or vinegar, and then continue the slow addition of oil till you have made the quantity you desire.

Suppose it separates? Stop immediately. Start another yolk in another bowl, and be *sure* to add the oil very slowly, drop by drop, till it amalgamates. You may then use the separated mixture as you would oil. Nothing is lost or wasted.

Making mayonnaise in a blender is even quicker and easier, though perhaps a little less refined, as you use the whole egg.

Once you have made and served your own mayonnaise, you will want to make plenty, and serve it often, because it's so good, and so easy to make, and because it keeps so well. But if you want to keep it wholesome, be sure to keep it tightly covered in the refrigerator.

In choosing the oil for mayonnaise, it will depend on what you are going to use the mayonnaise for. If you use all olive oil, it makes a very pungent mayonnaise. Half olive oil and half of any blending oil, such as peanut or vegetable oil, makes a very useful dressing. You may use mostly a bland oil and flavor it with a small amount of olive oil if you wish.

BASIC MAYONNAISE

1 egg yolk
½ teaspoon salt
¼–½ teaspoon dry mustard (optional)
1 cup oil
1–2 tablespoons vinegar or lemon juice

Mix the egg yolk, salt, and mustard if you wish together in the bottom of a bowl. Add the oil drop by drop while stirring. You may stir with a fork or rotary beater. When the mayonnaise begins to thicken, you may add the oil in a thin slow stream stirring constantly. If the mayonnaise gets too thick, add a little of the vinegar or lemon juice, and then continue the slow addition of oil.

(YIELDS 1½ CUPS)

BASIC BLENDER MAYONNAISE

1 egg
1 tablespoon wine vinegar or lemon juice
½ teaspoon salt
½ teaspoon dry mustard
¾ cup oil

Put the egg, vinegar or lemon juice, salt, and mustard in a blender. Add 2 tablespoons oil very slowly while the blender is at its lowest speed. Pour in the rest of the oil in a stream. The entire process of making the mayonnaise should not take more than a minute or two.

(YIELDS 1¼ CUPS)

MAYONNAISE VARIATIONS

To 1¼ to 1½ cups of Mayonnaise*, add any one of the following:

> ¾ cup chili sauce
> ⅛ teaspoon curry and ⅛ teaspoon paprika
> 1 tablespoon French Dressing* and ½ teaspoon dry tarragon
> 1 teaspoon curry and ½ teaspoon garlic salt
> 2 teaspoons curry and 3–4 drops lemon juice
> 2 teaspoons dry mustard and 1 teaspoon wine vinegar
> 1 teaspoon lemon juice and 2 tablespoons broth

CAPER MAYONNAISE

> 1 cup Mayonnaise*
> 2 tablespoons capers
> 1 teaspoon grated onion
> ½ teaspoon poultry seasoning

Mix all the ingredients together. The poultry seasoning may be omitted unless you are using the mayonnaise for poultry or cold veal salad.

CARAWAY MAYONNAISE

2 tablespoons vinegar
1 tablespoon grated onion
2 teaspoons caraway seeds
1 teaspoon sugar
½ teaspoon salt
⅛ teaspoon pepper
½ cup Mayonnaise*

Mix all of the ingredients together with the Mayonnaise.

CAVIAR MAYONNAISE

½ cup caviar
1 tablespoon onion or chives, chopped fine
1 tablespoon pimento, chopped
2 hard boiled eggs, chopped fine
1 teaspoon lemon juice
1 cup Mayonnaise*

Combine all of the ingredients with the Mayonnaise. For a special occasion use on soft greens or on any molded salad.

RED CAVIAR MAYONNAISE

¼ cup red caviar
Juice ¼ lemon
1 tablespoon prepared horseradish
1 cup Mayonnaise*

Mix all of the ingredients except the Mayonnaise, and then stir that in very gently. Wonderful for egg salad.

CHIVE MAYONNAISE

1 clove garlic
1 cup Mayonnaise*
3 tablespoons minced chives
1 tablespoon minced parsley
1 tablespoon minced pimento (optional)
¼ teaspoon freshly ground pepper

Rub a bowl thoroughly with the split clove of garlic. Mix the rest of the ingredients in the bowl. Good on tomato aspic.

BLENDER GREEN MAYONNAISE

5 leaves spinach
1 tablespoon fresh tarragon or 1 teaspoon dry
1 tablespoon chopped chives or green onion
1 teaspoon chopped dill
1 teaspoon minced fresh marjoram or parsley
1 egg
½ teaspoon salt
½ teaspoon sugar
1 cup olive or salad oil or half and half
2 tablespoons tarragon or wine vinegar

Mix all of the ingredients except the oil and vinegar in a blender. Keep the blender at low speed and add half of the oil very slowly, then the vinegar, and then the remaining oil. Exceptionally good for salmon or tuna salads.

GREEN GODDESS MAYONNAISE

2 tablespoons finely chopped anchovies or 1 table-
    spoon anchovy paste
3 tablespoons finely chopped chives or scallions
⅓ cup finely chopped parsley
½ cup heavy cream
1 tablespoon lemon juice
1 tablespoon tarragon vinegar
Dash of salt
Dash of freshly ground black pepper
1 cup Mayonnaise*

Mix all of the ingredients into the Mayonnaise, and let
stand in the refrigerator for several hours to blend
flavors. Use on crab or lobster salad, or any shellfish.

GREEN GODDESS MAYONNAISE
WITH SOUR CREAM

1 cup Mayonnaise*
1 cup sour cream
3 tablespoons tarragon vinegar, or 3 tablespoons
    vinegar and ½ teaspoon dried tarragon
1 tablespoon lemon juice
1 can anchovies
3 tablespoons chopped chives
¼ tablespoon chopped parsley
½ teaspoon salt
¼ teaspoon freshly ground pepper

Mix all of the ingredients together and put in a blender
for 2 minutes, or beat with a rotary beater.

GREEN MAYONNAISE

*1 cup Mayonnaise**
1½ teaspoons chives, chopped fine
1 teaspoon tarragon leaves, chopped fine
1 tablespoon parsley, chopped fine
½ teaspoon chervil, chopped fine
½ teaspoon dill, chopped fine

Blend all together. Traditional on cold salmon, good on all fish salads.

SHERRY MAYONNAISE

*1 cup Mayonnaise**
¼ cup pale dry sherry
1 cup whipped cream

Mix all the ingredients together. Use on fruit salads, especially for dessert, also on chicken or turkey.

SARDINE MAYONNAISE

*1 cup Mayonnaise**
4 tablespoons mashed sardines
1 tablespoon chopped pimento
1 tablespoon onion, chopped fine
2 hard boiled eggs, chopped fine

Mix all together, let stand in refrigerator for several hours to blend flavors. A tasty dressing for greens.

AVOCADO MAYONNAISE

1 medium-sized ripe avocado
1 tablespoon lemon juice
¼ cup Mayonnaise*
½ teaspoon salt
¼ teaspoon pepper
½ teaspoon chili powder
Pinch garlic powder
Pinch cayenne

Peel and mash the avocado with lemon juice until smooth, or buzz in a blender. Add Mayonnaise and all of the seasonings. Enhances any green salad.

TARRAGON MAYONNAISE

1 cup Mayonnaise*
2 teaspoons tarragon vinegar
1 teaspoon lemon juice
2 tablespoons catsup
1 teaspoon dry tarragon or 3 teaspoons chopped fresh

Mix all together and let stand several hours. Marvelous for poultry salads.

TARTARE SAUCE

1 cup Mayonnaise*
2 tablespoons finely chopped pickles
2 tablespoons finely chopped green olives
2 tablespoons finely chopped parsley
2 tablespoons coarsely chopped capers
2 tablespoons minced onion or chopped scallions

Mix all ingredients thoroughly. Use with fish.

THOUSAND ISLAND DRESSING

1 cup Mayonnaise*
3 tablespoons chili sauce
1 tablespoon cider vinegar
1 tablespoon cream
1 tablespoon minced green pepper
¼ cup chopped celery
1 hard boiled egg, chopped fine
¼ teaspoon salt
½ teaspoon paprika

Mix all the ingredients very thoroughly.

COOKED DRESSINGS

For a less rich salad dressing, there is always a smooth, zesty cooked dressing. A cooked dressing is calorie-wise, because its basis is milk rather than oil. Cooked in a double boiler, it is smooth and bland and as tasty or rich as you care to make it. It tastes so good on cole slaw!

COOKED DRESSING

1 teaspoon salt
¼ teaspoon white pepper
2 tablespoons sugar
½ cup flour
1 tablespoon mustard
1 cup milk
2 eggs
½ cup vinegar
1-2 tablespoons butter

Mix the dry ingredients. Add the milk and stir until smooth. Cook in a double boiler until thickened and smooth. Add the beaten eggs one at a time while cooking and heating. After 5 minutes, stir in the vinegar slowly. Remove from heat. Add a lump of butter, and stir well. Appropriate for cabbage salads.

BOILED DRESSING

¼ cup cider vinegar
1 teaspoon salt
¼ teaspoon pepper
3 egg yolks
¼ cup cream

Heat the vinegar in a double boiler and add salt and pepper. Beat the egg yolks in a bowl and pour the warm vinegar over while stirring. Return to double boiler and cook and stir till creamy. Remove from heat and add the cream. Chill. For fruit or cole slaw. Serve with mousses and aspics.

NOVA SCOTIA BOILED DRESSING

3 eggs, beaten
1 cup milk
¾ cup vinegar
2 tablespoons flour
2 tablespoons butter
1 teaspoon mustard
½ teaspoon salt
¼ teaspoon pepper

Heat the eggs and milk together. Heat the vinegar separately. Put the flour, butter, mustard, salt, and pepper in a bowl and stir in the hot milk. Cook until thickened and then add the warm vinegar. Use whenever you need a cooked dressing.

COOKED OIL SALAD DRESSING

2 tablespoons flour
1 teaspoon sugar
3 tablespoons oil
1 teaspoon salt
2 eggs
¼ cup cider vinegar
2 teaspoons prepared mustard

Mix flour, sugar, oil, and salt with 1 cup of water. Heat until thickened. Mix the slightly beaten eggs with the vinegar and add slowly to the mixture while stirring. Cook and stir until quite thick. Add the mustard.

COOKED FRUIT DRESSING

2 eggs
¼ cup sugar
⅓ cup lemon juice
2 teaspoons butter
⅛ teaspoon salt
2 tablespoons cream

Beat the eggs, add sugar, lemon juice, butter, and salt. Cook and stir until thick and fluffy. Cool. Just before serving, stir in the cream. Use on dessert salads. This is a sweet dressing.

WHIPPED CREAM FRUIT DRESSING

1 tablespoon butter
¼ tablespoon sugar
1 egg
Juice 1 orange
Juice 1 lemon
½ cup heavy cream, whipped

Put butter, sugar, and the slightly beaten egg in a double boiler. Cook and stir until smooth and thick. Add fruit juices and mix. Cool and fold in the whipped cream. For any dessert salad.

SHERRY DRESSING

1 egg, beaten
2 tablespoons sugar
¼ cup sherry
¼ teaspoon salt
2 teaspoons butter
¼ cup orange juice
2 tablespoons lemon juice
¼ cup heavy cream, whipped

Combine all ingredients except the cream in a double boiler. Cook until slightly thickened, stirring constantly. Chill. Fold in the whipped cream. Fine for fruits.

ROQUEFORT DRESSINGS

Roquefort cheese makes salad taste different, according to how it is blended. You can enjoy it in French Dressing* or Mayonnaise*; or you might smooth it in white wine; or try it in sour cream or in olive oil. Any way you blend it, Roquefort is special!

ROQUEFORT CHEESE DRESSING

¼ pound Roquefort cheese
¼ cup white wine
3 tablespoons olive oil
1 tablespoon lemon juice

Crumble the cheese and smooth it using the wine. Add the oil and lemon juice and mix thoroughly. Mixed greens are delicious with this flavorful dressing.

ROQUEFORT FRENCH DRESSING

*1 cup French Dressing**
¼ cup Roquefort or blue cheese

Crumble and cream the Roquefort cheese and then mix with the French Dressing. For mixed green salads, for a change.

ROQUEFORT LEMON DRESSING

½ pound Roquefort cheese, crumbled
½ cup olive oil
¼ teaspoon pepper
Juice 2 lemons

Mash the cheese and olive oil until smooth. Add the pepper and lemon juice and stir well. For any salads where cheese flavor is appropriate, greens, fruit, tomatoes, etc.

SOUR CREAM ROQUEFORT CHEESE DRESSING

1 cup sour cream
½ teaspoon salt
½ teaspoon dry mustard
½ teaspoon minced onion
⅛ pound Roquefort or blue cheese

Mix the cream, salt, mustard, and onion. Add to the crumbled Roquefort and stir until smooth. Use like any Roquefort dressing.

DAIRY DRESSINGS

Cottage or cream cheese makes a smooth creamy dressing with or without the addition of heavy cream, especially if made in a mixer or blender. You may smooth the cheese with a little milk or half and half. Yogurt and cottage cheese are valuable for low-calorie dressings.

CREAM CHEESE DRESSING

2 tablespoons Mayonnaise*
1 (3 ounce) package cream cheese
½ cup sour cream
1 tablespoon grated orange rind
1 tablespoon orange juice
¼ teaspoon salt

Blend the Mayonnaise into the cream cheese. Add the remaining ingredients and stir until mixed. Try with fruit or mixed salads.

COTTAGE CHEESE DRESSING

1 cup cottage cheese
⅓ cup milk
1 teaspoon chopped chives or scallions
2 tablespoons chopped parsley
½ teaspoon salt
¼ teaspoon freshly ground pepper
½ teaspoon Worcestershire sauce

Whip the cottage cheese with the milk until creamy. Add remaining ingredients. Refrigerate for several hours. Try on tomato or cucumber salad, as well as green salads.

COTTAGE CHEESE BUTTERMILK DRESSING

    ½ cup creamy cottage cheese
    ½ cup buttermilk
    1 teaspoon salt
    ¼ teaspoon pepper
    2 hard boiled egg yolks, mashed
    1 tablespoon minced green pepper (optional)
    1 tablespoon minced onion (optional)
    1 teaspoon caraway seed (optional)

Mix all of the ingredients together very thoroughly. Use like other cottage cheese dressings.

LOW-CALORIE COTTAGE CHEESE DRESSING

    1 cup cottage cheese
    ½ cup buttermilk or skim milk
    2–3 tablespoons wine vinegar
    ½ teaspoon grated onion
    ½ teaspoon salt

Combine the ingredients in a blender or mixer, or beat with a rotary mixer. Add a little artificial sweetener if this is to be used on fruit or dessert salad. About 2 calories per tablespoon.

SOUR CREAM DRESSING

1 cup sour cream
1 tablespoon minced olives
1/4 cup vinegar or 1/8 cup lemon juice
1 tablespoon sugar
1 teaspoon salt
1/4 teaspoon pepper
1 tablespoon prepared horseradish
1/2 teaspoon mustard (optional)

Mix all of the ingredients together; let stand to blend flavors. Good for molds, mousses, and aspics.

CAVIAR SOUR CREAM DRESSING

1/2 cup Mayonnaise*
1/2 cup sour cream
1 (2 ounce) jar black or red caviar
1 tablespoon catsup (optional)
1/4 teaspoon grated onion
2 teaspoons lemon juice

Mix all of the ingredients together. A distinguished dressing for chicken or fish salads.

YOGURT DRESSING

1 cup yogurt
1 teaspoon lemon juice
1/2 teaspoon finely minced chives
1/2 teaspoon salt
1/4 teaspoon pepper
1/2 teaspoon paprika
1/2 teaspoon dry mustard

Combine the ingredients and mix until well blended. Chill. Use whenever you want a creamy dressing.

CURRY YOGURT DRESSING

½ teaspoon salt
⅛ teaspoon paprika
⅛ teaspoon pepper
1 teaspoon sugar or 1 tablespoon honey
1–2 teaspoons curry powder
2 tablespoons lemon juice
1 pint yogurt

Mix all of the ingredients except the yogurt together and then stir in the yogurt. Good with fruit or poultry salads.

YOGURT FRENCH DRESSING

½ cup Basic French Dressing*
1 cup yogurt
1 teaspoon celery salt
1 clove garlic, crushed (optional)

Mix all of the ingredients together. Use with mixed or fruit salads.

LOW-CALORIE YOGURT DRESSING

1 cup yogurt
1 teaspoon salt
¼ teaspoon pepper
2 teaspoons prepared mustard
1 teaspoon salad herbs
1 teaspoon curry powder

Mix all of the ingredients gently together.

YOGURT MINT LOW-CALORIE DRESSING

1 cup yogurt
2 tablespoons honey
2 tablespoons minced fresh mint or 2 teaspoons
*   dried*
2 teaspoons lemon juice

Mix all of the ingredients together and let stand to bring out the mint flavor. Reseason to taste. Only about 15 calories per tablespoon.

BONUS DRESSINGS

If you've gone along with me this far, you deserve a bonus, and here it is, in the mixed bag of out-of-the-ordinary, one-of-a-kind, super-delectable dressings that follow. There is no reason why you too can't develop your own blue-ribbon *bonus dressings!*

SPECIAL SALAD DRESSING

1 clove garlic, crushed
½ teaspoon salt
¼ teaspoon pepper
⅛ teaspoon paprika
½ cup olive or salad oil or combination
1 egg
6 anchovies
¼ cup chopped water cress
3 tablespoons wine vinegar

Put the garlic in a bowl with salt, pepper, paprika, and mix. Add the oil slowly and the beaten raw egg. Mix the chopped anchovies, water cress, and vinegar, and beat in the oil mixture, and beat all together. Delicious!

ALMOND GARLIC DRESSING

12 almonds
2 cloves garlic
1 teaspoon salt
¼ teaspoon white pepper
¾ cup olive oil
¼ cup wine vinegar

Crush the blanched almonds with garlic. Add the salt
and pepper; beat in the olive oil in a thin stream. Add
the vinegar. Use on lettuce or mixed lettuces or greens.

CREAMY AVOCADO DRESSING

1 cup mashed avocado
1 teaspoon lemon juice
½ teaspoon salt
2 tablespoons powdered sugar
1 teaspoon onion juice (optional)
1 cup heavy cream, whipped

Season the avocado with lemon juice, salt, sugar, and
the onion juice, if you wish. Fold into the whipped
cream. Use with greens or fruit.

BACON DRESSING

6 slices bacon
½ cup vinegar
¼ teaspoon salt
½ teaspoon sugar
½ teaspoon pepper

Cook the bacon and remove from skillet. Add remaining ingredients to the bacon drippings. Heat. Crumble

the bacon, and add to the dressing. Serve warm over
lettuce or spinach for a wilted salad.

CHICKEN LIVER DRESSING

½ *pound chicken livers*
2 *tablespoons butter*
1 *medium onion, minced*
4 *hard boiled eggs*
¼ *cup Mayonnaise**
½ *teaspoon salt*
⅛ *teaspoon pepper*

Cook the livers in butter and add the onion. Reserve
pan drippings. Chop the liver with the eggs. Add the
pan drippings with the Mayonnaise and salt and
pepper. Taste for seasoning. Serve on lettuce or mixed
green salad.

BELGIAN CREAM DRESSING

¼ *cup olive oil*
1 *tablespoon lemon juice*
⅓ *cup heavy cream*
1 *teaspoon prepared mustard*
1 *tablespoon catsup*
3 *scallions or 1 small onion, minced*
2 *teaspoons minced parsley*
½ *teaspoon salt*
¼ *teaspoon vinegar*

Mix all of the ingredients and shake thoroughly in a
jar. Try on Belgian endive or other highly flavored
greens.

HORSERADISH HERB DRESSING

¾ cup sour cream
2 teaspoons tarragon or wine vinegar
2 tablespoons prepared horseradish
1 teaspoon sugar
⅛ teaspoon pepper
½ teaspoon salt
⅛ teaspoon paprika
1 teaspoon minced parsley
1 teaspoon minced dill or tarragon

Mix all of the ingredients together very thoroughly.
This is a highly flavored dressing. Use for a change on
appetizer salads and aspics.

CUCUMBER SALAD DRESSING

1 cucumber, grated
1 tablespoon grated onion
1 cup sour cream
½ teaspoon salt
¼ teaspoon pepper

Combine all of the ingredients. Especially good with
fish salads such as tuna or salmon.

LEMON DRESSING

¼ cup lemon juice
¼ cup sugar
1 egg, well beaten
1 cup heavy cream, whipped

Combine the lemon juice, sugar, and egg in a double
boiler. Cook until thick and smooth, stirring constantly.
Chill. Fold in the whipped cream. Use with dessert
salads.

HONEY LEMON DRESSING

½ cup honey
1 teaspoon salt
1 teaspoon mustard
1 teaspoon paprika
½ cup lemon juice
1 cup salad oil

Mix all of the ingredients in a blender at low speed. Add the oil slowly while mixing. Appropriate for dessert salads, and fruit.

LORENZO DRESSING

⅔ cup olive oil
⅓ cup vinegar
1 teaspoon salt
½ cup chili sauce
½ cup chopped water cress

Combine all the ingredients, and mix thoroughly. Wonderful on mixed salads of all kinds.

MINT SALAD DRESSING

1 cup olive oil
¼ cup cider vinegar
1 tablespoon minced shallots or scallions
2 tablespoons minced fresh mint
1 teaspoon salt
¼ teaspoon pepper

Mix all of the ingredients together and shake or stir thoroughly. Good on fruit salads or mixed greens.

MUSTARD DRESSING

1 tablespoon dry mustard
¼ cup dry white wine
1 egg yolk
½ cup salad oil
½ teaspoon salt
½ teaspoon sugar
1 clove garlic, crushed, or 1 teaspoon minced chives
2 teaspoons minced parsley

Mix all the ingredients together beating thoroughly. Add more mustard to taste. A strong dressing for a zesty salad.

POPPY SEED DRESSING

½ cup sugar
1 teaspoon mustard
1½ teaspoons salt
⅓ cup vinegar
2 teaspoons onion juice (optional)
1 cup salad oil
2–3 tablespoons poppy seeds

Combine sugar, mustard, salt, vinegar, and onion juice. Put in blender or mixer at low speed and add oil in a very slow stream. You may make this with a rotary hand mixer beating steadily. Add poppy seeds. A sweet dressing for dessert.

SPICY SALAD DRESSING

1 teaspoon dry mustard
½ teaspoon celery seed
½ teaspoon paprika
1 teaspoon salt
½ teaspoon freshly ground pepper
1 clove garlic crushed or ½ teaspoon garlic salt
⅓ cup cider vinegar
1 cup olive oil

Mix all of the dry ingredients together, and then add the vinegar and olive oil. A tasty dressing for vegetable salads.

RED SALAD DRESSING

1 teaspoon salt
½ teaspoon pepper
½ teaspoon paprika
½ teaspoon mustard
1 teaspoon sugar
¼ cup vinegar
1 teaspoon Worcestershire sauce
Few drops Tabasco sauce
¾ cup salad oil (or part olive oil)
3 tablespoons chili sauce

Mix the dry ingredients. Stir in the vinegar, Worcestershire sauce, and Tabasco. Add the oil slowly while beating, and the chili sauce. Shake thoroughly in a bottle. Try this on shellfish.

REMOULADE

1 teaspoon mustard
1 teaspoon anchovy paste
1 tablespoon vinegar
2 tablespoons sherry
½ clove garlic, crushed
3 tablespoons parsley
2–3 tablespoons capers
1 teaspoon onion juice or minced chives
1 cup Mayonnaise*

Mix all of the ingredients except Mayonnaise. Stir in the Mayonnaise. Let stand to blend flavors. Good with fish.

And if you aren't convinced by this time, there's no use telling you again

SALAD IS GOOD

INDEX

203

Gifts or Cash...from
Chesterfield Coupons

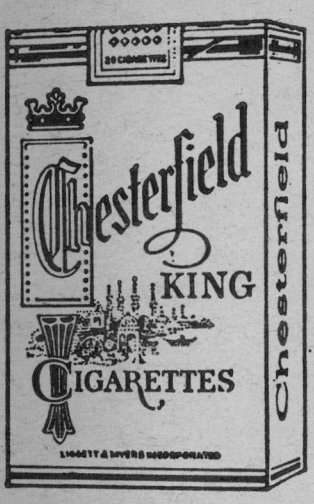

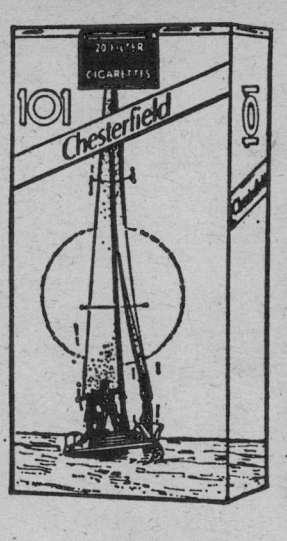

**See free coupons
for details when
you buy a carton.**

King: 29 mg. "tar", 1.8 mg. nicotine; 101 Filter: 19 mg. "tar",
1.5 mg. nicotine; av. per cigarette, FTC Report (Feb. '73).

The lady has taste.

Put some more flavor in your life.